MANAGEMENT OF RETIREMENT HOMES AND LONG-TERM CARE FACILITIES

MANAGEMENT OF RETIREMENT HOMES AND LONG-TERM CARE FACILITIES

JOHN H. COGGESHALL, B.S., M.H.A., F.A.C.N.H.A.

Administrator, Apartment Community of Our Lady of the Snows, Belleville,
Illinois; Coordinator-Instructor, Program in Long-Term Care Administration,
Belleville Area College, Belleville, Illinois; formerly Assistant Administrator,
St. Louis University Hospitals (Firmin Desloge Hospital and
David P. Wohl Memorial Mental Health Institute),
St. Louis, Missouri

ILLUSTRATED

THE C. V. MOSBY COMPANY

SAINT LOUIS   1973

Library of Congress Cataloging in Publication Data

Coggeshall, John H   1930-
    Management of retirement homes and long-term care facilities.

    1. Old age homes—Administration. 2. Nursing
homes—Administration. I. Title. [DNLM: 1. Extended
care facilities. 2. Long term care. 3. Retirement.
WT 30 C676m   1973]
HV1451.C56   362.6'15   73-4450
ISBN 0-8016-1008-7

Many people in everyone's life cause changes and offer needed encouragements in order for an individual to grow and meet his stated goals. I am indebted to many such people. Three people, however, perhaps have done the most toward helping me to realize my potential and helping to motivate me toward these goals. This book is dedicated to these people:

The Very Reverend Father Edwin J. Guild, O.M.I., Director of the League of Mary Immaculate, Belleville, Illinois, who had belief in me as an administrator.

Charles E. Berry, A.B., M.Sc., H.A., J.D., Associate Dean, School of Nursing and Allied Health Professions, St. Louis University, St. Louis, Missouri, who accepted me as a student and gave me early guidance.

My wife, Myra D. Coggeshall, who continually offered me encouragement and who has unselfishly accepted her obligation to often share me with those in need at times when many men would have been at home.

and

Special thanks is due to **Miss Marge Schuck,** who patiently struggled to read the handwritten manuscript in order to reduce these thoughts to readable print.

PREFACE

This book was written in the confusion of changing times. Twenty years ago little was done on a national level to meet the needs of the older person. Today so much has been structured that, at the present time, much of it is inappropriate and ineffective. We have just witnessed the creation of a professional position by federal law: the licensed nursing home administrator. No other professional has that to boast of or that cross to bear.

Today we have the anguish of misunderstood federal programs and misunderstood needs of elderly people. Although the Medicare and Medicaid programs have helped millions to receive needed health care, these laws and their application and interpretation have brought confusion to people who were expecting more, disillusionment to the professions and home owners, and even bankruptcy to a few.

We seem, at this time, to be in a state of suspended animation, waiting for the "other shoe to drop." The revisions to those great laws are still to come. There are charges, some proved and some unfounded, of misappropriation and misuse of the laws. There are accusations, again some proved and some untrue, of the inadequate care given to elderly people in nursing homes. Special investigating committees, task forces, class action groups, and home associations are all probing, suspecting, misinterpreting, charging, and damning each other. Some homes for the aged with long traditions of charitable service to older people are being forced to close for many reasons, primarily monetary.

Since the First White House Conference on Aging, some progress has been made. The Second White House Conference on Aging, just completed, has yet to prove its success. We are, indeed, in a transitional era in regard to the care of aged people. Let up hope that we find the answers soon.

John H. Coggeshall
November, 1972

CONTENTS

MANAGEMENT OF RETIREMENT HOMES AND LONG-TERM CARE FACILITIES

INTRODUCTION

This book deals with the administration and the management of long-term care facilities and facilities built to provide housing for the elderly.

Since the first White House Conference on the Aging in 1961, great attention has been focused on the housing and nursing care needs of the elderly. These needs range from simple housing units to highly sophisticated extended care facilities. Since the majority (about 95%) of the elderly do not require institutional care, specialized housing facilities and projects have been developed under the leadership of the government housing programs. Some of these programs have proved to be more problems than helps and some have been phased out to be replaced by new concepts.

In general, though, specialized housing projects for the elderly have mushroomed in the past decade. From 1960 to 1970 programs under government leadership have produced more than 336,000 subsidized units for the elderly.[1] Many more units need to be built, however. We also see programs approaching the needs from another angle by serving the elderly person in his own home; such programs are sponsored by voluntary agencies, some with federal funding.

The construction of housing facilities for the elderly results from several programs administered by the Department of Housing and Urban Development (HUD). Special features of the Federal Housing and the National Housing Act of HUD oversee several programs. Section 202 of the act was designed to provide direct loans from the federal government to nonprofit sponsors who desired to build specialized housing projects for the elderly and the handicapped. One hundred percent of the capital cost of construction was provided under this program with 50-year mortgages at 3% interest. In 1969 this program was transferred to Section 236. Section 236 was designed to provide housing on a subsidized basis for all ages, including the elderly. Instead of providing funds for this program, the government encouraged the borrowing of capital from the private money market with the government paying all but 1% of the interest on the borrowed capital. Other programs, including rent subsidy concepts, also have been developed to meet the need.

1

To all of these programs can be added the stimulated growth of extended care facilities, skilled nursing homes, and intermediate care homes that come about as a result of the Medicare and Medicaid programs initiated in 1965.

Consequently, the specialized field of professional administration of facilities for the elderly has been slowly developing. A requirement of the 1967 amendments to the Social Security Act is a licensing program for administration of nursing homes and extended care facilities. Under the original funding from the Older Americans Act, educational programs have been established at several universities throughout the country for training of administrators for housing facilities designed for the older person. By 1969, 48 grants had been awarded under this act.[2] Although most of the programs were designed to be multidisciplinary, many were specifically built around gerontological concepts and their application to housing administration and recreational programming. Studies authorized by other sections of the Older Americans Act were aimed toward determining the future needs of the elderly. The results of the study entitled *The Demand for Personnel and Training in the Field of Aging* were transmitted to the President and Congress in 1969. This survey showed that in 1969 there were 4,900 management personnel in the retirement housing field; that the need would nearly double to an estimated 8,000 personnel by 1970 and would advance to 32,000 to 42,000 by 1980; and that within ten years, more than 40,000 administrators of long-term care facilities would be required.[2]

This book, then, is designed to help those entering into the fields of retirement home management and long-term care facility management. Although most of the philosophy and techniques discussed in this book will apply to both fields, an attempt is made to separate, when necessary, the divergent approaches necessary in the two fields. As a case in point, the health and nursing care section is developed in two parts: one for the long-term care administrator and another for retirement home manager.

The other major areas of study are residential services, administrative services, and social components; in general, they are uniformly treated, and specific details are included, when necessary, for both fields.

The trend today in the care of elderly people is to keep them as independent as possible in their own homes, retirement villages, or specialized housing. The goal is to postpone as long as possible the need for institutional care. To make this concept work, alternatives to institutional care must be continuously expanded. These alternatives include formally organized home-help services or homemakers services, meal-on-wheels programs, adult day-care centers, transportation and escort services, and many others.

The trends, though, still point to an ever increasing need for more facilities for the elderly, each requiring some administrative or management personnel.

It is the goal of this book to help train the people who will serve these needs in the future.

NOTES

1. Tiven, Marjorie B.: Older Americans: special handling required. Prepared for the U. S. Department of Housing and Urban Development by the National Council on the Aging.
2. Aging, No. 175, May 1969, U. S. Department of Health, Education, and Welfare Social and Rehabilitation Service, Administration on Aging, U. S. Printing Office, Washington, D. C.

Chapter one

THE RESPONSIBILITIES OF OWNERSHIP

ORGANIZATIONAL STRUCTURES

In health care facilities there are three basic types of ownership. The first, and perhaps oldest, form is ownership vested in a group of religious or fraternal background. The second major form is ownership by governmental bodies. Ownership of the vast majority of the long-term care facilities is of the third type—proprietary—in which the facilities are owned by individuals and operated with the expectation of a financial gain.

The least complicated organizational structure and the most common is that in which the single proprietor operates a small home and acts as the administrator. The owner is on the scene daily, performing the management functions mainly by himself. Usually in this single-ownership form, little authority is delegated. The owner-administrator makes all the major decisions and, frequently, most of the minor ones. Since this type of home is typically a small one, the number of employees is low. There is little need for second-level management or department heads. The cook, the aide, the maid, and the handyman—all these come to the administrator for decisions. In directing the activities of the employees, the administrator acts in an autocratic manner, overseeing every minor detail of the operation. Just as the small farm is being replaced by the larger one, this type of home is slowly being replaced or overshadowed by the larger home in many parts of the country.

A more complicated type of organizational structure is that in which the individual who is the owner prefers to hire an administrator to run the facility for him. The owner delegates certain authority to the administrator and expects, in turn, successful results. As is the owner-administrator structure, this form is limited to proprietary facilities.

With facilities owned by religious and fraternal groups and with proprietary facilities owned by many people, such as through a corporation, the organizational structure becomes most complex. First, there is the corporate body of owners: the church group, the members of the fraternal organization, or the stockholders of

3

Fig. 1. Ownership structure type I of a retirement residence. Simple, least compli-cated.

Fig. 2. Ownership structure type II-A of a retirement residence. More complex, small facility.

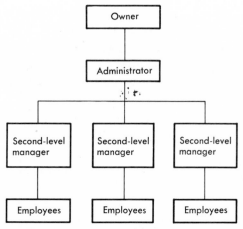

Fig. 3. Ownership structure type II-B of a retirement residence. More complex, larger facility.

the corporation. Typically, this body elects a board of directors empowered to act for the group. The board, then, in turn, hires the administrator to operate the facility.

The three organizational structures are graphically demonstrated in Figs. 1 through 4.

Through the organizational structures of types II and III, authority must flow to all levels so that the organization can function properly to carry out the goal of the ownership. This authority is given through formal written policy statements and through informal understandings, passed from level to level in a downward movement. This most essential aspect of management deserves more discussion and will be developed in depth later in this chapter, for the delegation of authority is one of the major duties or responsibilities of ownership.

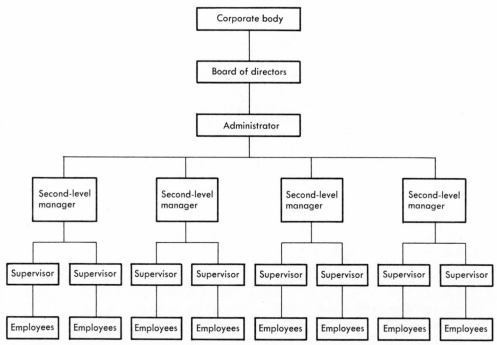

Fig. 4. Ownership structure type III of a retirement residence. Most complex, large facility.

RESPONSIBILITIES OF OWNERSHIP

A great deal of money is required for acquiring or constructing a building to be used for the care of the aging. Likewise, much capital must be invested in the essential equipment to be used in carrying out this care. Even a small home can have many thousands of dollars invested in the plant and its equipment. In larger homes, the many thousands become many hundreds of thousands.

Additional money is required for inventories of supplies and materials, such as foodstuffs, cleaning materials, paper goods, forms, linens, medical supplies (if it is the policy to provide nursing care in any degree), and many other "forgotten" incidentals that, when appearing on the financial statement, might astound the uninitiated person.

Cash must be available for meeting payrolls and for prompt payment of purchases. More cash must be available for meeting interest payments on the long-term debt (surely, one exists) and principal payments when necessary.

Quite possibly the home will have nonsalary cash responsibilities to its employees other than the legally required deductions for Social Security tax and payments for workmen's compensation insurance and unemployment insurance. For example, the home may agree to pay all or part of the employees' health insurance premiums. Also, the home may have established a pension fund as an added benefit for the employees. Cash must be available for all of these needs.

Taxes are no longer a strange entry in the ledger of the nonprofit home. It is an expected factor in the proprietary home. Money must be available for timely tax payments.

Furthermore, in the case of the proprietary facility, there must be a profit for ownership as a legitimate return on the investment.

All these points lead to the statement of three of the several basic responsibilities of ownership:

1. *It is the responsibility of ownership to assemble the resources to purchase the land and the facility or to construct a facility through public solicitation of funds, or borrowing, or both, or through the use of private capital, in order to provide a suitable facility acceptable by the governing licensing authority to provide the care the owners intend to give.*
2. *It is the responsibility of ownership to provide the necessary operating cash, including the sufficient "start-up" cash, by seeing that efficient management techniques are employed to ensure a constant flow of cash to meet the needs.*
3. *It is the responsibility of ownership to preserve the building and grounds by seeing that proper maintenance is performed as needed on the building to retard deterioration and obsolescence and to provide a fund for depreciation to cover the cost of renovation and replacement.*

Frequently, in a facility with a board of directors, a committee is developed to oversee these three responsibilities. It may be called the *building committee* or *development committee* or perhaps the *long-range planning committee*. After the initial work of assembling the resources for construction is successfully done, the responsibilities of this committee may be to work toward future building needs.

A second committee may be developed to oversee the cash flow requirements. It may be called the *financial committee*. Among this committee's duties will be the planning for both current and long-term financial needs.

A third committee that may be formed is commonly called the *physical plant committee*. Members of this committee will be expected to see that repairs of the building are made and that preventive maintenance is carried out.

How busy the members of these several committees will be depends, of course, on how good the administrator is. If the administrator is skilled and sufficiently capable of sound management and *is given the authority* to carry out these three responsibilities of ownership, the committees can rely on periodic reports and informal discussions. The administrator, in the ideal arrangement, will know that if he has a problem with the maintenance of the building, such as a need to replace some portion of gutter, he can pick up the telephone and discuss the matter with the chairman of the physical plant committee. Perhaps the chairman can give him the authority to proceed with the replacement, or perhaps it will have to go to the board for a decision; however, in either case, the administrator initiated the action.

If there is a question concerning the painting of a patient's or resident's room, this same administrator probably will have been *given the authority* to make this decision on his own, in keeping with a general budgetary allotment for this renovation procedure. This anticipated need would have been discussed previously with the financial committee and the physical plant committee when the administrator submitted his annual budget. He would have, at that time, been given the authority to spend a certain amount during the fiscal year for that purpose. If, through unforeseen events, it becomes necessary to spend more for painting rooms than had been budgeted, it would be necessary for him to seek approval from the board before proceeding with the renovation.

Since it is quite apparent that the members of the board must have a very capable administrator to carry out the details of the facility operation, another basic responsibility of ownership can now be stated:

4. *It is the responsibility of ownership to recruit and appoint a capable administrator to operate the facility.*

Selecting the administrator is a two-way street. Both the board and the administrator have to feel satisfied and comfortable that each has made a good decision. The qualifications of a good administrator will be explored in Chapter 2 in detail. In general, of course, the administrator must be a highly capable person well grounded in the needs of the elderly and must have a practical knowledge of management techniques. In certain facilities he must have a valid nursing home administrator's license.

The administrator, in order to be successful, must understand and accept the goals and requirements of the owner. He must have a complete grasp of all that will be expected of him and must be willing to work to accomplish all the aims of the owner. If the administrator is reluctant to totally accept all the policies and goals of the owner, he should not accept the job. It is a duty the administrator assumes when he takes the position to give the owner his complete loyalty to carry out these policies.

The owner, too, has a duty to the administrator. It is imperative that this duty be carried out for the successful function of the organization, and it, then, is another responsibility of ownership:

5. *It is the responsibility of ownership to delegate sufficient authority to the administrator for him to perform, with freedom, the necessary management functions required for the successful operation of the facility within the policy guidelines established by the owner.*

The owner expects the administrator to carry out successfully the general goals established. The owner holds the administrator responsible for these successful actions.

In order for the administrator to live up to these responsibilities, he must be given sufficient authority to conduct all the aspects of the facility. The owner does not blindly give the administrator absolute authority. The owner establishes broad policies to act as guidelines for the administrator, who is given the authority to act within those policy guidelines. Through the establishment of these broad policies, the owner retains certain controls. The owner, in establishing these policies, is setting up boundaries that say to the administrator: "You are free to act within these boundaries, but you must seek permission from me before extending beyond them."

Of course, these boundaries must be wide enough to enable the administrator to act and to conduct the day-to-day business of the facility without seeking permission for every act. The idea is to give the administrator sufficient authority that his permission-seeking needs are minimal. Specifically, for example, the administrator must have the authority to select his employees, to manage them, to discipline them (in accepted ways), and to discharge them without owner interference.

For the facility operation to be successful, the administrator must be given the right to hire and fire. If the owner overrules the administrator's decision to discharge an employee, the administrator no longer can function adequately as the manager, for the owner has assumed one of the management functions. Of course, the owner has the right to do this; however, in doing so, he has become the administrator and has seriously diluted the ability of the appointed administrator to carry out the expected duties.

Another management function for which the owner should delegate sufficient authority to the administrator is the right to purchase in the name of the facility. Again, the owner must establish guidelines that set the limit of the administrators' authority and yet allow him to act on his own within the guideline. For example, the administrator may be given the authority to purchase minor equipment with value of up to $100 without owner approval, within the limits of the established budget. If, at the time of the budget making, the administrator projects the need to spend $2,000 in the fiscal year for minor equipment replacement, he should be given the authority to buy a replacement lawn mower for $90 or a new vacuum cleaner for $85 when he determines it to be necessary, without specific approval. This purchasing policy, however, would prevent him from buying a $450 carpet shampoo machine without first receiving specific approval from the owner.

Another administrative responsibility requiring the delegation of authority to the administrator is the right to contract in the name of the facility. Of course, a specific guideline is indicated here also. It is obvious that the owner cannot allow the administrator to contract for a loan from a bank without specific authority. However, the owner must delegate the authority to sign standard agreements with residents or to sign short-term purchase agreements or individual purchase orders within established budgetary guidelines.

In exploring the appointment of the administrator and the delegation of authority to him, I have been referring to the goals of ownership and the operational policies of the facility. This brings me to two more of the responsibilities of ownership:

6. *It is the responsibility of ownership to develop and clearly define, in writing, the goals and objectives of the facility.*

7. *It is the responsibility of ownership to develop and clearly define, in writing, the broad operational policies necessary to achieve the stated goals.*

The discussion of the responsibilities of ownership could have begun with these two statements. Before the owner begins to assemble resources for the facility, he must know the general purpose of the facility. Therefore, the owner obviously must, quite early in the planning stages, develop the goals and objectives of the facility. It must be decided to whom the care will be given and what kind of care will be given. This planning must be done in detail.

The owner must decide what *level of care* he intends to provide. This becomes one of the goals or objectives of the facility. In the case of a home for the aged, all levels, excluding care of patients with acute conditions, are frequently developed. Usually the proprietary facility will limit the program to one or two major levels. The levels of care are the degrees of intensity of the health and nursing aspects of care. Extended care is at one end of the scale and residential or housing facilities at the other. In between are at least three other levels: skilled care, intermediate care, and personal care.*

---

*On October 30, 1972, Public Law 92-603, the Social Security Amendments of 1972, brought significant changes to the long-term care field. Among these is the change in definitions of the terms *extended care facility* and *skilled nursing home*. The law stipulated that wherever these two terms appear in Title XVIII (Medicare) or Title XIX (Medicaid), the term *skilled nursing facility* should be substituted. Therefore, wherever the term *extended care facility* is used in this text, it should be understood that I am referring to a facility approved for care of patients under Title XVIII (Medicare); and wherever the term *skilled nursing facility* or *skilled nursing home* is used, I am referring to a facility approved for care of patients or residents under Title XIX (Medicaid).

On March 5, 1973, the Department of Health, Education, and Welfare Social and Rehabilitation Service published some proposed rule-making in the Federal Register (Vol. 38, No. 32). This proposed rule-making specifically identified an intermediate care facility for the purposes of Title XIX of the Social Security Act, as a facility that provides "on a regular basis, health related care and services to individuals who do not require the degree of care and treatment which a hospital or skilled nursing facility is designed to provide, but who because of their mental or physical condition require care and services (above the level of room and board) which can be made available to them only through institutional facilities." Therefore, wherever the term *personal care facility* or *shelter care facility* is used in this text, it should be understood that this refers to a facility qualifying under this definition.

I do not intend for the terms *residential facilities, residential care facilities,* and *specialized housing for the elderly* in this text to meet this definition even though I suggest that a degree of health care be provided in this latter classification.

In the extended care facility there is a very high degree of emphasis on nursing and medical care to meet the needs of the patient who, having been transferred from a hospital, is recovering from his ailment. This facility provides continued nursing care under the supervision of a physician for an illness, and not a custodial situation.

The skilled nursing home also provides a high degree of health care emphasis, with professional nurses in charge and licensed nurses on duty each shift. Frequently, extended care facilities and skilled nursing homes are combined, using the *distinct part* concept; a physically identifiable separate unit with its own nursing station and utility areas might be considered the extended care part, and the balance of the home's beds, also with adequate ancillary facilities and appropriate staffing could be considered the part providing a lower level of care such as skilled care.

Intermediate care facilities provide care for those patients who do not require a high degree of skilled nursing and yet do require that their care be supervised by a nurse at least during part of the day. There is still physician contact but, as determined by the needs of the patient, it is less frequent.

Personal care facilities, also classed by the Social Security Act as intermediate care facilities, are designed to meet the residents' needs of assistance with their activities of daily living. Each patient can be assisted in such activities as dressing, bathing, feeding, and walking, according to his individual requirement. Usually a high emphasis is placed on his psychological and social needs. There are activity programs and rehabilitation programs designed to keep him physically and mentally active. No nursing care is given at this level except in temporary illnesses. Usually no professional nurse is in regular attendance, although it is expected that the new federal guidelines will require a professional nurse on the staff.

Within the last ten years a new level of care has emerged, that is, *specialized housing* for the elderly. Sparked by the spin-off programs stimulated by the 1961 White House Conference on the Aging, scores of housing projects for the aging have been developed in the United States in the last few years. Through various federal housing programs, facilities are being subsidized in both construction and operation to provide low-cost rent-subsidized housing for the elderly. These programs are sponsored by civic, church, or fraternal groups and are nonprofit.

The health emphasis found in these programs may, at one end of the scale, be minimal to nonexistent or, at the other end, a highly organized health service. The extent of health service that can be provided is determined by the sponsor.

These levels of care are explored in greater detail in the introductory remarks of Chapter 5.

The owner must also make the following decisions: Who is he going to care for? Is this care to be available to all who need it? Are there going to be minimal financial requirements established? Is he going to limit the care to one sex only? Is he going to set admission age limits? Is he going to admit primarily only those who are members of a fraternal, religious, or ethnic group? (Some of these qualifying considerations cannot be allowed if the facility is receiving Medicare, Medicaid, or other federally rooted funding.)

The owner must decide these and many other questions prior to the construction and operation of the facility. These are the *goals and objectives* of the organization. They should be set out in writing so that the administrator clearly understands the direction of his efforts. These goals and objectives will be the basics used in writing the admission policies. They will determine the qualifications and number of staff members to be hired. They will determine how the building is to be constructed and the equipment is to be purchased. Deciding the goals and objectives, then, is indeed a major responsibility of ownership.

Along with the goals and objectives, the owner must also establish *broad opera-*

tional policies necessary to achieve the stated goals. Earlier I pointed out some areas in which the owner might give the administrator broad financial policy. Through this policy development, the owner is able to delegate sufficient authority to the administrator and still retain a high degree of control. Policies indicate conduct, boundaries, guidelines, and direction. They provide the administrator with assistance in decision making. When the owner gives the administrator authority, he must also give him the policies to guide him.

These broad, general policies express the objectives and goals of the facility that the owner has established. They will express the owner's intentions in regard to such matters as qualifications of residents for admission; benefits for personnel; and relationships with other health agencies, physicians, relatives, and the community.

Of course, from these broad general policies, the administrator, and perhaps the department heads, will develop specific policies within the limits set by the basic policy.

Policies must be thoroughly established by the owner, put in writing, and made available to the administrator in order for the facility to be successfully operated.

At the beginning of this chapter, I mentioned the owner's responsibility concerning protection of the assets of the facility. In order to keep the facility balance sheet healthy, the owner also has an obligation to minimize the liabilities.

8. *It is the responsibility of the owner to maintain the liabilities of the facility in proper balance with the assets.*

The owner should minimize potential liabilities through an adequate insurance program. Insurance should be planned to protect the assets and thus prevent unnecessary liabilities from loss due to fire, windstorm, and similar hazards. If there is no insurance coverage, a windstorm damaging the assets could create liabilities for replacement of the area destroyed.

Insurance for malpractice, public liability, and product liability also should be provided to prevent a liability resulting from a lawsuit against the facility.

The owner must also be cautious in the borrowing of capital for either operation or additional construction. This borrowing creates a liability that eventually must be paid. If sound planning is not employed, too large a liability can seriously harm the financial health of the organization and possibly bring about bankruptcy.

It is apparent that the owner needs advice in order to successfully carry out many of the responsibilities highlighted so far. This need brings me to the next responsibility of ownership:

9. *It is the responsibility of the owner to obtain special expertise to provide him with proper guidance.*

The matter of the proper kinds and amounts of insurance that should be provided calls for the skills of a good insurance broker. This person should study the operational aspects and also inspect the facility's physical plant. He can then advise the owner about the types of insurance that should be carried.

This broker should be invited, regularly, to review the insurance portfolio to detect any need for change in the coverage. Operational practices change and building and equipment replacement values change. A good broker will discover these changes and recommend necessary insurance changes.

An attorney familiar with the business is essential for a long-term care facility today. This is another type of expertise the owner needs to have for guidance. The attorney should be on a retainer. The owner should see that the attorney is constantly kept up to date with trends in the field. The owner should educate the attorney in the concepts of the care of the aging and see that the attorney knows the details of the operations of the facility. Advice from the attorney should be obtained in the designing of contracts for resident admissions. The owner and the administrator should consult him when reviewing contemplated policy for such things as accepting residents' valuables for safekeeping. Of course, he is called at the hint of any legal troubles. If the home owner has kept the attorney up to date on the goals of the facility, when trouble comes, the attorney is better equipped to help.

Another specialist the owner should have as a member of his consultative team is a certified public accountant (CPA) who is familiar with the long-term care field. This service should not be limited merely to a periodic audit of the books. The CPA should be asked to assist the administrator, if needed, to develop better management techniques or, at least, to offer comments on them. Good financial guidance from a knowledgeable CPA firm can help to prevent financial difficulties and possibly increase the facility's potential to make a profit or to keep charges from advancing. The owner should see that the CPA is up to date on the trends in the field. The CPA firm should make a report to the owner, although in preparing the facts for the report, it is accepted practice to discuss the details with the administrator in order to be sure that all facets are explored.

The owner also has the obligation to be knowledgeable about caring for the aging.

10. *It is the responsibility of the owner to keep informed of the changing concepts and trends in the particular branch of the long-term care field in which he is engaged.*

Although the owner relies on his administrator and the administrator's staff to keep up to date on matters in the field, he, too, has an obligation to do the same. The administrator also has an obligation to assist the owner in this by sending him various association news items that come to him. The owner has the primary obligation, however. He should see that the facility becomes a member in the national and state associations that best mirror their objectives. The proprietary groups should consider joining the American Nursing Home Association and the state chapter of the association. Although nursing homes are mentioned in the association name, it does serve the needs of the other levels of proprietary care. Those facilities that do not operate for profit would find their objectives best served by joining the American Association of Homes for the Aging and the corresponding state association. These association memberships offer many advantages for up-to-date education. They provide institutes, conventions, newsletters, and other services designed to keep their members up to date on the field's ever changing needs and advancing skills.

The home owner should encourage the home administrator to join the American College of Nursing Home Administrators. This is the national professional organization for administrators in the long-term care field. Its purpose is to serve the continuing educational needs of administrators of both proprietary and nonprofit facilities. Among other goals, the college has the aim to help advance the quality of patient care, to work with other agencies and government to this end, and to certify the professional growth of the administrator.

There are professional journals that will help the owner broaden his knowledge of the care of the aging. Membership in the Gerontological Society provides such a journal to keep him up to date. This society also conducts educational programs at its annual meetings. Various agencies of the federal government offer educational literature, newsletters, pamphlets, and reports on the needs and care of the aging. The Administration on Aging publishes a monthly magazine *Aging* that can keep the owner abreast of the many federal programs for the aging. Newspapers and newsmagazines regularly publish articles concerning the field of caring for the aging. These articles should be read and circulated if they are of value.

The owner must be aware of the needs and trends in the field so that he can better make policies and assist the administrator. With good knowledge of the business, the owner is better qualified to judge the administrator's work. He can better determine if the goals and objectives are being met to the degree that he expects. He will also be better able to anticipate the need for changes in service, programs, or structures.

As well as being aware of the trends in the field, the owner must keep up to date on the specifics of his own home.

11. *It is the responsibility of the owner to maintain sufficient liaison with the administrator of the facility to be able to provide informal guidance when necessary and to be sure that the goals and objectives of the facility are being met adequately.*

A successful operation requires that the owner be kept informed. An owner who is lax in his duty may soon find that his facility is in deep trouble, perhaps beyond help. Even if the administrator is most competent and there is apparently little danger, under his guidance, of financial difficulty, there may be other problems of insidious nature below the surface. The owner who keeps in touch with his administrator regularly has a better opportunity to detect problems such as high personnel turnover, poor public concepts of the home, gradual deterioration of the plant, and less-than-desired care for the residents.

The owner should not be content merely with a quarterly financial statement showing a profit. He should keep in regular touch with the administrator, keep informed, and be ready to give the administrator backing or guidance when needed. Of course, he should not interfere with the administrator. The administrator must be allowed to manage without interference. The point is, however, that the owner should know what is going on and be on hand when the administrator needs him.

Regular meetings with the administrator on a scheduled basis provide an excellent channel for communication on a formal basis. These meetings should be held at least once a month. The administrator should be asked to have certain statistical and financial reports available for these meetings. Ideally, a monthly financial statement should be provided. A statistical report should provide helpful data such as resident days, admissions, discharges, transfers, meal counts, and personnel hours. Comparison of these data with figures from the previous year is also enlightening.

Informal discussions via the telephone should be encouraged by the owner. He should make himself available to receive these calls or to return them promptly if he is not available at the time. He should maintain a friendly atmosphere with the administrator, conveying complete trust in the administrator's ability.

The owner should ask the administrator to accompany him on a tour of the building occasionally. The owner should always ask the administrator to go with him and should give him sufficient notice prior to the trip. Exceptions to this imply distrust. There is nothing more unnerving to the administrator than to have the owner make an inspection without first inviting him to go along.

Ownership involves many other responsibilities, duties, and obligations. One more that should be mentioned in this discussion is the owner's responsibility to the residents and to the community the facility serves.

12. *It is the responsibility of ownership to ascertain that the residents or patients of the facility are receiving the care they require and for which they are paying.*

The owner receives this information from many sources, primarily the administrator. Occasionally he may receive a letter or a comment indicating the possibility of a problem. Although he must investigate this, he should go to the administrator for the answer.

The owner is responsible to see that he has an adequate, safe physical plant that meets the state or local standards for the level of care provided. If he is more interested in the profit picture than in providing a good, safe environment for his residents, he is in the wrong business.

The owner must be sure that the administrator is competent and that the budget is adequate to provide for sufficient staff with proper qualifications. He must see that the standards of the licensing authority, if there are any, or the qualities that produce good care are met. To do less than any of these things is to be merely an operator of a human warehouse.

Owning a long-term care facility is not a simple matter. It is a business venture. Whether for profit or not for profit, the facility must operate economically with good management. It is increasingly more important today for the nonprofit facility to at least reach the break-even point financially. No longer do there exist the vast funds of endowment to allow deficit financing.

The long-term care facility is a *human care* facility. It may offer only residential care, or it may offer extended care. Either type of facility provides care for people. The owner's responsibility is great when thinking in terms of human well-being.

The owner does not have to go into this business; the church group can elect to support missions instead; the fraternal group can help with other local or national community needs; the businessman can use his capital to build a motel or a service station. If they elect to go into the field of the care of the elderly, however, they commit themselves to the care of human beings, and the obligations they assume are of great weight.

Chapter two

THE ROLE OF THE ADMINISTRATOR

The role of the administrator in a long-term facility will differ from facility to facility, depending on such things as size and level of care. In the small facility, the owner-administrator may double as the repairman of the laundry equipment and the purchasing agent for foodstuffs and supplies; he may accompany a resident to a physician's office; he may keep the financial records; and he may even change a resident's bedclothes. Even though encumbered with these extra chores, the administrator in a small facility does the same thing as the administrator of a large facility: he *manages* it.

The administrator of the long-term care facility should be considered a *manager:* one who gets things done through other people. Even in the smallest facility, the administrator needs many hands to help him care for his residents. He recruits, screens, hires, and trains his staff members. He plans and organizes their work efforts. He motivates and directs their activities, and he controls the results of their endeavors. Whether or not the administrator recognizes these functions as formal management techniques, he is, indeed, performing them. His success as an administrator depends on how skillfully he exercises these techniques.

Since these techniques can be identified and described, I will discuss each management aspect in considerable detail to give a better understanding of how the administrator manages the facility.

There are many terms employed to describe these elements of the administrator's job. Gulick and Urwick developed the memory word *POSDCORB*, which is used as a reminder of their concepts of management.[1] POSDCORB stands for planning, organizing, staffing, directing, coordinating, reporting, and budgeting. These are the techniques the administrator uses to manage, they believe. McQuillan prefers to describe the managing techniques as assembling resources, planning, delegating responsibility, organizing, establishing controls, directing, and evaluating.[2]

One traditional approach to this management process recognizes only five basic management functions, however.[3] I will confine the discussion to these functions, which are, simply, *planning, organizing, directing, controlling,* and *staffing.* All the other labels given above, I believe, can easily be grouped under one of these five functions.

Every administrator must employ these special techniques, with whatever label, in order to manage his facility. This is true regardless of the size or the level of care of the facility. They are, in fact, the same methods a manager uses in the operation of a drive-in restaurant, a resort hotel, or any other business venture.

The field of long-term care, however, involves caring for people. The emphasis and approach of the administrator of a long-term care facility in utilizing these techniques are different from those of the drive-in restaurant manager.

PLANNING FUNCTION OF MANAGEMENT

Planning is predicting future events and preparing to manage them. The word *planning* can convey several different meanings. Consider the following synonyms: designing, projecting, proposing, scheduling, preparing, and arranging. A plan can be considered a sketch, a skeleton, an outline, a layout, a policy, or a conduct. These words should expand your thinking to accept the word *plan* in its broadest concept.

In long-term care management there are long-range plans and short-range plans, plans constructed through the use of broad policy formulated to act as guides to properly direct and control future circumstances, financial plans, resident or patient care plans, and fire and disaster plans. The role of the administrator in planning for the needs of the facility in these and other areas is paramount. The administrator must spend much of his time in planning, and much of his planning must be done for events far in the future. Although some time is given to planning the forthcoming events of the day and the week, much more time is usually spent on planning events that will take place in a month, several months, or several years in the future. If the amount of time the administrator spends in planning for current and future events could be graphed, it might appear as in Fig. 5.

If the time spent in planning by the cook in the same facility could also be plotted, it would appear to be quite different. The cook is projecting ahead several weeks in menu planning and in ordering food and supplies. He is, however, devoting much more time to planning the next meal and the meals for the next day. Perhaps the graph of his planning time would look like that in Fig. 6.

Policies as plans

The American Heritage Dictionary of the English Language defines the word *policy* as "any plan or course of action adopted by a government, political party, business organization, or the like designed to influence and determine decisions, actions, and other matters."[4] It must be understood from this definition that a

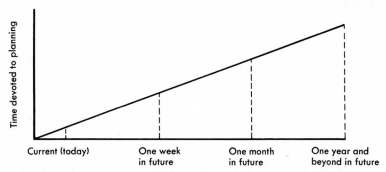

Fig. 5. Administrator's time devoted to planning for current and future events.

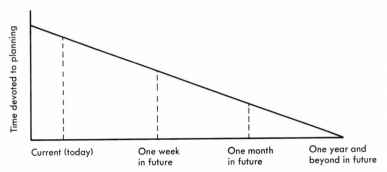

Fig. 6. Cook's time devoted to planning.

policy *is* a plan and that policies are products of planning. Through the formulation of policy, one is planning actions to govern expected repetitive events. Lasser says that a policy explains an attitude or course of action that should be followed by employees when predicted events occur.[5] He points out that through the use of policy, the administrator can feel free to delegate authority and yet still have control over decisions made by subordinates, since the policy sets the guidelines and boundaries for their decisions.

It is essential that policies be written. Moreover, they should be available to those who are expected to use them. When policies are not reduced to writing, the application of them can become fuzzy. Decisions may not be consistent. The original goals and objectives can become distorted, and all expected benefits of the plan can be lost.

It is important, then, for the administrator, to develop a *policy manual* covering these many anticipated needs. In large facilities, the administrator will ask his department heads to assist him with this project. Along with the policies, the administrator will develop or have his subordinates develop written *procedures* on how to carry out these policies. Procedures are instructions developed with much care, telling of the methods to be used step by step in applying the particular policy. The manual then becomes a *policy and procedure manual.*

The benefit of the administrator's having written policies and procedures is that they provide standard guides to thinking and decisions for his employees so that he can delegate authority and yet still retain his broad management control.

Job description as a planning mechanism

The job description is an offshoot of the policy and procedure concept and is, therefore, a planning mechanism. The job description is a record on paper of what is expected of the employee in the performance of his duties. Since development of the job description is properly a function of staffing, it will be discussed in detail in that section.

Budget as a basic planning technique

In the broadest sense, budgeting can be considered to be the setting of goals that management believes can be met, the establishment of methods for meeting them, and then the testing of the results with the goals set. Therefore, the budget can be considered to be both a *planning* and a *controlling* function of management. A budget may be a plan of the *time* needed to accomplish objectives, or it may be a prediction of *financial* activities.

The financial budget is a prediction of income and an estimate of the expenses

Budget year _____   _____ Department

Job title	Budget number	Employee's name	Current wage	Anticipated wage increase	Annual budgeted hours	Annual budgeted wage

Fig. 7. Personnel budget planning form.

involved in obtaining the income. The preparation of the budget, then, necessitates planning for the future. The financial budget is prepared for a certain period of time, usually a year, and it must be compiled before the period is begun. The administrator should begin constructing his budget by first examining the previous year's budget and comparing it with actual events. This will give him an overview of his previous planning and the results. He should then begin examining in detail the previous year's expenses by accounts. This will remind him of expenses that are routine and more that will not recur. He should consider any predictable factors that will call for changes in future expenses. He should consider methods that can help to reduce expenses. For example, the purchase of a certain piece of equipment might bring about a more efficient utilization of man-hours. Budget preparation forces one to think about income and expense and therefore provides an excellent opportunity to discover ways of improving the financial stability of the organization.

   Specifically, the administrator should consider three major areas of his financial budget: the personnel budget, the supplies budget, and the equipment budget.

   Personnel budget. In facilities providing nursing or personal care, the payroll will be the largest single expense. It is important, then, to review it carefully and to establish a tight budgetary control to be used throughout the year.

   In large facilities with department or supervisory heads, the administrator should prepare each section's personnel budget jointly with that section's supervisor, who through involvement in the planning function, can better appreciate the necessity of his providing intelligent, efficient staffing assignments. It also provides an opportunity for the administrator and the submanager to form an informal appraisal of each employee.

   Certain financial facts should be recorded for each employee. A form such as that shown in Fig. 7 can be used to collect these details.

   The budget number is a good control tool for larger organizations with many employees. When vacancies occur, they are filled by the use of the vacant budget

Budget year _____   _____ Department

Item	Unit of purchase	Cost per unit	Number of units needed	Annual cost

Fig. 8. Supplies budget planning form.

number and not by the name of the employee who previously held the job. This helps prevent confusion and prevents the possibility of adding employees over and above the budgeted amount.

The annual budgeted hours figure also is an excellent control tool. I will discuss that later in examining the technique of control.

On the personnel budget form at the bottom, the administrator can calculate the departmental total and add the cost of the projected fringe benefits and payroll taxes. Although both of these costs will be included in two other expense accounts, they can be computed by department and grouped later.

Supplies budget. In preparing this budget also the administrator should work in detail with the section leader. Even though the administrator may do the purchasing himself, he should seek the opinion and assistance of his submanager, who through involvement can feel his responsibility in controlling the cost of supplies through careful utilization.

Much detailed work spent on this budget will prove to be beneficial. For example,

Budget year _____   _____ Department

Item requested	Cost — show freight and installations separately	Why item is needed

Fig. 9. Capital equipment budget planning form.

it may be evident that it is possible to save supply costs through larger purchases with less frequent deliveries. If the administrator anticipates a sufficient cash flow, he can seek opportunities to do this within the limits of his storage capabilities.

The detailed data for this area can be collected on a predesigned form. Utilizing this technique, the administrator can have uniformity in his approach with each department or section. A simple form can be used such as that shown in Fig. 8.

Equipment budget. New and replacement equipment should be included in the equipment budget. Depending on the accounting approach, equipment having a unit price over a certain dollar value—for example, $50—is put into a *capital* account rather than an *expense* account. Routine replacements of items such as china and silverware are treated by accountants as expenses and should be included in the supplies budget.

The administrator should meet with his submanager to plan the equipment needs for the year. For uniformity these are also listed on a form such as that shown in Fig. 9. It is quite likely that the administrator will have to take each specific equipment item to his board for its approval. In the list of items, each item should be accompanied with an explanation of why it is needed.

•   •   •

The budget is a very basic financial plan. It is also a valuable control mechanism and will be discussed later in this regard.

Submanagers and their relationship to planning done by the administrator

Even in the smaller facilities, many administrators find it good practice to discuss ideas with subordinates while formulating plans that will require cooperation from the subordinates. If, as in the larger facilities, the administrator has submanagers with a department head status, he will no doubt hold regular staff meetings to discuss the day-to-day needs of the home. These staff meetings can provide an excellent opportunity for group planning of activities or methods involving two or more departments. The administrator retains control and may guide the thinking if he needs to. He can allow in-depth discussion of the subject and arrive at a solution during the meeting, or he can retain the right to study the several ideas presented and to make his decision later.

Group planning techniques are successful if the administrator is skillful in handling the type of session. He should announce at the onset of each meeting that all ideas should be presented. He should take care not to dampen enthusiasm by being negative toward an idea. If the suggestion is a bad one, frequently another member of the group besides the administrator will detect the problem and will point it out.

Group planning is one method of motivation, a technique of management that I will discuss in more detail later in this chapter. At this point in the discussion, however, it should be understood that if the individuals who are expected to oversee or carry out the details of the plan are actually involved in its development, they will feel that the plan is *their* plan. They will be committed to its success. They will respond, then, to their roles in the plan much better than if the plan is formulated by the administrator alone.

The submanager's ideas are essential to the administrator's formulation of a plan involving the submanager's particular area. For example, if the administrator wishes to develop a plan for cleaning certain sections of the building at night, he will have much more success if he discusses this with his housekeeping supervisor *before* he formulates the plan. The same motivational force applies individually as it does with the group. The housekeeping supervisor will feel more committed to the success of the plan if it is *their* plan, not the administrator's plan. If they jointly develop the plan, the administrator also utilizes the supervisor's expertise in house-keeping. As administrator, he is an expert in management, not in housekeeping.

Committee approach to planning

Frequently, planning requires much detailed study and research. When this is necessary, the administrator may wish to appoint a committee to search out and review these details. When this is done, it is quite important that the purpose of the committee be fully explained. The administrator should appoint a chairman who he feels will keep the committee's attention on the subject matter and will not allow them to drift into other areas. It is wise to set a deadline for the completion of the committee's work. The administrator should make it clear to the committee members that he is retaining the right to accept and implement their findings, to modify them, or to reject them.

Planning for problems

A fire and disaster plan is an example of planning for problems. Every facility, regardless of the level of care, must anticipate the possibility of a fire or some other disaster. A written fire plan must be developed. This plan outlines the specific duties that must be done by the employees to save the residents and summon the fire department. A plan of building evacuation is also necessary in anticipation of any disaster to the structure or an expected danger to the residents such as a nuclear attack. Fire and disaster plans are examined in detail in Chapter 4.

Plans or procedures for other anticipated problems should be drawn up also. For example, a facility without an emergency electrical power generator should have a written plan to cover the possibility of a power failure. Proper preplanning will foreshow the need for battery-powered emergency lights mounted in stairwells and corridors. Employees should have written directions of steps that should be carried out if this occurs.

Planning for change

The long-term care field is changing. Government spending has focused the attention of legislators on the field. Standards are being raised. Owners of obsolete facilities are being forced to remodel them, change them to a lower level of care, or close them.

There are more old people today than at any other time in the history of our country. There are more older old people too. Therefore, more residential retirement facilities are needed. More personal care and nursing care beds are needed for the older old people. Population statistics point to a continuing increase in these needs for years to come.

Large communities are changing their makeup. The urban centers of many cities are losing their more affluent citizens, who are moving to the suburbs. The residential retirement center in the "downtown" area, which just a few years ago may have been an exclusive section, may now be surrounded by vacant buildings. The streets may no longer be safe to walk on at night or perhaps even in the daylight.

These and many other factors make long-range planning for the expected needs of the facility necessary in order to preserve its future.

ORGANIZING FUNCTION OF MANAGEMENT

Organizations have three basic features. First, the organization has goals and objectives. It exists for certain purposes. Second, the organization has people—

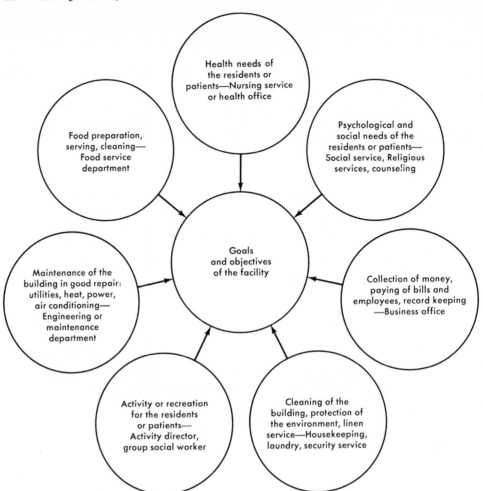

Fig. 10. Work-producing centers of the facility.

managers, supervisors, and workers—who are present to produce the work to accomplish their goals. Third, there is a structure, either formal or informal, that is necessary to indicate the working relationships that exist among the people.[6]

The function of organizing is *grouping* these people into certain *work-producing centers* in order to better accomplish the organization's goals. Each work-producing center has its own goals and objectives. All of the people in a specific work-producing center do the same general work. Subworking centers are developed when the work efforts can be shown to be generally the same but specifically different.

This grouping into work-producing centers is called *organizing*. The producing center itself, in the health care field, is usually referred to as a *department*. Even in the smallest facility, grouping into work-producing centers exists. Although they may not be considered departments in the sense of having separate managers— the administrator himself acts as the center's supervisor—they are still separate in that they do different things. Thus the maids form one work-producing center, the kitchen personnel another, the office staff a third, and so forth. In simple form it can be expressed graphically as in Fig. 10.

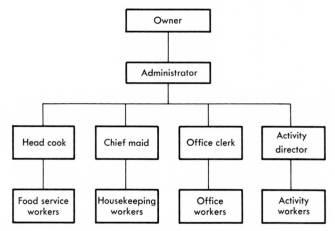

Fig. 11. Line supervision illustrated by a simple organizational chart of a small home providing no health care.

Major work-producing centers of a long-term care facility and their coordination by the administrator

The diagram in Fig. 10 illustrates that each center has its own goals and objectives but is directed toward achieving the facility's goals and objectives. The administrator acts to integrate these individual directions toward the central direction. Without this integration of work effort, each work-producing center would attempt to meet its objectives without regard for the needs of the other centers. Chaos would result. The food preparation group, for example, without this integration, could consider its function so important to the success of the organization that the need for cooperation with the group that is responsible for cleaning the building is not considered. Feuding between the two groups would result in production of inferior service by both groups. The administrator, therefore, must see that all work-producing centers work together in cooperation with each other in striving for the central goal.

When a new administrator comes to an existing facility, much of this organizing function may have already been accomplished. However, organizing is not static. It must be reviewed and changed as the facility or its needs change. Also as sub-managers grow in their jobs, more responsibility can be given them, thus changing the organizational structure. When a strong manager leaves a facility, it may be necessary to change the structure until the new manager learns his job.

The larger the facility becomes, the more complex the organizational structure becomes. The same is true with levels of care. The organizational structure of a 100-bed extended care facility is highly complex compared with that of a 100-room retirement hotel. Regardless of the size and the level of care, though, there is the need for this organizing function.

Organizational chart

As work-producing centers are identified and grouped with similar centers, it is possible to show on an *organizational chart* how each center is a part of the total organization. The chart will show the flow of authority and responsibility from the facility owner, through the administrator, to the leader, manager, or department head of the specific work-producing center or department. It shows the relationship of one department to another and the relationship of both to the administrator.

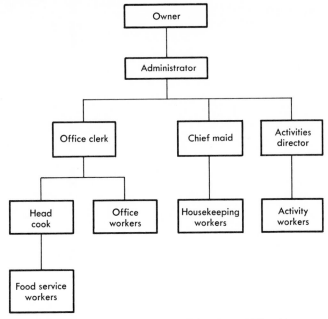

Fig. 12. Administrative modification of Fig. 11.

A major benefit from the use of an organizational chart is that the people in the organization can visualize how they individually fit into the total structure. They can see the channel of authority. There are two generally accepted types of positions in organizational charts: the *line position* and the *staff position*. In this concept authority flows down a line from the top to the bottom of the organization. Each *line supervisor* directly controls the personnel below him. This is shown graphically in Fig. 11 for a simple retirement complex without health care. The lines in the graph show the flow of authority. The graph points out that the head cook is responsible to the administrator for the results of the dietary section. In this example, the office clerk has no authority over the head cook. If the administrator wanted the office clerk to supervise the head cook, the flow of authority could be shown graphically as in Fig. 12. In this example, the administrator has organized the facility differently and, for certain reasons, has placed the office clerk as supervisor of the dietary function.

The person in the *staff position* does not exercise authority over other members of the organization except his own section personnel. The person in the staff position is an *adviser* set up to assist the administrator and the several line supervisors. In the long-term care facility, examples of staff positions are departmental consultants in food service, physical therapy, medical records, pharmacy, and social service; an advisory physician; perhaps a personnel director; an accountant or auditor; and an attorney. The staff position is shown on the organizational chart in Fig. 13 by a broken line. This broken line indicates advisory capacity and not authority. In this particular illustration a consulting dietitian has been employed to advise the administrator and the head cook on dietary departmental affairs. The consultant has no authority over the head cook, and the head cook reports to the administrator for direction of the department. The head cook may use the suggestions made by the consultant. He may also disregard them unless ordered by the administrator to follow them.

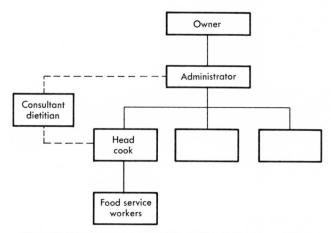

Fig. 13. Line supervision with staff (advisory) position.

Span of control

It is obvious that in organizing a work-producing center, a leader or manager must be appointed. This leader has the responsibility for all the activities in this center. The personnel in this center come to him for direction in their work. If the section is large, the supervisor will have many people to direct. If the work activities are routine, repetitive, and closely related, the supervisor can handle a large number of people. As an example, in a manufacturing plant a foreman might successfully supervise 20, 50, 100, or more people doing assembly work. This is not usually the situation, however, in the long-term care field. Direction of activities of the workers is more complex, since their work is with people, not things. A single supervisor in a long-term care facility can successfully direct only a limited number of people. The optimum number of people ranges from 5 to 15. The number of workers supervised by one manager is called the *span of control*.

Delegation of authority and the obligation of responsibility

Managing is getting things done through other people. In order to give the "other people" the opportunity to "get things done," the administrator *delegates* or passes down part of the *authority* given him by the owner. Authority is the right of one person to require a subordinate to do certain activities.[7] In accepting authority from the owner, the administrator also accepts the *responsibility* for his and his subordinates' administrative actions. However, when the owner delegates authority below to the administrator, the owner cannot delegate his responsibility. Both the owner and the administrator are responsible for the acts of the administrator. Responsibility for delegated authority means *accountability* for the results of actions stemming from the use of this authority.

It follows, then, that one cannot be legitimately held responsible for performance without having authority to control. The administrator, therefore, must give sufficient authority to his department heads or supervisors so that he can hold them responsible. The more authority the administrator can delegate, the more decisions the department heads may make without coming back to the administrator. Thus more efficiency is developed and the organization moves ahead.

In larger long-term care facilities, several levels of authority may exist. The administrator may delegate wide areas of authority to his assistant administrator.

To his director of nurses also he may delegate wide latitude of authority in the nursing area, but this authority will not be as broad as that given his assistant. The director of nursing, in turn, delegates specific and narrower areas of authority to the nurses in his charge, and so on.

The organization chart can show this delegation of authority quite clearly. People can see the areas for which they are responsible and can see the source of this authority.

When authority is delegated to a department head by the administrator and so on down the line, the one who delegates should not interfere without grave reasons in the decisions of the person given the authority. If the administrator is displeased with a department head's actions, he should approach him in private conference. If the administrator openly interferes, he is seriously diluting the effectiveness of the department head for future direction of his department.

The policy and procedure manual is a very effective way of delegating authority to subordinates. The manager can point out these written plans for action to his subordinates. They can be told that they may act within these policies without returning for further direction. However, the manager also points out that when circumstances develop that are not covered by the policies, the subordinate should return for advice. Through the use of the policy and procedure manual, therefore, the manager can delegate authority to his subordinates to make decisions within these boundaries and yet can still retain control.

DIRECTING FUNCTION OF MANAGEMENT

The *leadership* function of the manager is the process of getting people to perform the activities desired in a manner that will accomplish the goals of the organization. Leadership implies communication and motivation. The leader must be convinced of the integrity of the objectives and goals of the organization. He must have a flexible personality and the ability to utilize a variety of leadership styles. The latter is particularly true for the administrator of a long-term care facility, who must be a leader not only of his employees, but also of his residents, their families, and the various "outside" people, such as physicians, consultants, inspectors, and the general public.

I will begin the discussion of the direction function of management by considering the three leadership styles the administrator might employ. It should be emphasized that usually the successful leader will utilize more than one of these approaches. Seldom does an administrator use only one style exclusively in all his contacts.

Leadership styles

Most authorities agree that there are at least three individual leadership styles used by managers. They may be described as autocratic or leader centered, democratic or group centered, and free rein.[8]

There is disagreement between the traditionalist and the modernist schools of management theories as to the style the successful leader should employ most of the time. In the long-term care facility, an administrator will find all three styles helpful in varying situations, depending on the strengths and weaknesses of his department heads or the particular problem at hand.

Autocratic or leader-centered style. In the autocratic, or leader-centered, style the administrator retains strong control of every aspect of the situation. Decisions are made only by him. Subordinates are required to seek him out to review each problem and get his direction. The subordinate's dependency on the administrator is quite apparent in their relationship. McGregor's "Theory X" demands the autocratic concept of direction.[9] Theory X implies that employees have an inherent dislike of work; must be coerced, directed, and threatened to put forward an adequate work effort; and wish to avoid responsibility, preferring to be directed.

Autocratic leadership, although usually negative, has its place in the administrator's overall technique of direction. There are certain functions the administrator may wish to control closely. In many homes, admissions of residents or patients may be one aspect of the home management that the administrator will personally oversee. The administrator may prefer to employ autocratic directions when introducing a new policy and procedure. He may, in this instance, monitor all phases of the new idea until he is satisfied it is workable.

In the very small home, there may not be sufficient submanagement or supervisory talent available for the administrator to feel free with any style except the autocratic approach in most instances.

Democratic or group-centered style. When the administrator exercises the democratic, or group-centered, style of leadership, he asks for participation by his department heads in making decisions about their sections. He seeks out their ideas and listens to their suggestions. He freely delegates authority and gives the department heads more freedom in running their sections. When changes are necessary, he discusses them with the subordinate and is prepared to use the subordinate's idea on occasion if it is better than his own.[10]

The administrator keeps his department heads fully informed of the home's activities. Projects are mutually discussed and plans are made jointly. He reviews their departmental activities regularly with them, discussing their reports and giving them information such as the actual expenses versus budgeted expenses. He holds them responsible for keeping him informed of their problems, but he expects them to handle the routine matters alone.

Frequently, a regular staff conference attended by the department and section heads is led by the administrator. The administrator uses this for making announcements and receiving informal verbal reports from the department heads. The thrust is to keep all heads informed of each other's efforts and goals. This meeting, however, is more for giving information than for solving problems, unless a specific problem affecting all the departments is broached.

For problem solving, the administrator using the group-centered approach will often work jointly with the two or three department heads together in a special meeting. He will attempt to have the department heads solve the problem themselves, while acting as a moderator giving only final approval to the joint decisions or presenting an occasional suggestion.

This leadership style is most effective in developing submanagers who are productive and creative, according to those who support this modern view of direction.[8] McGregor's "Theory Y" supports this premise. Theory Y is that work is as natural as play and that if a man is committed to an objective or goal, he will exercise self-direction and self-control in his activities to achieve that goal. Theory Y also states that under the proper conditions (group-centered leadership, for example), the average man will seek and accept responsibility and is capable of exercising imagination and problem-solving techniques with ingenuity and creativity.[9] The commitment to objectives that McGregor mentions is one of the keys to the truth of this theory. If a department head has played a major role in the formulation of a plan of action, he is more likely to be committed to its success. He will be committed because it is *his* plan of action. I will discuss why this can be a successful practice in the section on motivation as a practice of direction.

Free-rein style. In large health care organizations such as a university-based teaching hospital, the free-rein style of leadership is quite successfully practiced by the administrator. It is not frequently seen as the major style in the long-term care field, however. Although there is central leadership given by the administrator using this style, in which he allows most of the department heads a great deal of freedom to operate their departments, he requires them to stay within the broad general policies established for their sections and to maintain their operations within financial budgetary limits. But the departmental operational decisions are in the hands of the department heads. They sink or swim on the results of their decisions. Weak department heads are weeded out and are replaced. The strong leaders survive and pattern their departmental operations according to what they believe best serves the facility.

In directing this facility, the administrator thinks of himself as a coordinator or coach. He recognizes that the nurse, physician, scientist, engineer, dietitian, and housekeeper have a greater technical knowledge of their field than he does. He allows them to practice their art with little influence, on the assumption that they are better qualified to make departmental decisions. He integrates their efforts toward the facility's goals. He interferes only when they act contrary to the broad policies he has established.

Although an administrator will likely lean toward one of the basic style, usually he blends them together. He may use an autocratic approach for certain matters and a democratic approach for others. He may also use the free-rein method if he has a strong department head who needs incentive for development. Which technique he uses is not as important as how and when he employs the specific style best suited.

Motivation and leadership

In recent years motivation as a science of management direction has become widely accepted. Early studies conducted by Whitehead and his associates at the Harvard Graduate School of Business Administration proved it possible to enhance the productivity of workers when they are given a feeling of being important. These studies, conducted first in 1923 and then in subsequent years, were made at the Hawthorne plant of the Western Electric Company. They are popularly known as the Hawthorne experiments.[10] These studies opened an entirely new approach to management, the so-called human relation management. Employees' attitudes toward their jobs and their supervisor and the supervisor's attitude toward the employees became recognized as important factors in the success of the organization. The concept of human motivation was discovered as a necessary leadership technique.

Attitude motivation is considered to be the most positive and longest-lasting form. The attitude motivational approach implies *changing* the employee's attitude. In applying this method of motivation, one must discard the traditional theory that man is inherently lazy, shuns responsibility, and must be given ever increasing financial rewards in order to do his day's work.

Cohen of the University of Chicago has written a paper entitled "Getting the Staff to Pull Together (in the Same Direction)." In his paper, Cohen stresses that the home administrator must concern himself with his attitude toward his staff. He points out that personnel perceive quite quickly whether or not they have the administrator's trust. If he holds negative concepts of them (Theory X), they will react negatively toward him and, consequently, toward the ultimate goals he establishes for the home.[11]

If, on the other hand, the administrator approaches his personnel with a positive attitude, teaching and training them; giving them trust, authority, and responsibility; and upholding them when they receive unjust criticism, he will stand a much better chance of motivating them to pull together to accomplish the home's goals. Cohen suggests that the administrator can best express this attitude by getting his staff members involved actively and meaningfully in the pursuance of the home's goals. He should invite them to express their ideas about the development of methods of carrying out these objectives. Moreover, Cohen points out, the administrator should show sincere concern about the needs of the staff members for adequate wages, benefits, and a good, safe working environment. He should also demonstrate that the home cares about them. Proper attitude motivation develops teamwork and creates a high staff morale. If the staff members are considered important by the home's administrator, they will respond by being important and acting with greater responsibility.[11]

CONTROLLING FUNCTION OF MANAGEMENT

Controlling is that function of management that involves looking back. Just as planning involves looking ahead to forecast, controlling involves auditing the results and altering the course when necessary. In applying this function, the manager can utilize many controls, some of which are the financial summaries, statistical summaries, verbal and written reports, and personal interviews and inspections made by the administrator. The administrator can determine through these methods whether or not what has occurred is what was planned.

Because of their importance to the financial and quality-of-care standards of the home, controls must be *timely*. To learn at the end of a year that the home is losing $1.80 a patient-day because of inadequate charges or runaway expenses, could prove to be too late to keep the home from bankruptcy. With timely monthly or quarterly financial and statistical statements, however, the administrator could learn about the problem quickly enough to make corrections.

Controls must also be *accurate*. Incorrect information used for the basis of decisions or changes also can prove to be disastrous. In establishing a statistical report for the meal count, for example, the administrator and the food manager should agree on statistical terms, units of measure, methods of counting, and an acceptable reporting mechanism. This report is quite essential to the development of a meal cost figure that can be a guide to the administrator as he reviews his job costs. Meals not counted would distort the cost figure. Snacks and nourishments counted as meals would pull the cost picture below the actual cost.

Controls must be *consistent*. For comparing statistical or financial data reports with previous reports, the same unit and methods of measurement must be used. For example, the guest meals should not be counted one month and omitted from the count the next month. If the way facts are gathered is not consistent, the report, too, will be distorted.

Controls must be *worth their cost*. Financial controls are expensive, of course. The cost of the recording function and the cost of the auditing function must be considered. But the expense is justified by the necessity of having complete, accurate, and timely financial information. A control, however, should be considered in the light of its cost. Stationing a man at the door of your home to count the daily visitor traffic would provide you with an interesting report but would hardly be worth its cost. Controls should be considered in regard to their cost compared with their value. Overburdening an office clerk by requiring him to take a daily count of the supplies to the point that he cannot do his regular work, is another example of a costly control. By the utilization of a perpetual inventory control system, the office clerk can do his inventory on supply day and accomplish the same result with much more efficiency.

Controls must be *meaningful*. At a certain point it might be quite important for the administrator to know certain facts about his home regularly each month. All too often over the years these facts become less important, but the data requested by the administrator keeps coming regularly, accumulating in his files. When a report is no longer of consequence, it should be discontinued.

Some examples of controls and their uses follow.

THE BEST NURSING HOME, INC.

Revenue and expense statement for the month ending January 19____

Income

Room, board, and nursing care $_____

Medical supplies   _____

Stock medications   _____

Oxygen therapy   _____

Physical therapy   _____

Personal laundry   _____

Beauty shop   _____

Guest meal charges   _____

Special services   _____

Total income $_____

Expenses
Nursing

Payroll $_____

Supplies   _____

Other   _____

Subtotal $_____

Dietary

Payroll   _____

Food   _____

Supplies   _____

Subtotal   _____

Housekeeping

Payroll   _____

Supplies   _____

Other   _____

Subtotal   _____

THE BEST NURSING HOME, INC.

Expenses—cont'd

Maintenance

Payroll _____

Supplies _____

Utilities _____

Other _____

Subtotal _____

Activities

Payroll _____

Supplies _____

Other _____

Subtotal _____

Linen service

Payroll _____

Supplies _____

Other _____

Subtotal _____

Administration

Payroll _____

Supplies _____

Other _____

Subtotal _____

Nonoperating expenses

Debt service _____

Depreciation _____

Property taxes _____

Other _____

Subtotal _____

Total expenses $_____

Net income before taxes $_____

Income and expense statement

Ideally, this should be prepared monthly, as soon after the end of the month as possible. This report, as its title suggests, shows the administrator the profit or loss picture for the period reported. By showing income and expense in categories (*accounts*), the report defines the financial activity of the home by separate classifications. See the form on pp. 30 and 31.

This report shows, in a very general way, the income in relation to expenses. The report needs to be more detailed, however, to be of full benefit to the home owner and the administrator. The generalized report should be accompanied by a detailed examination of activity for the time period in each category, an example of which is shown below.

	Actual	Budgeted
Expenses for January 19____		
660 Administration		
01 Payroll	$_____	$_____
02 Contract labor	_____	_____
03 Fees, legal	_____	_____
04 Fees, accounting	_____	_____
05 Fees, other	_____	_____
06 Office supplies	_____	_____
07 Postage	_____	_____
08 Printing and forms	_____	_____
09 Promotional activities	_____	_____
10 Telephone service	_____	_____
11 License and registration fees	_____	_____
12 Association dues and assessments	_____	_____
13 Education and training fees	_____	_____
14 Insurance expense	_____	_____
15 Travel expense	_____	_____
16 Special consultants' fees	_____	_____
17 Payroll expense (administration)	_____	_____
18 Employee benefits (administration)	_____	_____
19 Miscellaneous expenses	_____	_____
Total administration	_____	_____

The general accounting area is identified by the account code 660 Administration. Each account has a separate page in the *general ledger* with a subaccount number; thus the ledger sheet for the administrative payroll would be headed 660-01 Payroll.

The report shown on p. 32 details the expenses of the home by departmental accounts and compares these expenses with the amounts budgeted for that period. Income is likewise reported by categories and is compared with the budgeted or estimated income.

It is obvious that this report would give the administrator the essential information to see whether or not his budget (plan) is on course. The report might show that his office supplies account is out of line for the period and for the year to date. This could result from a one-time volume purchase of supplies that will last several months, or it could result from uncontrolled use and purchasing of supplies. The administrator should use this as a signal of something that is out of the ordinary and thus investigate the reason.

Budgeted hours and payroll report

When the financial budget is prepared, each individual position should be charted; detailed information should be recorded in order to arrive at the personnel cost for the year. An example of a form for collecting these essential data is shown on p. 34.

One of the facts reported on this form is the annual budgeted hours figure for each department. These data can be used as a control to see that the actual number of hours worked by the personnel of the section or departmental unit is what was expected. Without this control and its proper application, poor supervisory scheduling of staff can soon erode any financial budget. For example, a part-time employee for whom three days of work a week are budgeted could, because of filling in during holidays, vacations, or sickness of other employees, be legitimately called in to work more than the budgeted three days. As long as the total number of departmental budgeted hours remains the same, there is no problem. Sometimes, because of inefficient scheduling, however, a supervisor may schedule more employees for a shift than is necessary. This type of error can be detected by this control method. The problem of unnecessary overtime also can be pinpointed with this type of control.

To prepare a control form, the administrator takes his budgeted hours by department and divides the total by the number of pay periods. Thus, if an annual total of 26,000 hours is budgeted for his housekeeping department employees, he would divide 26,000 by the number of pay periods. To make this illustration simple, let us assume that the home pays every other Friday, or 26 times a year. For each pay period the housekeeping department personnel should be paid for 1,000 hours of work. If the budgeted hours report indicated that the total number of hours paid was 1,075, the administrator would have some investigating to do.

This same control can also incorporate financial data to document similar statistics on the financial aspect of the payroll for the same period. The report can show the gross amount paid compared with the budgeted amount. One advantage of the budgeted hours payroll report is *time*. This report is prepared immediately on completion of the payroll. The administrator can respond at once to discovered problems without waiting for the monthly or quarterly income and expense reports.

Daily, weekly, or monthly report

The daily, weekly, or monthly report is a collection of statistical and other data on the activities of the home for the period covered. The report could be designed

PAYROLL REPORT

Biweekly pay period ending_____

Department	Hours budgeted/actual	Gross pay budgeted/actual	Hours Benefits/overtime			Comments
Nursing	___ ___	$___ $___	V___	H___	S___ OT___	
Nursing relief	___ ___	(Included above)				Balance available ___
Transportation	___ ___	___ ___	V___	H___	S___ OT___	
Dietary	___ ___	___ ___	V___	H___	S___ OT___	
Housekeeping	___ ___	___ ___	V___	H___	S___ OT___	
Maintenance	___ ___	___ ___	V___	H___	S___ OT___	
Administration	___ ___	___ ___	V___	H___	S___ OT___	
Switchboard	___ ___	___ ___	V___	H___	S___ OT___	
Switchboard relief	___ ___	(Included above)				Balance available ___
Gift shop	___ ___	___ ___				
Totals	___ ___	$___ $___	V___	H___	S___ OT___	___Total benefit hours
						___Total overtime hours

to compare the data with that of the same period of the previous year. The report could document such facts as the total number of beds or rooms occupied as of a given hour or date, the percentage of capacity this occupancy represents, the occupancy and percentages of occupancy of the various levels of care, and the number of admissions and discharges for the period. The report also could include the names and addresses of the new patients admitted and the names and disposition of the patients discharged or transferred.

The value of this report is that it graphically displays the patients' or residents' movements for the period and the actual percentage of occupancy for the home. The report also supplies the administrator with information about the patients' or residents' needs for special care by levels. The home addresses of the patients admitted can supply the home with important geographic statistics indicating the home's drawing area. The historical significance of the data can provide a basis for planning for future needs. Comparing current data with that compiled for the same period of the previous year can also be useful to gauge the current activity.

Other reports

Other statistical information that can be collected for a specific period and compared with data for the same period of the previous year might be *resident- or patient-days, meal count, total cost per meal* (frequently recorded as cost per day), *raw food cost per meal* (frequently recorded as cost per day), *housekeeping costs by square foot of building, linen costs by patient-days,* and *nursing-hours-to-patient ratio.*

An administrator should make sure that a statistical control is begun for any area he believes needs monitoring. When the control is no longer necessary, he should cancel it, however.

Inspections as a controlling mechanism

The administrator can also use the technique of inspection as a control feature. He should frequently leave his office and tour the facility. He should look at the remote areas of the building periodically to see if fire and safety standards are being practiced. During these tours he should watch for hazards and for deterioration of the building and the equipment. He should also use this time to talk with and *listen* to the patients and residents of the home. He should open closed doors and look into cabinets, refrigerators, and storage drawers. He should read the medical records of patients in the nursing section and examine subsidiary records such as medication or drug logs. He should inspect the power plant to look at the maintenance logs and to verify such things as temperatures of the domestic hot water and the boiler pressure. He should drop in to the kitchen to watch the food preparation and the cleaning techniques and to check the temperatures of the dishwashing machine.

•   •   •

The controlling function can vary according to the directing style the manager employs. Although the controls described in this section are the ones most managers of health care facilities would rely on heavily, a manager using the autocratic style of direction might insist on more rigid controls.

STAFFING FUNCTION OF MANAGEMENT

The staffing function of management refers to the methods of dealing with the personnel of the facility. This function involves, minimally, personnel administration, training of staff, and wage administration.

Personnel administration

Although most long-term homes cannot afford a personnel manager, most of the functions this person carries out in larger facilities and in industry must be done in every facility. Personnel administration covers such functions as recruitment, selection of workers, hiring and discharging of workers, development of job descriptions, counseling, retiring of employees, and record keeping.

Since the personnel costs represent the major expenditure in most facilities, recruitment and selection of workers are very important.

Also, each employee represents the image of the facility to the patients, the relatives, and the public. This makes choosing the right people for employees essential to success.

In interviewing prospective employees, one should keep in mind that it takes patience and empathy to work with older people, especially those who are no longer able to care for their normal body functions. Not everyone is suited for this field. Questions such as Why do you wish to work with older people? or Why do you think patients (residents) come to live here? might help to open up a frank discussion with the applicant.

Employment application. The employment application form should be completed by the applicant prior to the interview. It is used as a tool by the interviewer to stimulate questions. After the interview, the interviewer should make an informal note of his impressions of the applicant and attach it to the form. This may prove to be helpful to someone going through the files later to find a suitable replacement.

The application should include places for listing previous work experience and names of personal references. Before the employee is hired, written verification of employment history and comments on the applicant's character should be obtained from these work and personal references. It is absolutely necessary that this be done. The administrator has a duty to see that his personnel are properly qualified and of good character. Furthermore, in the case of licensed personnel, such as nurses, technicians, therapists, dietitians, social workers, pharmacists, and physicians, there is a greater duty to verify the qualifications, registrations, licenses, and past history. The administrator must be certain that the applicant is who he says he is.

The employment application is one of the basic documents in the individual's personnel file. This form is prepared before the employee is accepted, but it becomes a permanent record when the individual is hired. Each facility will want to design an application best suited to its needs, but several essential facts must be found in every application.

Identifying information comes first. Name, address, former address, telephone number, marital status, name of spouse, person to notify in case of emergency, date of birth, and Social Security number are the minimal requirements.

The next section should be devoted to *general information* such as position applied for, salary expected, shift desired or availability for all shifts, desire for full-time or part-time work, dependents living at home, and other special responsibilities.

The next major area should be *education and certification*. License or registry data, including license numbers, special training courses, refresher courses, and the like, should be requested also. The application should call for full addresses of schools and licensing or certifying agencies so that the data can be verified.

Space should be provided on the application for the recording of *social reference data:* names and addresses of personal references should be requested. Some facilities believe that credit references also are essential.

A separate section of the application should be provided for the applicant's *work history.* Depending on the position applied for, the facility may desire to check the applicant's work history for several years back or to request his entire past work history. At least the last five years of the employee's work history should be recorded and verified. With the applications of professional licensed personnel, such as nurses, therapists, and dietitians, who will hold the more responsible positions, the facility administrator has a duty to be more cautious. He should request a full work history and verify it along with all other given data.

It is a good idea to include a statement on the last part of the application as shown below.

With this application, I herewith request the Best Nursing Home, Inc., to consider me for

the position of _____. I submit the above information with

the belief that it is true and correct to the best of my knowledge and I authorize the administrator or his representatives of Best Nursing Home, Inc., to verify this information in any way deemed necessary.

_____	_____
Date	Signature of applicant

Reference checks. These may be made over the telephone to expedite the process, but they must be followed up in writing. In the case of licensed personnel, a letter must be sent to the registering agency, and the verifying answer must be placed in the employee's file.

A form letter can be used for prior work verification, as is illustrated on p. 38.

Interviewing and hiring. During the interview with the prospective employee, if it becomes apparent to the interviewer that the applicant is suitable for the position and, pending a satisfactory reference check, he expects to hire him, he should thoroughly discuss the job with the applicant. He should review the job description in detail. They should visit the work site, and introductions should be made. The interviewer should point out the negative factors (if any) of the job. He should also explain the personnel policies and give the applicant every opportunity to understand the benefits and requirements covered in the policies. The applicant should be given a copy of the policies to keep. The interviewer should mention the wage range for the job. It is wise to tell the employee at this point how the wage system works so that he knows what to expect in the future.

In the smaller home interviewing and hiring probably will be done primarily by the administrator. In accordance with the philosophy of delegating authority, however, whoever would supervise the employee actually should perform this function. Even in the smaller home, for example, the head cook or whoever is the leader of the food production phase should do the hiring of the kitchen helper. Of course, the administrator should be involved. He may interview this person too. However, if he is comfortable with his knowledge of the head cook's supervisory ability, he will probably delegate the final decision to him. In the larger home, the administrator may speak only briefly with the new employee when the deparment head brings him into his office to introduce him after hiring him. In this case, there would be an established procedure for the administrator's office staff to handle the checking of the references.

Personnel files. The individual's file should be begun at the onset of his employment. Initially it will contain his application and his reference verifications. Later this individual file will grow as other records are acquired, such as copies of

BEST NURSING HOME, INC.

ANYTOWN, U. S. A.

To: (Name of company)

Address   _____

Date

_____, nee _____

Name of applicant   Maiden name, if any

whose Social Security number is _____ has made application for the position

of _____ at the Best Nursing Home. Your agency's name was given

as a former employer. Dates of your employment were given as from _____ 19 ____

to _____ 19___. The reason for leaving your employment was given as:

_____

Would you kindly complete the following statements in regard to the applicant's ability
and personal qualification so that we might make a fair evaluation of the applicant's
qualification toward our requirement. Your reply will be kept in strict confidence.

Thank you for your cooperation.

Sincerely yours,

_____

Position _____, Salary _____, Employment dates _____

From

_____, Reason for leaving_____.

To

Technical competence _____, Dependability _____.

Initiative _____, Cooperation _____, Attendance record _____.

Punctuality _____, Personal appearance _____, Honesty _____.

Character _____, Personality _____.

Health _____, Physical handicap _____.

Financial obligations: Credit complaints _____, Wage assignments _____.

Would you reemploy? _____, If not, why not? _____, Other remarks _____

_____

_____   _____   _____

Date   Signature   Title

EMPLOYEE PERFORMANCE APPRAISAL

Name _____

Date _____ Evaluated by _____

Attitude toward job:

    Works in a highly responsible manner.

    Usually is conscientious toward responsibility.

    Has careless approach to duties.

    Seldom seems interested in work assigned.

Relationship with staff and residents:

    Is cheerful and friendly at all times.

    Is usually polite and usually cheerful.

    Occasionally seems to appear uncooperative.

    Presents a negative attitude toward staff and residents.

Appearance:

    Always is well groomed and has fresh uniform.

    Usually has good appearance.

    Frequently reports for duty in less than best appearance.

    Seldom has adequate appearance.

Punctuality:

    Is always on time.

    Occasionally is late for duty.

    Frequently is late.

    Is almost always late.

Work stability:

    Absences are infrequent and for justified reasons.

    Absences are regular and/or for unexplained or unjustified reasons.

Work ability:

    Excellent performance of assigned task.

    Better than average performance.

    Below average performance.

    Unsatisfactory performance.

Comments: _____

_____

_____

Recommendation for merit increase:

    Approved.

    Hold for now; review in _____ days.

    Disapproved.

_____

                                 Supervisor

I have read this performance appraisal and have had my supervisor explain its effect on my work record.

_____

                                 Employee

correspondence, memoranda of promotions, records of disciplinary actions, records of accidents, and rating sheets.

Employee rating sheets. These are used by many homes for recording the positive and negative aspects of the employee's working ability and attitude. These are usually written at the time the employee is being considered for a merit increase in salary. The employee's supervisor, using this form, grades the employee in several specific categories. The employee is then shown the sheet by the supervisor, who discusses it with him. The purpose of the form is to help the employee grow in his job. A negative use of the form is to document dissatisfaction over work effort that may not at the time be sufficient grounds for discharge. By documenting this dissatisfaction, a supervisor is better able to defend himself if challenged subsequently for discharging an employee at a later date for further problems. The supervisor thus can prove that the employee was given sufficient warning and counseling. An example of this form, called an employee performance appraisal, is shown on p. 39.

Discharging an employee. This is always an unpleasant task. It involves emotional conflicts between at least two people. Since it is disturbing, sometimes a weak supervisor will put up with a problem employee long past the time he should have been fired. The administrator should be alert to this possibility.

Discharges should always be done with *cause*, and the employee should be informed of the reason. Frequently, the personnel policies will specify a working test period of several weeks during which the employee is on trial. If he fails to meet the supervisor's expectations after reasonable attempts to train him, he can be discharged for failure to meet the expected standards of the job. After the working test period has been completed, more concrete grounds should be required for discharge. These grounds should be spelled out in the personnel policies and should include insubordination, excessive absence, drinking or using drugs on duty, theft, abuse of a patient or fellow employee, and misuse of the home's property or facilities.

Job description. The job description is a phase of personnel administration. It is a record of the details and qualifications of each type of job in the facility. It is commonly divided into sections such as job title; job summary; job description, purpose of job, or performance requirements; job specifications or qualifications; degree of physical difficulty; and pay range. Following is an example of a job description:

JOB DESCRIPTION OF MAID

Title: Maid.

Job summary: Under the direct supervision of the housekeeper, cleans, dusts, vacuum-cleans, polishes, and sanitizes areas assigned. Empties trash containers, replaces paper supplies, and does related tasks as assigned.

Daily tasks:

1. Dusts furniture.
2. Vacuum-cleans floors.
3. Empties all trash containers.
4. Polishes mirrors and glass.
5. Cleans bathrooms, including all fixtures.
6. Replaces supplies.
7. Mops tile floors.
8. Sanitizes stools and urinals.
9. Does other related duties as assigned.

10. Reports to the housekeeper all hazardous situations, broken equipment, damaged furniture, and similar unusual items.

Weekly tasks as scheduled by housekeeper:
1. Washes inside of patient room windows.
2. Uses special bowl cleaner on stools.
3. Attends weekly staff meeting.
4. Does other related special tasks as assigned.

Job specifications:
1. Education—minimum of eighth grade.
2. Ability to get along with others.
3. Some previous work experience that evidences good character and stability.
4. Good physical condition. Ability to work on feet with moderately heavy equipment. Able to work with detergents.

Degree of physical difficulty:
1. Works with hot water and strong detergents.
2. Lifts and carries moderately heavy equipment such as vacuum cleaners and pails with water.
3. Is exposed to hazards such as broken glass in trash and chemical irritation.
4. Is frequently exposed to soils of human waste during daily cleaning tasks.

Pay range:
$0.00 to $0.00 an hour over three-year period.

This example is not meant to be all inclusive. Each administrator will develop his own style in creating the job descriptions to suit his needs.

Training of staff

In-service training, the training of staff members while they are on the job, is a requirement of the standards of licensure of nursing homes in many states. This is an ongoing educational program for each section or departmental group of personnel to help them learn more about their job, the patients they serve, the goals of the home, and how the home's staff members work together to meet these goals.

Each departmental section should have its own in-service program. The food service department, for instance, should have a regularly scheduled session once a week in which all its personnel hear a talk on sanitation, see a movie on the subject of food poisoning, learn of a new food product, see the operation of a new piece of equipment, or discuss the importance of temperatures in the serving and preserving of food products.

Occasionally the administrator should have a total staff educational program that is devoted to a topic of interest to the whole. Fire safety is always an excellent group topic. Films on the problems of aged people to help the staff members better understand their roles are usually effective for total staff work.

Wage administration

Using the job description as a starting point, the administrator should develop a *wage range* for the various jobs of the home. Much of the pattern for wage ranges will come from the study of wages paid employees in comparable jobs in other local homes, hospitals, and industries. The federal minimum wage law will be a major consideration, too. If the home employees are represented by a union, this alone may be the determining factor.

Good, fair wage administration is necessary to the success of an agency. The employees must receive an equitable wage in keeping with their value to the organization. Regular *merit increases* should be scheduled for all the staff. This raise should be geared to the employee's meriting it. He should be given it if he is performing his job satisfactorily, and he should be denied it if he is working below his expected quality.

The merit increase should be geared to a formal employee evaluation. When the time comes for the increase, the employee should be evaluated on a special employee rating sheet or evaluation form by his supervisor. This form should indicate how the employee is doing in his work and areas of improvement needed. The supervisor should discuss the evaluation with the employee. If the supervisor is not going to recommend the employee for his pay increase, the employee should be told why and shown where he can improve to merit the increase in the future.

The evaluation sheet should become a part of the employee's record. A typical evaluation sheet is shown on p. 39. It is just one of many excellent forms developed for evaluating employees. Each is subjective, of course, and is not perfect.

Sometimes supervisors fail to be truly honest, not wanting to confront an employee. In this situation, the supervisor may tend to rate the employee higher than he really should be rated.

The last selection in each category is meant to indicate an intolerable situation that will lead to discharge if immediate upgrading is not done by the employee. When an employee is discharged, previous rating sheets can be studied to see if the employee was given an adequate warning and a trial time for improvement. Although the employee may refuse to sign the rating sheet, it is wise to attempt to get his signature to document counseling of situations less than desirable.

NOTES

1. Durbin, Richard L., and Springall, W. Herbert: Organization and administration of health care, St. Louis, 1969, The C. V. Mosby Co.
2. McQuillan, Florence L.: Fundamentals of nursing home administration, Philadelphia, 1967, W. B. Saunders Co.
3. Koontz, Harold, and O'Donnell, Cyril, editors: Management. A book of readings, New York, 1968, McGraw-Hill Book Co.
4. From American Heritage dictionary of the English language. © Copyright 1969, 1970, 1971 by American Heritage Publishing Co., Inc. Reprinted by permission.
5. Lasser, J. K.: Business management handbook, New York, 1968, McGraw-Hill Book Co.
6. Hershey, Robert L.: Organizational planning, Business Topics 10(1):29-40, 1962.
7. Shubin, John A.: Business management, New York, 1957, Barnes & Nobel, Inc.
8. Golembiewski, Robert T.: Three styles of leadership and their uses, Personnel 38(4):34-45, 1961.
9. McGregor, Douglas: The human side of enterprise, New York, 1960, McGraw-Hill Book Co.
10. Heyel, Carl: Changing concepts of human relations. In Management for modern supervisors, New York, 1962, American Management Association.
11. Cohen, Stephen Z.: Getting the staff to pull together (in the same direction). In Directions '70, American Association of Homes for the Aging, Washington, D. C.

Chapter three

THE ORGANIZATION AND ADMINISTRATION OF THE FACILITY

INTEGRATION OF DEPARTMENTAL WORK EFFORTS BY THE ADMINISTRATOR

The success of a long-term care facility depends on many things. The integration of the work efforts of the various departments or work centers toward the goals of the agency is one of the main factors in a successful program. This integration of work efforts is, indeed, a major duty of the administrator. He must blend together the individual goals of the several departments, keeping them in balance so that no one department overshadows the others to the detriment of the total needs of the residents. For example, a strong or forceful leadership in the health services department is necessary; however, if the food service or housekeeping efforts are thwarted by an overpowering health services department head, the total goals of the agency may not be met. It is the administrator's job to help to keep all the departments' efforts in the proper perspective.

DEPARTMENTS OF THE FACILITY

In most long-term care facilities, the departmental services can be grouped into four general service areas: health services, residential services, social services, and administrative services. Depending on the goals of the facility, these four broad service areas vary in degrees of sophistication.

Health services are the departments or functions relating to the medical, nursing, and health needs of the resident. In a skilled nursing home these service areas may include nursing service; pharmacy service; medical consultation, such as advisory committee or advisory physician, and medical director; medical records; physical therapy; x-ray and laboratory service; and other ancillary services.

In a residential center, at the other end of the scale, in which the health services are minimal, this function might include only a health office with a nurse on duty during the day. It might be even more minimal, with the administrative staff assuming the obligation of contacting the resident's physician when the resident is unable to do this himself.

Residential services are necessary in every facility program. They include mechanical maintenance, such as heat, light, and air conditioning power and repairs; housekeeping services; laundry and linen service; grounds maintenance; food service (optional, but preferred); security and fire safety; and transportation (optional). Depending on the goals of the agency, these services are available either by inclusion in the daily or monthly rate or by fee for service or are not available at all.

Social services include social casework and group social work, such as activity programs, religious services, and counseling.

Administrative services include the business office and all its functions, communications such as paging and telephone service, and administrative supervision.

Departmental development—degrees of emphasis

The four service areas are found in almost all long-term care facilities. The sophistication and development of each function is in direct proportion to the goals of the facility. If this thought were diagrammed on a pie-graph, with the administrative service as the binding, the degrees of emphasis could be graphed as shown in Figs. 14 and 15.

In the skilled nursing home, the emphasis is usually fairly evenly divided among the four service areas. Occasionally more emphasis is placed on the health needs than on the other areas in some nursing homes; these are facilities with the goal of providing nursing care with medical supervision to patients who may be recovering from serious illness or injury after the acute phase is treated in the hospital, or to patients who have deteriorated physically to the stage at which professional nursing care is required.

At the other end of the scale in the long-term care field is the facility providing shelter care or residential care with the greatest development of the social, recreational, and religious service and/or counseling services. The health care service may be minimal or not even present. It is almost always a preventive or emergency service when present. The goal of the residential or shelter care facility is usually the development of services to meet the psychological, social, and religious needs of the older person: activity programs are well organized; social casework is usually available; and religious counseling and services are often on hand for those who

Fig. 14. Services of skilled nursing home. (Courtesy Neil L. Gaynes, Neil L. Gaynes and Associates, Chicago, Ill.)

want them. The residents in this type of care facility are generally well aged people.

In the remainder of this chapter and in subsequent chapters, I will discuss these four areas by departments, sections, and functions. Few facilities have *each* department developed to the extent discussed in this book. Every facility, however, has many of the departments or functions as necessary and integral parts of the organization.

ADMINISTRATIVE SERVICES
Business office

Functions of office manager. The business office manager's job description will depend on assigned duties. Following is one example:

JOB DESCRIPTION OF BUSINESS OFFICE MANAGER

Title:	Business office manager.
Hours:	8:00 A.M. to 4:30 P.M.; however, working beyond these hours is frequently necessary, depending on office needs.
Work area:	Main business office.
Job summary:	Under the direct supervision of the administrator, the business office manager supervises, manages, and directs the personnel working in that office; keeps and/or oversees all the accounts; oversees cash control procedures; and prepares the statistical and financial records and reports.

Job description:
1. Supervises the office assistants and any part-time office help, plans their work schedules, and assigns work projects.
2. Supervises the chief switchboard operator and the function of communications (optional).
3. Keeps all financial records of the home, including accounts payable, accounts receivable, and payroll. Delegates most of the details of these tasks.
4. Keeps the general ledger.
5. Prepares monthly financial statements, including the balance sheet, income and expense summary, and other regular or special reports that may be requested by the administrator.
6. Audits cash receipts and bank deposits.

Fig. 15. Services of personal care home or residential complex. (Courtesy Neil L. Gaynes, Neil L. Gaynes and Associates, Chicago, Ill.)

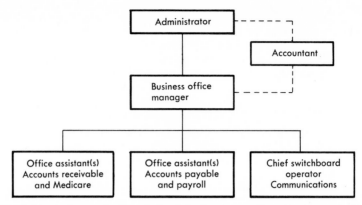

Fig. 16. Typical organizational chart for business office of a larger facility.

7. Supervises the writing of all checks after bills are authorized for payment by the administrator. (The administrator should sign the checks or control the key-operated signature machine.) Is responsible for check signature machine. Keeps all records of use of machine. (The administrator controls the key and audits the records.)
8. Keeps administrator informed regularly of the balances of the several checking and savings accounts of the home.
9. Keeps the petty-cash fund. (May delegate this duty with adequate supervision.)
10. Checks postage machine balance and purchases postage when necessary. (May delegate this duty.)
11. Keeps all personnel documents, including applications, letters of reference, merit ratings, records of physical examinations, and all other individual personnel records. Keeps records of vacations, sick leaves, and holidays taken. Files employee accident reports with insurance company and maintains the recording and reporting of accidents in accordance with the Occupational Safety and Health Act. Interprets and explains the benefits due employees for sickness, vacations, and holidays. Explains home's health insurance program to employees and files claims for employees. Confers with administrator regarding difficult questions of interpretation of the personnel policies.
12. Supervises the ordering of office supplies.
13. Has access to office safe.
14. Assists the administrator in the annual development of the facility budget.
15. Revises and redesigns business and office forms when necessary.
16. Prepares and files employer's quarterly federal and state tax returns.
17. Reconciles all the bank statements monthly.
18. Maintains liaison with the facility accountant, assisting him with the audit and preparation of tax returns and seeking his advice on accounting matters when necessary.
19. Assumes the responsibility of the facility in the absence of the administrator. *Note:* someone must be assigned this responsibility. However, it might be assigned to someone else such as the assistant administrator (if any) or the director of nursing (if any).

The business office manager holds a key position in the facility. The very survival of the program and of the administrator may depend on how this person conducts the office. Obviously, there is always the possibility of fraud, embezzlement, and other dishonest practices that could destroy or damage the agency. (Insurance must be obtained for protection against these possibilities.) More likely, though, the failure of the office manager to perform his duties with skill and promptness will be the cause of financial problems for the facility. If the production of the monthly income and expense statement falls behind several reporting periods, the administrator loses a vital control necessary to watch the financial soundness of the program. If many months have passed before the statement is finally received for a certain month, it may be too late to correct a damaging and heretofore unknown financial problem.

Each of the functions the office manager is assigned carries with it great responsibilities. Failure to perform adequately in any one of the many of these tasks could result in a major problem for the agency. Because of this, great care must be taken in the selection of this individual. The administrator may wish to have his accountant help him with the selection of this person, since it involves the need for technical knowledge and ability. The applicant's background, including his prior work history, must be thoroughly investigated.

Functions of subgroups. The employees in the business office who handle the *accounts receivable* and *Medicare* and *Medicaid* (public aid) can be considered as one subgroup in the office. Possibly the work could be performed by one person. In some facilities with high patient turnover and a large volume of Medicare or Medicaid work, more than one person may be necessary. Some of the duties that are assigned this subgroup are as follows:

1. Maintaining records of accounts receivable by posting charges and credits on the patient's ledger.
2. Receiving cash, using the proper procedure.
3. Preparing monthly statements.
4. Balancing accounts receivable ledger monthly.
5. Discussing and explaining bills, charges, and credits to patients and/or their families and third-party agencies responsible for the account.
6. Preparing insurance forms for patients on request.
7. Preparing all Medicare reports and maintaining liaison with the fiscal intermediary.
8. Explaining Medicare procedures and decisions of the fiscal intermediary to the patients and/or their relatives. Obtaining appropriate signatures.
9. Preparing all reports for and maintains liaison with the state department of public aids or similar state agency responsible for Medicaid.
10. Preparing office files and records for all newly admitted patients. Preparing admittance advice forms for all departments.
11. Obtaining proper signatures on financial agreement forms. (This may be the task of the administrator.)
12. Contacting patients or their relatives when information is needed to complete office records.
13. Answering office telephones.
14. Securing office at end of day according to the written procedure.
15. Preparing cash receipt report daily.

The one selecting persons to occupy these positions should remember that frequent public contact is required. These employees act for the agency in many business matters. They maintain contact between the agency and the patient or relatives regarding the bill and charges; contact with the fiscal intermediary for Medicare needs; and contact with the state office for public aid. Tactfulness and patience are frequently needed.

The employees in the business office who handle the *accounts payable* and *payroll* can be successfully combined into another subgroup. Some typical duties that are assigned are as follows:

1. Maintaining the records of accounts payable and voucher register.
2. Seeking the approval of invoices from persons ordering and receiving.

3. Vouchering approved invoices and assigning account numbers.
4. Contacting the various companies to check bills when items are questionable.
5. Preparing checks for approved vouchers.
6. Maintaining paid bills file.
7. Auditing employees' time cards approved by various supervisors.
8. Maintaining the payroll records and registers.
9. Computing wages due and preparing the paychecks for signature.
10. Preparing the tax records and reports.
11. Preparing the paychecks for the payroll taxes and forwarding them to the proper fiscal depositories.
12. Computing the proper payroll deductions for employees' share of cost of benefits and other miscellaneous items of deduction, such as United Fund and payroll savings, and preparing and forwarding the accumulated money by check to the proper agencies.

Since this job also has a great deal of fiscal responsibility, caution must be thoroughly exercised in selecting a person to fill this position.

Policies and procedures of the business office. As in every department, the development of policies and procedures in the business office is necessary for smooth, efficient operation. The accountant should be asked to help the administrator and the office manager in this development. He also should provide ongoing management consultation to see that the developed policies and procedures are workable and should aid in their revision from time to time. The office manager

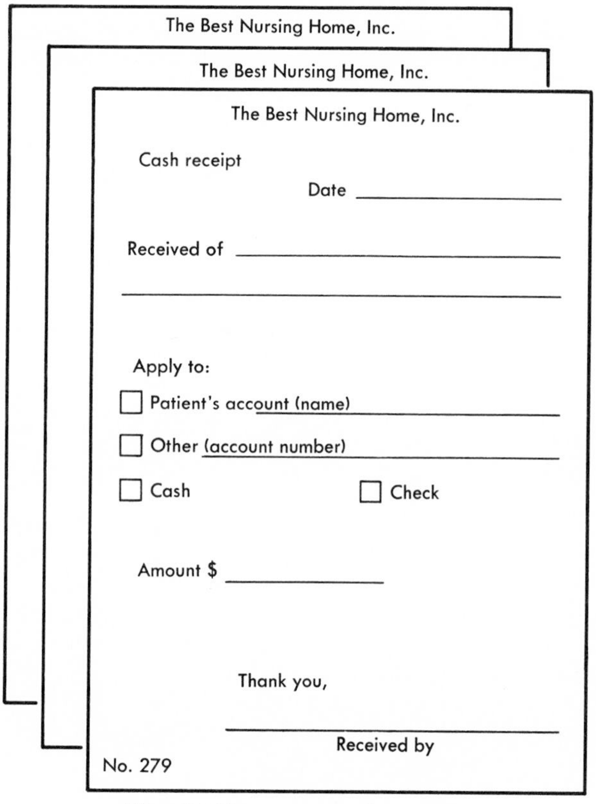
The Best Nursing Home, Inc.
The Best Nursing Home, Inc.
The Best Nursing Home, Inc.
Cash receipt
Date ______
Received of ______
Apply to:
☐ Patient's account (name) ______
☐ Other (account number) ______
☐ Cash ☐ Check
Amount $ ______
Thank you,
______
Received by
No. 279

Fig. 17. Three-part cash receipt.

should be free to contact the accountant for advice when his technical knowledge would be helpful.

Let us examine some areas in the business office that require written policies and procedures.

Handling of cash. A policy statement is needed indicating who is to be held primarily responsible for the cash received in the office. Ideally it should be the function of one person—for example, the accounts receivable clerk. If the policy allows for several people, such as the office manager, the administrator, and the office workers, it is more difficult to trace an error and to spot a fraudulent action.

A prenumbered three-part receipt form, preferably contained in a receipt-writing machine, should be used. The original is given to the person rendering the payment, the first copy is retained for posting, and the second copy is held in the machine and later used for auditing purposes. All cash should be received by this method.

If it is necessary to void a receipt, the word *void* should be written on all three copies. All three copies are retained, stapled together, and filed in proper numerical sequence with the auditing copy. It is important that all three copies of a voided receipt be retained. This is a protection; for a dishonest clerk could, theoretically, give the original to the payer, void the remaining copies, and pocket the cash. See Fig. 17.

Cash receipts report. This is a summary of the cash received during a given period. It may be made daily if there is a good deal of cash flow, or it may be done when the deposit is made up for that period. It should be timed to correspond with the deposit, however. It should be prepared by the person responsible for receiving cash and turned over to the person responsible for making up the deposit.

Let us assume that the Best Nursing Home, Inc., normally makes deposits twice a week except during the first week of the month, when patients' payments are received. The accounts receivable clerk gives the office manager the cash receipts he has in his cash drawer on the day of deposit, together with the completed cash receipts form. The office manager and the accounts receivable clerk together count the cash and verify the total of the report with the cash turned in. At the same time, the clerk gives the office manager the control copies of the receipts together with all copies of any voided receipts. The second copies of receipts are held for posting by the accounts receivable clerk. The office manager is then able to make up the deposit that will balance with the accounts receivable total posted to the several accounts by the accounts receivable clerk; this total thus can be verified by audit. An example of a cash receipts report is shown on p. 50.

Petty cash. A policy statement and procedures detail is needed for the handling

Date	Paid to	Account number	Amount	Balance
Nov. 23	J. Smith—travel	666-27	$25.00	$ 75.00
Nov. 30	Postman—postage due	666-17	.38	74.62
Dec. 4	Ace Freight Co.	413	13.50	61.12
Dec. 5	City Hardware—miscellaneous supplies	664-19	2.97	58.15
Dec. 6	T. Brown—car wash	661-85	2.00	56.15
Dec. 7	Postman—postage due	666-17	.14	56.01
Dec. 12	City Hardware—screening	664-19	14.25	31.76
Dec. 12	Reimbursed by check number 746		(68.24)	100.00

THE BEST NURSING HOME, INC.

Cash receipts report

Date of report _____

Date of deposit _____   Deposit number _____

Cash receipts tickets from # _____ to #_____

Are all tickets accounted for? _____

Do all voided receipts have all copies attached? _____

Detail account number	Description	
560	Nursing home care	$_____
561	Drugs, medicines, vitamins	_____
562	Supplies	_____
563	Physical therapy	_____
564	Beauty or barber shop	_____
565	Rental of special equipment	_____
566	Laundry	_____
570	Guest meals	_____
571	Reimbursed costs—dietary	_____
580	Vending equipment sales	_____
581	Sales in gift shop	_____
590	Reimbursed cost—miscellaneous	_____
591	Donations	_____
592	Miscellaneous	_____
	Other	_____

Total cash received $_____

Cash over (short) $_____

Total deposit $_____

Signature of clerk _____

of petty cash in the business office. A fund should be established and recorded on the books for petty cash. The fund, say $100, is to be replenished from time to time by check in the exact amount of the cash used. To account for the cash dispersed, a petty-cash voucher or a petty-cash daybook is used. When it is necessary to replenish the petty-cash fund, the check is written for the certain amount, and the expenses are recorded by accounts from the vouchers or the daybook. An example of a page in a petty-cash daybook is shown on p. 49.

When check number 746 was written, the expenses were summarized by account and spread to offset the amount of the check.

Safe storage of cash on hand. The petty-cash fund and daily cash receipts that are not banked immediately should be secured safely at the end of each working day. The administrator should see that a practical written procedure is developed for this safety practice. Some kind of a safe should be provided for this purpose. When considering the size and type of a safe, the thoughtful administrator will also consider the need to store ledgers, records, and other important documents in a secure fireproof storage vault; the safe should be large enough to include some of these vital business records.

Receiving and safeguarding valuables of residents. Frequently it becomes necessary for the facility to receive the valuables of residents for safekeeping. If such a policy is established, a sound procedure must be written to govern this practice. When the facility representative receives these valuables, an unwritten *contract of bailment* arises. The facility is contracting to exercise due care in keeping the property safe and to deliver the same property to the resident or his designated agent and to no one else.[1]

The use of a *valuables envelope* that can be sealed is good practice. The envelope can be manufactured so that it has a prenumbered receipt on the flap that can be removed and given to the depositor; the number matches the number on the envelope. The envelope can be printed so that its contents can be listed on the front.*

A *valuables log* also should be used. It is a master schedule of the items received and returned. A sample of a page in such a log is shown below.

Envelope number	Deposited by	Received by	Date	Returned to (signature)	Returned by	Date
61	Mary Smith	Bill Jones	12/8	Mary Smith	A. T. Shard	12/10
62	George Black	A. T. Shard	12/9			
63	Steve Sims	A. T. Shard	12/9	Steve Sims	Bill Jones	12/14

Custody of possessions of residents who die. The administrator of a facility has a duty to see that the personal possessions of a deceased resident are turned over to the duly authorized legal representative. As a practical procedure, he may give items of minimal value to the family after getting a receipt.[1] Often, however, the remaining possessions are quite valuable. Jewelry, furniture, television sets, documents, and money are frequently found in the resident's quarters. In certain homes for the aged and in residential and apartment facilities, these items can include valuable bric-a-brac, antiques, stocks, bonds, and similar securities. The facility administrator must be cautious before letting relatives or friends go through these items. He should consult the facility attorney for specific guidelines to follow in

---

*The Physicians' Record Company, Berwyn, Ill., can supply such an envelope.

these matters. These guides should be tailored to the type of facility and the particular state laws. In general, the administrator should receive a certified copy of the appointment of the executor or administrator of the estate. It should be remembered that the one named as next of kin is not necessarily the one who will be authorized to take the valuables.[1]

Banking—checking and savings accounts. At least two checking accounts should be established for the facility. One known as the general fund is a checking account used for all receipts and for the payment of all bills. The other is an *imprest fund* set up for the payroll. This fund is solely for the paychecks. Each payday one check is written from the general fund for the total amount of the employees' paychecks. It is deposited to the second account, and then the individual employee checks are written against this deposit. It is important to separate these two accounts. One major reason is to have ease of reconciliation; another is to have a limit on attempts to steal from the facility through the payrolls.

Sometimes it is useful to establish another checking account for the *plant fund*. This fund would receive checks from the general fund for depreciation of the plant at regular accounting intervals. In life care facilities with membership fees, the funds collected would be credited to the plant fund account. Expenditure from this account would seldom be made, except for investments and principle and interest payments. Other expenditures would be made for major plant renovations, such as roof repairs.

Often a facility finds it useful to establish a savings account for future lump-sum payments that can be predicted, such as tax payments and insurance premiums. Each month one twelfth of the payment is made to the savings account from the general fund. The interest earned would be recorded as income to the general fund.

One person should be appointed to handle the bank deposits. The total of a particular deposit should be the total of the cash receipts report that indicates the details of the receipts. Each individual cash receipts report should have a corresponding deposit slip with the same total. The deposit slip should be made in duplicate and itemized by checks, with some useful identification for rechecking. Both deposit slips are sent to the bank, and a receipted copy is returned for filing with the cash receipts report.

Accounts payable. Earlier in this chapter I gave a description of the duties involved in handling accounts payable. Let us now examine in detail some of the procedures that are necessary.

VERIFYING INVOICES. There are elaborate, sophisticated methods of verifying invoices to prove that the merchandise was actually received. In large facilities the use of a *purchase order* and a *receiving report* should prove to be quite helpful. The home's accountant should be asked to develop the best system for verifying invoices. In the smaller home, the accounts receivable clerk can oversee this function adequately without the use of elaborate forms. When an invoice is received, the clerk contacts the department head who placed the order, to verify it before making payment. The several questions that must be answered are as follows: When was this received? By whom? Were all the items satisfactory? and Were the prices correct?[2] He then gets the person who ordered to initial the invoice in approval; assigns the proper account number to it; and presents it to the administrator, who will give final approval for payment.

Bills should be paid only if there are approved invoices that show in detail the items received. Statements that are routinely presented monthly by companies are summaries of the several invoice totals but do not show necessary details. Statements, therefore, are not adequate documentations of the expense and should not be the basis used for payment.

VOUCHERING. Vouchering is a major feature of the *accrual* method of accounting. The purpose of vouchering invoices is to record the expense in the proper accounting period, usually the month in which the expense occurred. The invoice may be paid at a later date, but the expense is vouchered and thus recorded when it occurred. This gives proper perspective to the financial reports for the period.

In this system, a voucher form is attached to the invoice permanently. The form has two parts: the original sent with the payment and the carbon copy used for posting to the voucher register, which records the vouchers consecutively as the invoices are received. At the end of the month, the total of the voucher register must be in agreement with the total of the accounts payable ledger.

PAYING THE VOUCHERS. When the accounts payable clerk receives final approval to pay the bill, he can prepare the checks for signature, address the envelopes, and give the checks with the vouchered invoices to the administrator for signature. Good accounting practice calls for someone other than the one preparing the vouchers to sign the checks. The administrator may delegate this task to the office manager through the use of a check-writing-and-signing machine. However, proper checks and balances should be developed by the agency's accountant; for example, the administrator should keep control over the key that operates the signature machine and should keep a control record by check number.

Accounts receivable. The major portion of revenue is generated by service to the clients of the agency. The source of payment may, in many cases, be a third party; the state welfare department or the fiscal intermediary of the Medicare program may well be the main sources of payment. The individual residents' or patients' accounts, in any case, must be adequately maintained and documented. This is one of the duties of the accounts receivable clerk.

A separate ledger must be kept for each resident. The ledger should have identifying information, including resident's name, room or apartment number, daily or monthly rate, Medicare number, and name and address of the person or agency responsible for the bill.

Posting to the ledger is done at least monthly. Charges for the normal care are posted automatically. Special charges are accumulated and posted at the time the normal care charge is recorded. In short-term care facilities such as a hospital and perhaps in some extended care units, posting must be done daily, since charges accumulate faster and the patient's stay is much shorter. In a long-term care facility, however, monthly posting is quite adequate.

Special charges made depend on the type of program operated. Special charges may be made for services of the barber shop, beauty shop, laundry, and telephone, and for gift shop purchases, guest meals, and special services such as extra housekeeping or personal care. In many facilities most of these special charges are included in the basic monthly rate.

Billing cycles may be necessary in large homes, but they are not popular with the residents who receive their Social Security checks shortly after the first of the month.

The administrator should ask the accounts receivable clerk to keep him informed of any delinquent accounts.

Payroll

METHODS OF PREPARATION. The payroll can be prepared in a number of ways. In the small home, the administrator will probably handle the preparation himself. However, as the number of paychecks increases with the size of the home, the administrator should delegate this task. The preparation of the payroll can usually be assigned to the accounts payable clerk or the office manager.

Often the payroll is prepared by hand. Hand preparation of a fairly large number of checks with a commercially available payroll preparation system can be efficient. When done in this way, paychecks can be issued as soon as the next day after the time cards have been received.

In larger facilities, however, sometimes preparation is automated and a local bank or payroll preparation service prepares it on data-processing equipment. This latter method has distinct advantages: the preparation of quarterly tax summaries is a by-product of the system, and the office staff is freed of a time-consuming task. The disadvantages are as follows: There is a time delay, often of several days, between the time the time cards are approved and the day the employee receives his check. Charges are added for changes in the data given originally for each employee, such as rate changes, and for the addition of employees due to turnover. Also, time must be spent in preparing the data to be sent to the processor and in checking the results prior to distribution of the checks.

PAY PERIODS. Pay periods can be on a cycle of 7 days, 14 days, the first and fifteenth days of the month, or a month. Employees might prefer a 7-day cycle, but that requires 52 payrolls. Management might prefer a monthly cycle, since it requires only 12 payrolls. A happy compromise is often a 14-day cycle such as every other Friday; this requires 26 payrolls a year.

The administrator should establish written policy on the methods of payment covering such details as the time when checks are issued, who distributes the checks, what is done with the checks for employees not on duty that day, and requests for early release of paychecks. A policy should be carefully developed regarding someone other than the individual employee sent to pick up the check.

METHODS OF RECORDING HOURS WORKED—THE TIME CARD. The use of the time clock is an efficient method of controlling employees' hours worked. There is always the possibility of an employee's punching another's time card dishonestly, but a good supervisor can quickly detect this practice. Therefore, the supervisor must be given the responsibility of verifying all his employees' time cards prior to submission to the payroll department. Time cards should be saved for future reference. Work schedules compiled by the supervisor prior to the work period should be submitted along with the time cards for that same period. These schedules likewise should be saved for future needs. These records can serve as proof of adequate scheduling to inspecting agencies and can settle possible future complaints from employees concerning past paychecks.

Hand posting can be done efficiently also. Control in this method as well rests with the supervisor.

PAYROLL SUMMARY RECORDS. Individual payroll summary records must be maintained for each employee. This record should show such information as the employee's name, address, telephone number, person to notify in an emergency, Social Security number, dependents claimed for federal and state withholding taxes, rate of pay, premium rates for night work (if applicable), record of pay increases, and the recording of special deductions such as United Fund pledges, insurance premiums, and retirement contributions. The card should be designed to strike quarterly balances for federal income tax deductions, state tax deductions, and Social Security contributions. These records should be preserved.

Telephone and communications

Two types of telephone service should be discussed: facility telephone service and resident telephone service.

Facility telephone service. During the preliminary planning stages of the facility, decisions should be made concerning the type of service needed. An unsophisticated single- or double-line telephone with an extension or two might be quite adequate for a very small home. A full switchboard with several incoming and outgoing trunks and banks of extensions might be the best answer for a large facility. The call director system is another method frequently used. The telephone company can provide technical advice at the onset of the program development and should be asked to do so. Proper telephone planning so that there are sufficient conduits for telephone wires will save major headaches later.

Procedures should be written concerning the facility telephone service. They should cover details such as who is to answer the telephone (for example, during the day shift, one office, and during the other shifts, a second office), how the telephone is to be answered (for example, "Good morning, Best Nursing Home"), and who is authorized to give out certain information (such as patient information, rate information, and employment verification).

Since the telephone plays a major role in building the facility's image, care should be taken to see that the personnel assigned to use the telephone are properly trained in telephone courtesy. The telephone company can assist the administrator in this task.

The telephone plays a vital role in the fire emergency procedures. The fire department's telephone number should be posted near the telephone, and the reporting procedure in the event of fire should be well known by all of the staff members. The police telephone number also should be posted nearby.

Resident telephone service. In some facilities that offer telephone service for the residents (usually for an extra service fee), the central switchboard might prove to be advantageous from the standpoint of control and added security. This is especially true in a retirement complex for independent well aged people. It is less complicated to use a switchboard service for large facilities than to constantly refer calls to other telephone numbers if persons call the facility to speak to certain residents. Switchboards, however, are costly. There must be space set aside, too, for remote equipment that serves the board. The least expensive way is to allow the resident to have a telephone installed in his own name, with the bill coming directly to him. Pay telephones also should be installed in convenient locations, since some residents may prefer to use this method.

Reception of visitors

If the building is properly designed, the business office can double as the reception center for visitors. It is wise to have some screening control placed over those who enter the building. The receptionist–office workers can exercise this function if the office is open to the entry way.

After-hours reception should be arranged. The door should be locked to visitors at a definite time, and there should be a written policy for answering a knock or bell ring. Various methods can be employed to offer some degree of security. A telephone extension can be placed at the door with an automatic ring to the night telephone desk; a two-way speaker can be installed; or a more elaborate remote television system can be utilized.

Receipt of mail and packages

Business mail should be opened by the office manager or the administrator if he has no office manager. All mail addressed simply to the facility is business mail. Vendors should be advised to mail the invoices and statements to the facility in general and not to one individual.

Mail for patients or residents can be a problem if guidelines are not laid down. In a residential complex, separate mail boxes for each resident apartment are ideal. They can be served directly by the postman. In facilities providing care, however, this is not practical. Patient mail can be sorted in the business office and taken to the nursing station for delivery. In certain cases in which the patient has demonstrated incompetence, arrangements must be made for a responsible person to handle his business needs; this can be a relative or a court-appointed conservator.

NOTES

1. Hayt, Emanuel, Hayt, Lillian R., and Croeschel, August H.: Law of hospital, physician and patient, ed. 2, New York, 1952, Hospital Textbooks Co.
2. Carson, A. B., Sherwood, J. F., and Boling, C.: College accounting, ed. 7, Cincinnati, 1967, South-Western Publishing Co.

Chapter four

RESIDENTIAL SERVICES

Every facility has the need for most of the following residential services: housekeeping, mechanical maintenance, ground and building maintenance, laundry and linen service, food service, and fire safety and building security. Each of these services will be discussed in considerable detail.

CONTRACTING FOR SERVICES

It should be pointed out that any or all of the services mentioned except fire safety can be contracted for by the administrator of the facility. Fire safety is the responsibility of all departments, and a master plan using all facility personnel should be developed for it.

In contracting, the administrator, with adequately developed specifications, calls for bids for residential services. Housekeeping services, for example, can be contracted on the basis of cost per square foot, taking into consideration such variables as frequency of cleaning; time of cleaning (night service for office and nonpatient areas); job specifications and job descriptions of the maids, janitors, and supervisors; responsibility for ownership and repair of equipment; responsibility for purchasing and inventorying supplies; and special services such as exterior window washing and snow removal.

Laundry service can be contracted on several bases: for example, the facility can own its own linen and contract for a laundry firm to wash the linens or the facility can rent finished linens that are owned by the laundry, and the facility can contract to pay for the service by the finished piece or by the finished weight. Smaller facilities usually find contracting for linen service quite advantageous. Under the subsection concerning linen service, I will discuss contracting pros and cons in more detail.

Contracting for food service is not an unusual function for hospitals, nursing homes, other health care facilities, and residential facilities. Many hotels and motels also contract for this specialty. There are many excellent food management firms established on a local, regional, or national basis. Methods of compensation vary.

The food must be paid for, the employees must be compensated, and the contractor must be paid for his management service.

When considering negotiating for food service, the administrator must keep in mind the nutritional needs of his charges. The facility, especially one providing any degree of health care, is subject to licensing by state authorities. Certain state and federal minimum guidelines must be met in regard to adequacy of diet; supervision by a professional dietitian; special therapeutic dietary needs; and the need for sanitary food preparation, serving, storing, and cleaning of equipment. Contracting for this service does not relieve the facility of its responsibility to satisfy all these needs.

Basics for contract considerations, including food standards and grades and qualities of foods to be served, must be determined. Other decisions also must be made prior to negotiations, such as (1) who will pay the food service employees; (2) who will control the purchasing of foodstuffs and supplies and thus pay for and own the inventory; (3) who will supply the dietary consultative service; (4) who will prepare the menus, the recipes, and the special diet lists; and (5) what the management fee will be. Usually the facility provides the space and equipment.

A typical food service contract might be constructed so that the facility gives the responsibility to the food management firm for purchasing food, employing personnel, paying salaries, supplying professional dietary supervision and daily management services, preparing menus according to agreed standards, and keeping all records. The contract should specify that all these services are to be performed in accordance with all local, state, and federal codes and regulations and are to comply with specific licensing requirements imposed on the facility by the state. The administrator should require the submission of menus for periods of at least 90 days prior to the beginning of each quarter of the year. He should see that substitutions are kept to a minimum. Payment for a contract like this might be based on a total cost of salaries, supplies, and food, plus a 5% to 8% management fee, provided that the firm keeps the daily cost of food per patient-day within previously agreed contractual limitations.

Similarly, contracts can be developed for building and equipment maintenance, grounds and garden care, security patrol systems, and transportation service.

The administrator should make sure that the home's licensing standards and goals are being properly upheld in a contracted service. He should make sure that the needs of the residents are thoroughly met. The contract should be flexible so that the home can terminate it without danger to the program and so that if the company terminates it, the proper amount of time can be taken to provide a continuity of service. For example, if the home has a contract with a food service management company, sufficient changeover time (perhaps 90 days) should be written in the termination clause. This would allow for selecting and training personnel, making purchasing arrangements for food supplies, and preparing recipes and menus. Changeover from contracted service to home-controlled service is never easy. In my experience, changeovers can be done with mutual, friendly cooperation. Usually a reputable contractor, although sorry to lose the account, does not want the reputation of supplying bad or undesired service and assists during the transition.

I will now consider the departments or subsections in detail as if the home were doing the service itself.

HOUSEKEEPING

The goal of the housekeeping department should be to provide a clean, safe, and pleasant environment for the residents and the personnel.

Organization of the department

Executive housekeeper. The person with the title of housekeeper-supervisor, chief housekeeper, executive housekeeper, matron, or senior maid or some similar assigned title is necessary in every home. Responsibility for the home environmental safety program rests to a great degree with this department head. Odors, dangerous bacteria levels, and fire and safety hazards can be eliminated if this department head is vigilant. The home's public image can be greatly helped if he sees that the home is clean and well decorated, with the furniture and accessories arranged in good taste.

Following is an example of a job description of a housekeeper in a large retirement complex.

JOB DESCRIPTION OF EXECUTIVE HOUSEKEEPER

Title: Executive housekeeper.
Hours: 8:00 A.M. to 4:30 P.M. (on call at other times).
Days: Monday through Friday (unless work load demands attendance on week-ends).
Work area: Entire home interior.

Major duties: Under the direct supervision of the administrator, the executive house-keeper has the following responsibilities:

1. Manages the maid and janitorial employees: hires, fires, counsels, trains, supervises work performance, lays out work assignments, schedules work hours, checks employees' time records, inspects finished work.
2. Supervises receipt of clean linen from the laundry service contractor, maintaining a count of clean linen received and soiled linen returned; issues clean linen to maids; maintains liaison with the linen service contractor to handle problems.
3. Supervises transportation service and chauffeur: schedules chauffeur for residents' trips to physicians and other special trips; prepares charge tickets for this service; supervises other duties of the chauffeur, such as seeing that the automotive equipment is maintained properly and that it is kept clean.
4. Coordinates housing needs of the residents: supervises each new resident's move in, assigning members from his staff to help with arranging furniture, hanging pictures, and storing trunks and luggage; greets each new resident, orients him to his room, and explains the operation of the kitchen appliances, the emergency call system, and the intercom; gives each new resident his copy of the resident handbook.
5. Supervises the placement and change of placement of furniture and decorative accessories in the public areas of the home; sees that these items are in good repair, and requests replacements when they are worn; on authorization to replace, shops for and selects the items.
6. Keeps master file on each apartment, recording repairs, fixture replacements, redecorations, wall washings, carpet replacements, and similar data.
7. Interviews salesmen; selects cleaning products and supplies and places orders for same.
8. Coordinates schedules for use of all public meeting rooms.

A job description of this nature would imply an organizational structure of the housekeeping department as shown in Fig. 18. This organization chart is for a 172-unit residential apartment complex accommodating 200 well aged residents, with each apartment receiving weekly maid service. The facility has an area of over 127,000 square feet, over 95% of which is carpeted. It has seven apartment complexes connected by covered corridors to a central high-rise building with an attached community area containing dining facilities, chapel, auditorium, offices, health service area, and shops. This is a typical retirement residence. Although lifetime care is given its residents, the facility provides no on-site nursing care.

Maids in retirement residence. The specific duties of maids in the residents'

apartments are as follows and are performed weekly unless otherwise indicated:
1. Replenish bath linens.
2. Make the beds with fresh linen.
3. Dust all furniture and woodwork, and dust pictures once a month.
4. Vacuum-clean the floors.
5. Wash insides of windows monthly.
6. Wash bathroom walls.
7. Clean bathroom mirror.
8. Clean bathroom fixtures.
9. Polish bathroom fixtures.
10. Scrub bathroom floor.
11. Sweep patio, and scrub when necessary.

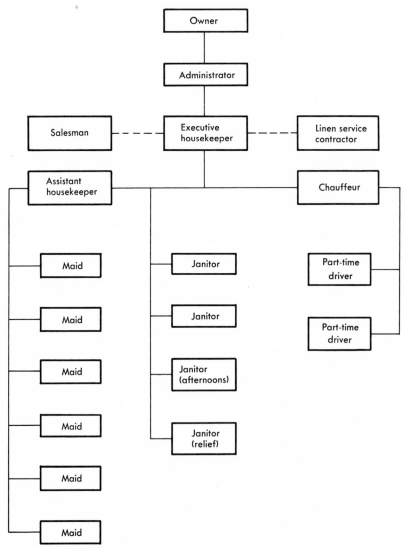

Fig. 18. Typical organizational chart of a large residential complex housekeeping department.

Maids in a nursing home. The maids' tasks in a nursing home setting are similar to those in a retirement residence except that the linen service, including the making of the bed, is traditionally performed by nursing service personnel. The tasks, however, must be done daily instead of weekly.

A different dusting technique must be employed also. In the residential setting, with each resident occupying a private apartment furnished with his own furniture, more emphasis is placed on preservation of the integrity and appearance of the furniture and less emphasis is placed on bacterial control. A solution with a lemon-oil base might be used for dusting in the residential complex. A germicidal damp-dusting technique must be used in the nursing home setting. Germicidal damp-dusting is geared totally to the maintaining of a low bacterial count and to prevention of the spread of bacteria that can occur with dry dusting or dusting with oil-base solutions.

Greater attention must be devoted to the toilet and the floor around it to thoroughly remove spillage. Supplies such as toilet paper, paper towels, and hand soap must be replenished, whereas in an apartment complex this is the residents' responsibility. Damp-mopping with germicidal solutions must be done frequently, at least daily, in a nursing home.

One of the first signs of poor cleaning techniques in a nursing home is a lingering offensive odor. The maid, through performance of her assigned duties, can help to counteract this problem. Although much responsibility rests with the nursing personnel, too, keeping the patients' rooms and corridors clean is one major factor in keeping odor under control.

Departmental management

Motivational techniques. The executive housekeeper must be a good motivator of personnel. He must be able to build a faithful esprit de corps within his department. He must be tough minded and able to discipline, yet softhearted and able to sympathize. He must be able to lead his personnel through difficult duties and help them to understand the sometimes complaining and fault-finding attitudes of some of the residents or patients. He must instill in his personnel a feeling of pride in their work, which is often unpleasant and distasteful.

Following is a list of the qualities necessary in the makeup of a good housekeeping employee:

1. He must be well groomed at all times.
2. He must be careful of offending odors.
3. He must be cheerful (a smile can do wonders).
4. He must be courteous.
5. He must be attentive (the residents need him).
6. He must not repeat anything he sees or hears in the residents' homes or in the offices.
7. He must not gripe or gossip to a resident.
8. He must not gripe or gossip among other employees.
9. He must not use a resident's apartment or belongings in any way except to clean or to move an object as requested.

These also are the necessary ingredients of a good employee in any department.

Housekeeper's responsibility for training. Each facility requires certain methods of cleaning suited especially to the type of care being rendered. It is the responsibility of the housekeeper to see that the personnel under his supervision understand the proper and safe working procedures that are necessary. The job description should state what is to be done, and the procedure manual developed by the housekeeper should tell how it is to be done. However, these two tools are not sufficient.

Training of a new employee might begin with the housekeeper's assigning the beginner to work alongside another employee who has proved himself to be knowledgeable in the specific work methods. When the housekeeper is satisfied that the new worker has a sufficient grasp of the tasks, he can assign him to work alone. The housekeeper should make frequent checks until he is assured of the worker's ability.

The housekeeper should also hold several training conferences with the new employee during his first few weeks on the job. During the first week, two to three hours of individual conference may be required, but thereafter an hour a week should suffice. The first conference or two should be spent on discussion of the goals of the facility and of the department, personnel policies, special departmental policies, timekeeping, and methods of payment for service. The remaining private sessions should be devoted to the details of the procedures and the job description. The employee should be given a thorough indoctrination in the methods expected to be used in his assignment.

Regularly, at least monthly, the housekeeper should gather his staff together for a special in-service training program, which can feature a movie, a talk by someone well qualified in the field, or a demonstration of new equipment by a sales representative. The housekeeper should look for help for these programs from sales representatives. Many companies selling cleaning chemicals will supply personnel to assist with these programs.

Films on cleaning techniques, safety practices, fire safety, and simple bacteriological instruction are available.

Simple instruction booklets can be obtained from companies selling cleaning products and from the United States government. One publication entitled *Principles of Inspection Control in Health Facilities* developed by the Public Health Service is an excellent individual programmed course for housekeeping personnel.[1] It was developed to fill a need for training materials in housekeeping principles and techniques. A similar publication is *The Care and Cleaning of Housekeeping Equipment and the Storage Room in Health Facilities*.[2] It, too, utilizes the programmed instructional approach. These two publications are phrased in very simple terms. Since they are programmed courses, the employee can work at his own pace by himself. They can also be used by the housekeeper to teach by group discussion.

Hazard prevention and fire safety

The housekeeper plays a key role in the facility safety and fire prevention program. There is probably no other person in the facility who regularly sees every part of the building. He should spot potential fire safety dangers and see that they are corrected. He should see that trash is not accumulated in remote areas, that stairwells are clear, and that fire doors are not propped open. He should find and report hazards or potential dangers in the building structure, furniture, and floor covering. He should instill this awareness of potential dangers in his staff members so that they will report them to him.

Prompt disposal of packing and boxes should be the rule. Trash containers should be emptied at least daily. In certain cases they should be emptied several times a day. Old newspapers should be discarded regularly and not accumulated to remain in stacks for possible sale to scavengers.

All the housekeeping personnel should be thoroughly trained in the details of the facility fire plan and should be given instruction in the operation of the several types of fire extinguishers on hand. One of the in-service programs each year should be devoted to the actual use of these extinguishers. A good time to conduct this program is the day the service company comes to make the annual inspection of the fire extinguishers. The personnel can discharge them, and they can be refilled and placed back into service immediately.

Control of pathogenic bacteria. In very simple terms, pathogenic bacteria require at least five ideal conditions before they can multiply: *food, the proper temperature range, the right pH range, moisture,* and *sufficient time.* Although other factors are necessary also, I will concentrate on these.

Many bacteria enjoy the same foods we do. Ham, turkey, custards, moist puddings, and certain vegetables are especially good growth media. Other bacteria use human and animal wastes for their food. When bacteria are present in dangerous forms in such foods and are taken into the body through the mouth, either through eating or through careless hand-washing techniques, serious problems can result.

However, in order for bacteria to grow to dangerous levels, the proper temperature range must be present for a sufficient time. The bacteria will stop growing when the temperature range falls below 40° F. Most bacteria are killed at temperatures above 180° to 190° F. if the temperature is held for a sufficient time. The ideal growth temperature for most bacteria is 98.6° F., our body temperature. This is why food sanitarians caution us to keep hot foods hot and cold foods cold.

Time is necessary for growth. Bacteria divide when growing. Under proper conditions, one bacterium will become two in about 20 minutes, and two will become four in an additional 20 minutes. In a few hours a small group of bacteria can multiply to a dangerously potent count of millions.

Moisture is another necessary factor in the growth of bacteria. Most foods have moisture in them to begin with. Food dried on a table can become a growth medium again if it becomes moistened by spillage. Bacteria will not grow on clean, dry surfaces; this points up a major reason for good, thorough cleaning techniques.

The pH range refers to acidity or alkalinity. Bacteria are very selective. Some prefer acid media and some like alkaline media. In order to be certain that the bacteria is being killed as the staff members clean, the housekeeper must see that proper techniques are utilized.

Bacteria are everywhere and are always present in a nursing home environment. The goal of the housekeeping department in the nursing home is to keep the bacteria at a safe level so that they are of little danger. Constant odor present in a nursing home is indicative of bacteria growing. It indicates poor housekeeping and nursing techniques.

To control the pathogenic, or disease-causing, bacteria, the housekeeper must see that a correctly manufactured *bacteriostatic* substance is used in the cleaning solution. It is good practice for him to ask the home's advisory physician or consulting pharmacist to review the literature produced by the several manufacturers and to provide advice about the best type to use.

The representative of the company selected as the supplier of the basteriostatic compound should provide guidance to the housekeeper, indicating the proper mix with water in order to provide the correct strength. Improper mixing can cause impotent solutions or solutions so strong that they are harmful to finishes or to personnel using them. Also the use of too much of the solution is wasteful.

Refuse disposal. The housekeeper must make sure that there is an efficient method of disposal of trash. A system for regular removal of waste from the building is an important part of the fire safety program.

The decision must be made about what to do with the trash once it is removed. Incineration in or near the facility was a common solution at one time. Air pollution controls prohibit this practice in many municipalities now. Built-in incinerators may cause odor problems, and as they age, danger of fires becomes a real possibility. Incineration requires personnel time for feeding the trash into the firebox and for removing and discarding the residue. Sorting must be done prior to burning, since some items, such as tin cans, pressurized containers, and metal, should be disposed of without burning.

The housekeeper should contract for trash hauling service. Modern bins that can be dumped into a compactor truck provide the most practical collection method. Lids can be kept closed on the bins so that the trash does not blow about.

Compactors are available for use by the home staff. They can crush bulky items before they are put into the disposal bin. This saves space, of course, and allows for more trash to be stored. The trash can then be picked up less frequently, and since the contracting hauler charges by the binful, this can result in a saving. However, personnel time is required for loading, operating, and unloading the compacting equipment. Even if the home does not have a compactor, bulky boxes and large cans should be crushed to save space.

Since the area of the building where the trash is collected will be the most unpleasant in appearance, it should be screened off as well as possible from public view.

Extermination of vermin. Another contract that should be let is one for regular visits by an exterminating service. Efficient, professional service done with consistency will keep the home free from unwanted visitors. Of course, the housekeeper may elect to have his staff do this. But if it is not done with regularity and done properly, the results may be unfavorable. There are special chemicals that should be used; moreover, they must be used with skill so that foodstuffs, equipment, and supplies are not contaminated. Since this is a very technical procedure, it is best assigned to a professional exterminator rather than to a staff person.

Decoration

Nothing can be more depressing than a poor choice of colors. The housekeeper should do research so that he can advise the painter about the color schemes to be used. White walls should be avoided. They can remind the resident of the sterile hospital atmosphere, and they also tend to produce a boring atmosphere for the employees. Light shades of peach, salmon, and yellow can be used to make dark areas of the facility cheerful. Color should be carried into ceilings in order to give the appearance of spaciousness and to be relaxing to patients who are bedfast.[3]

Departmental master work schedule

Following is the detailed work schedule or outline developed for the housekeeping department of the typical apartment community described earlier in this chapter that illustrates the depth of organization needed in any department in a long-term care or retirement facility. It is not a procedure manual; it does not state how to perform specific functions. This would be included in another section of the department's manual. It could best be described as a master schedule of work or services needed to be done by the maids, janitors, drivers, and the housekeeper and his assistant, as assigned by the administrator. It should be developed jointly by the administrator and his executive housekeeper. It should be revised frequently, at least yearly, to keep it meaningful. It is used to help the housekeeper organize and assign the staff in the most efficient manner. It illustrates what must be done by the department and what responsibilities and authorities have been assigned to the housekeeper and his staff.

HOUSEKEEPING DEPARTMENT RESPONSIBILITIES
TYPICAL RETIREMENT RESIDENCE WITH A HEALTH SERVICE

I. Resident apartments

The maids provide weekly cleaning of the residents' apartments; this includes the following responsibilities:

A. Bathroom. The maids will provide complete bathroom cleaning as outlined as follows, with the following exception: they will not replenish the supplies (soap and toilet tissues); this is the responsibility of the resident.
   1. The maids will wash the walls around the shower and bathtub, washbasin, toilet, and heating unit. The shower curtain will be washed and dried to prevent water spotting and mildew. The shower curtain rod will be washed and polished, and the curtain will be spaced evenly on the rod so that it may air properly. Once a month the tile walls will be completely washed.
   2. They will polish all mirrors and wash and dry bathtub, washbasin, and toilet.
   3. After checking to see that they have not missed anything, they will scrub floor, using a germicidal detergent.
   4. They will then place fresh bath linen neatly on towel bar.
B. Complete change of bed linens. The maids will change both top and bottom sheets and pillow slips, replacing them with fresh linens, and make the bed. (This will be done according to each resident's specifications.)
C. The maids will empty and clean all waste containers, including ash trays, and then return them to their proper places.
D. Dusting. The maids will clean all mirrors and dust furniture, pictures, walls, sills, doors, and other trim. Upholstered furniture and draperies will be thoroughly vacuum-cleaned.
E. Glass areas. Smudges and fingerprints will be removed from all glass areas, including patio doors. Metal trim around doors and windows will also be kept free from smudges and fingerprints. The screens will be vacuum-cleaned as necessary.
F. Disposal unit. The garbage disposal will be checked to see if it is operating correctly.
G. Floor care. The maids will vacuum-clean the floors and remove all stains from carpeting, being careful to vacuum-clean under and behind all furniture and doors. All door frames and window frames will be vacuum-cleaned.
H. Other services in residents' apartments. Except for minor requests not demanding much of their time, the maids will refer requests for additional services by the resident to the housekeeping office.
II. Lounges, game rooms, club rooms, and lobbies
  A. The maids will dust all furniture daily.
  B. Maids will vacuum-clean floors twice weekly, or as needed. Stains and heavy soil will be removed with approved methods in procedure manual.
  C. Game equipment. Any game equipment left out by the residents will be assembled and returned to storage cabinets when not in use.
III. Corridors
  A. Floors. The janitors will vacuum-clean all corridor floors two times each week. They will remove heavy soil and stains when necessary, with approved methods in procedure manual.
  B. Sand urns and ash trays. The janitors will clean all sand urns and ash trays twice daily or oftener if they see paper or any other combustible materials in them. The maids will wash the sand urns and ash trays as needed.
  C. Waste containers. The janitors will empty all waste containers at 8:00 A.M. and at 4:30 P.M. They will be emptied between these hours if the containers are full. When a resident places large items such as boxes, papers, or bottles near the trash container or in the corridors, they will be removed as soon as they are noticed.
  D. Walls, sills, doors, and other trim. The janitors will do all high dusting.
  E. Drinking fountains. The maids will clean and polish drinking fountains daily and oftener when needed.
  F. Glass area. The maids will remove fingerprints and smudges from all glass areas, including doors, daily.
     The janitors will wash all windows and doors inside in corridors, dining

room, high-rise building lounges, card room, music room, sewing room, pool-room, auditorium, solarium, and all other lounges once a month and oftener if needed. The janitors will wash the outside of all the glass areas three times a year (ground level only).

  G. Main entrances.
    1. The maids will polish the glass area immediately surrounding the outside of the entrance daily.
    2. The rubber mat on inside of door will be removed and cleaned weekly, or oftener during bad weather.
    3. Fingerprints and smudges will be removed from glass doors daily.
    4. The outdoor carpet at front entrance will be vacuum-cleaned weekly and shampooed as needed. A broom will be used daily to keep leaves off the carpet if necessary.
    5. The chat from the driveway will be pushed from curb back into driveway with the broom as needed.

IV. Office service (daily)
  A. The maids will dust furniture and desk tops.
  B. Floors will be vacuum-cleaned and spots removed.
  C. Office equipment and machines will be dusted when not in operation.
  D. All ash trays will be cleaned.
  E. No papers, records, letters, reports, or anything on the desks will be examined by the maids during this procedure.

V. Library
  A. The maids will dust furniture and tables once a week thoroughly. They will dust lightly daily.
  B. All floors will be vacuum-cleaned once a week thoroughly, and oftener when needed.
  C. All ash trays will be cleaned daily.
  D. All waste containers will be emptied twice each day.
  E. Books and shelving will be dusted weekly.
  F. Walls, sills, doors, and other trim will be dusted weekly.

VI. Nurses' office
  A. The maids will dust furniture and desk tops daily.
  B. All floors will be vacuum-cleaned daily. Stains and heavy soil will be removed as needed, with approved methods in procedure manual.
  C. All ash trays will be cleaned daily.
  D. Walls, sills, doors, and other trim will be dusted weekly.
  E. Sinks will be cleaned and all stains removed daily.
  F. Lavatories will be cleaned thoroughly daily, with approved method in procedure manual.
  G. No papers, records, letters, reports, or anything on the desks will be examined by the maids during these procedures.

VII. Beauty shop (weekly service)
Daily cleaning is the responsibility of the beauty shop operator.
  A. The maids will dust the furniture and hair dryers.
  B. Sinks and counters will be cleaned thoroughly.
  C. All floors will be vacuum-cleaned. Stains and heavy soil will be removed as necessary, with approved methods in procedure manual.
  D. Ash trays will be cleaned
  E. Walls, sills, doors, and other trim will be dusted.
  F. Waste containers will be emptied daily.

VIII. Gift shop
  A. The maids will dust showcases, display racks, and counter tops as necessary.
  B. Furniture will be dusted and tables washed and dried daily.
  C. All sand urns and ash trays will be emptied twice a day.
  D. All floors will be vacuum-cleaned once a week thoroughly. Stains and heavy soil will be removed by approved methods in procedure manual.

E. Walls, sills, doors, and other trim will be cleaned once a week.
IX. Basement areas
  A. Employees' locker rooms and rest rooms (daily service)
    1. The maids will clean the locker rooms thoroughly, including the floors, lockers, the tops of lockers, mirrors, and furniture.
    2. The rest rooms will be cleaned thoroughly according to the established procedure in procedure manual.
  B. Other areas (weekly service or more frequent service if needed). The maids' work in other areas of the basement will consist primarily of the cleaning of the floors. In most cases these may be swept with a compound in order to keep the dust down, with the exception of the stairwell and tiled area.
    1. The tiled area will be waxed once a year; wet-mopped twice a month, or oftener if necessary; and dust-mopped weekly.
    2. The stairwell area will be scrubbed weekly. The handrails will be dusted weekly and washed and polished monthly.
X. Self-service laundry rooms (daily service)
  A. The maids will clean the floors daily.
  B. The exterior walls of the washers and dryers will be cleaned. Waste soap and other stains and blemishes will be removed.
  C. The lint will be removed from filters in dryers, and filters will be returned to dryers.
  D. Sinks will be cleaned.
  E. Walls, sills, doors, shelves, and other trim will be kept clean.
XI. Janitors' and utility rooms
  A. Floors will be cleaned as needed.
  B. Sinks will be cleaned daily.
  C. Shelving will be cleaned and maintained in a neat and orderly fashion.
  D. Supplies will be kept in suitable containers, with lids and labels. Supplies of a hazardous nature will be so labeled and kept in safety containers. No flammable supplies will be kept in these areas in quantities over one pint. The flammable supplies will be stored in safety containers with labels.
XII. Exhaust and intake air vents
Vents, both intake and air exhaust, located throughout the building will be kept clean. The maintenance department will be responsible for changing the filters. The housekeeping department will be responsible for keeping the exterior surface of these vents clean at all times.
XIII. High dusting
High dusting is the cleaning of areas of the building beyond the normal reach of a maid who is standing on the floor. High dusting will be done by a janitor. It is necessary for a janitor to use a safety ladder when high dusting. High dusting will be performed as necessary, but will be done no less than once a month, as assigned.
XIV. Public rest rooms (daily service or oftener as needed)
  A. Washbasins and sinks will be scoured and the chrome polished.
  B. Toilet seats, toilets, and urinals will be completely disinfected according to procedure manual.
  C. Mirrors, partitions, other bathroom equipment, and walls will be cleaned and the mirrors polished.
  D. Floors will be mopped with a germicidal solution according to procedure manual. This will be done more than once a day if necessary.
  E. Paper, soap, and sanitary dispensers will be filled with supplies as needed.
  F. Waste cans will be emptied twice daily.
Note: The housekeeping personnel must make several inspections of the public and employee rest rooms throughout the day. More frequent cleaning of the rooms may be necessary in order to keep them in spotless condition at all times.
XV. Dining room
It is the responsibility of the kitchen personnel to do the daily cleaning of the

dining room, but the housekeeping department performs the following tasks:
A. Windows will be cleaned monthly.
B. Sills, doors, walls, and other trim will be cleaned monthly.
C. The dividing wall will be cleaned (washed down) and the tile floor mopped weekly around coffee urns.
D. Carpets will be vacuum-cleaned thoroughly once a day.

XVI. Auditorium
A. Windows will be cleaned monthly and smudges, fingerprints, and the like removed daily.
B. Furniture, game tables, and the like will be dusted daily.
C. Employee coffee break tables will be cleaned after each use.
D. Floors will be stripped and waxed once a year. They will be buffed only when necessary and damp-mopped after each party where food or drink is dropped. They will be dust-mopped daily.

XVII. Parties, plays, dances, bingo, tours, and movies
A. Before each of these activities, the janitors will place furniture such as chairs, card tables, and piano in a preplanned manner, under the supervision of the housekeeper or housekeeping assistant.
B. After the festivities
1. After the parties are over, the janitors will stack the chairs and tables and then return them to the proper area.
2. They will sweep up all crumbs and lint or dust and then damp-mop the floor.
3. They will buff the floor if it looks dull, to bring back the shine.

XVIII. Elevators
A. Elevator walls will be washed weekly and fixtures polished.
B. Lights will be cleaned when necessary and light coverings washed and polished and then replaced.
C. Carpets of elevators will be vacuum-cleaned daily; they will be shampooed as needed, but no less than once a month.

XIX. Stain removal
Stains will be removed as soon as they are noted. Removal of stains from carpets, furniture, desk tops, floors, and other objects will be done only in the approved manner. Always consult the procedure manual. If the maids or janitors think a stain will present a removal problem, they will discuss this with the housekeeper before proceeding.

XX. Exterior window cleaning
A separate contract will be negotiated with a window washing firm for the washing of the outside of all windows of the high-rise building twice each year (spring and late fall). The janitors will wash all the glass areas on the lower level (corridors) as assigned. The maids will wash all glass, inside and outside, on the residents' apartments (lower level) as assigned. They will wash inside only of the windows of the residents' apartments in the high-rise building, as assigned.

XXI. Mechanical maintenance
The housekeeping personnel are not required to perform any mechanical maintenance, including the installation of fluorescent lamps. The housekeeper will refer all mechanical and electrical maintenance needs to the maintenance department immediately.

XXII. Art objects, paintings, sculptures, statuary
The maids will dust these objects weekly unless told otherwise, using no cleaning agent, including water, unless otherwise directed.

XXIII. Linen service
A. Receiving clean linen from linen contractor
1. The responsibility of receiving clean linen will be assigned to the housekeeping department personnel. This will be done specifically by the housekeeper or housekeeping assistant.
2. The housekeeper will see that the linen is counted when it is received from

the linen contractor. The totals of the linen count will be recorded in a ledger by date received.

B. Transportation of clean linen. The bulk of the clean linen supply will be transported from the receiving area to the storage area in trucks provided by the linen contractor. These trucks will be lined with paper and covered to protect the clean linen from soil.

C. Storage. There will be a central storage area for all clean linen receipts. This room will be locked at all times. The housekeeper and assistant housekeeper will have access to this room. Either one will issue clean linen supplies from this storage area.

D. Issuing of clean linen
  1. It will be the responsibility of the housekeeper to issue clean linen.
  2. The housekeeper or assistant housekeeper will issue the number of items needed to each maid for her daily needs. This will be computed from the number of units and number and size of beds in the units that the maid will clean that day.
  3. Each apartment will be issued a predetermined amount of linen, by item, which will be constant. This standard for each apartment will be recorded permanently so that the housekeeper or assistant housekeeper will know what items and quantities of linen to give the maids and so that the amount of linen in the apartments at inventory time can be determined at any time without the need for an actual count.
  Normal apartment weekly linen quota:
  a. Per bed—2 bed sheets; 1 pillowcase per pillow.
  b. Per bath or per person—2 large bath towels; 2 hand towels; 2 washcloths; 1 bath mat; 1 shower curtain.
  4. Extra linen will be given to residents in cases of emergency or if they have company. There will be a small charge for extra linens given to the resident for guests' use. The charges will be computed by the housekeeper.

XXIV. Dry cleaning and laundry service
The housekeeping department will be responsible for the dry cleaning and laundry service.

A. The resident will take his soiled personal things to the housekeeping office. The housekeeper or housekeeping assistant will count the items and enter the correct amount with the names of the articles and descriptions on triple-copy sales slips. Two copies will be placed in the bag with the soiled clothes, and one copy will be retained for the retirement residence records.

B. When the cleaners return the dry cleaning and laundry to the retirement residence, the housekeeping department will distribute it and see that the charge tickets are taken to the office for posting to the residents' accounts.

XXV. Transportation
There is no charge for transportation to local physicians or for regularly scheduled transportation.

A. Physician appointments. When a resident has a physician's appointment, he will tell the nurse in advance, who will complete an appointment slip and give a copy to the housekeeper to make the transportation schedule. The housekeeper will give the assignments to the drivers, after writing the departure time on the slip. The chauffeur supervisor will decide which driver will take the resident to the physician.

B. Regularly scheduled transportation (bus or limousine service)
  1. To local town:

DAY	DEPART	RETURN	DESTINATION AND PICKUP
Monday	9:00 A.M.	10:45 A.M.	Downtown
Tuesday	1:00 P.M.	3:30 P.M.	Downtown
Wednesday	10:30 A.M.	12:00 noon	Shopping plaza

| | Thursday | 9:00 A.M. | 12:00 noon | Downtown |
| | Friday | 9:00 A.M. | 10:45 A.M. | Downtown |

2. To more distant large city:

DAY	DEPART	RETURN	DESTINATION AND PICKUP
Monday	9:30 A.M.	2:30 P.M.	Large department store
Tuesday	(No bus)		
Wednesday	9:30 A.M.	2:30 P.M.	Large department store
Thursday	(No bus)		
Friday	9:30 A.M.	2:30 P.M.	Large department store

3. Special bus to large city last week in the month:

DAY	DEPART	RETURN	DESTINATION AND PICKUP
Monday	9:30 A.M.	1:30 P.M.	Large department store
Tuesday	(No bus)		
Wednesday	11:30 A.M.	5:00 P.M.	Large department store
Thursday	(No bus)		
Friday	9:30 A.M.	2:30 P.M.	Large department store

C. Charge for special transportation

If a resident wants special transportation service on an individual basis, he will make transportation arrangements with the housekeeper. There will be a charge for this extra transportation according to time and mileage, to defray the costs of the driver, gasoline, oil, and the like. The charges will be computed by the housekeeper and given to the office for posting.

XXVI. New residents

A. Coordination of the move in. When a new resident moves in, the housekeeper will assist him in arranging the furniture and will give suggestions, when asked, about the hanging of pictures or color schemes. When the resident is ready to have the pictures or mirrors hung or has any maintenance problem, the housekeeper will refer the work to the maintenance department. The housekeeper will orient the new resident to the apartment, including the operation of keys, locks, doors, and windows; kitchenette, including the operation of refrigerator, garbage disposal, exhaust vents, and lights; the special features of the bathroom, including the fixtures, exhaust fan, light, and emergency call system; and operation of the heating control and the intercom. He will give the resident the resident handbook and point out special highlights such as meal times and fire safety.

B. Flowers for new resident. After the new resident has moved in and become settled in his new home, the housekeeper will order flowers as a gesture of welcome. When they arrive, the flowers will be delivered by the housekeeper.

XXVII. Total home decor

The housekeeper on authorization from the administrator will shop for and buy furniture, pictures, and accessories for the retirement residence public areas and display apartments. The housekeeper will arrange the furniture, pictures, and accessories in the public areas, corridors, alcoves, and club rooms as he sees the needs.

Furnishings and capital equipment log

One of the suggested duties of the housekeeper is the responsibility of placement of furniture in public areas and the selection of new or replacement items of furniture with administrative approval.

For appraisal and accounting purposes, all furniture and capital equipment items should be recorded in a log. This task may be delegated to the housekeeper. Some administrators may prefer that it be maintained by the bookkeeper, however, for better financial control of depreciation.

The purpose of the log is to maintain an up-to-date list of equipment, furniture, and decorative accessories that, for accounting purposes, are classed as capital equipment items. The accountant should specify the dollar breaking point used to determine if an item should be capitalized or charged to expense. For example, items with a value of $50 or more and an expected life of one year or longer may be classed as depreciable assets. Pertinent data about each such item should be maintained in a subsidiary record such as the furnishings and equipment log. The general ledger should have an asset account for furniture and equipment. Such purchases are thus charged to this account rather than charged as an expense of operation.[4]

This log is valuable for determining depreciation schedules and also for providing records for insurance claims if proof of loss due to theft, fire, or the like is necessary.

The log is also valuable for providing some method of control for keeping the item in the proper location and for providing a method of tagging or labeling the item as the property of the facility. A prenumbered metal identification label with an adhesive backing can be affixed to the item. The label could state as follows: Property of Best Nursing Home, Inc., Item no. 468. When a piece of equipment to be capitalized is purchased, the property tag can be affixed to it, the tag number can be recorded on the invoice, and the item can be entered in the log.

The log could be divided into subgroups that best fit the needs of the facility, such as (1) kitchen and dining room equipment and function; (2) power plant and shop equipment and function; (3) housekeeping department equipment and function; (4) office equipment and furniture; (5) medical, nursing, and patient room equipment and furniture; (6) lobby, lounge, and corridor furniture; (7) exterior grounds equipment and yard furniture; (8) automotive equipment; and (9) miscellaneous items.

It is obvious that this will require a great amount of detailed work and effort when the home first opens. However, it will provide the administrator and the owner with valuable information to document depreciation and valuations for accounting and insurance purposes.

As the home continues in operation, the purchase or disposal of each item of equipment should be entered in the log. See form on p. 72.

MECHANICAL MAINTENANCE

In this section I will discuss the care of the building and its equipment from another point of view. I will cover *preventive maintenance, repair and renovations,* and *general upkeep* of the physical plant and its equipment. Often the word *maintenance* means general cleaning; with this concept, a maintenance man might be thought of as a janitor assigned to do building cleaning. I prefer to use the term *maintenance man* to refer to a person assigned to the care of mechanical equipment, including its repair or preventive maintenance programs; repair of broken or worn equipment or building appearances; supervision of the power plant; oversight of the electrical, ventilation, and plumbing systems; and oversight of contractors called in for major repairs or specialized maintenance of sophisticated equipment.

In the small home, a handyman is often the one who does many of these necessary tasks. Frequently it is the administrator himself who repairs the washer when it breaks down or who returns from home to get the furnace going again.

Today, however, with the trend of the larger modern nursing home or residential

FURNISHINGS AND CAPITAL EQUIPMENT LOG
DEPARTMENT: *Kitchen and dining room*

Item	Location	Tag number	Cost	Date purchased	Serial or model number	Manufacturer	Date of disposal	Cash received at disposal
Ice cube machine	Subkitchen, nursing wing, south	293	$475.00	2/1/68	4-M-132	Cold Products Company		
Meat slicer	Main kitchen	294	240.00	2/1/68	K-33	Gray Co.		
Toaster	Main kitchen	295	75.00	2/1/68	—	Gray Co.	3/1/72	No value—discarded
Dining room table	Dining room	296	80.00	2/1/68	—	Stevens Furniture Co.		
Dining room table	"	297	"	"		"		
Dining room table	"	298	"	"		"		
Dining room table	"	299	"	"		"		
Dining room table	"	300	"	"		"		
Dining room table	"	301	"	"		"		
Dining room table	"	302	"	"		"		
Dining room table	"	303	"	"		"		
Chair, dining	"	304	55.00	"		"		
Chair, dining	"	305	"	"		"		
Chair, dining	"	306	"	"		"		
Chair, dining	"	307	"	"		"		
Chair, dining	"	308	"	"		"		
Chair, dining	"	309	"	"		"		
Chair, dining	"	310	"	"		"		
Chair, dining	"	311	"	"		"		
Chair, dining	"	312	"	"		"		
Chair, dining	"	313	"	"		"		

complex, a well-structured maintenance department is a necessity for the protection of the safety of the patients and the preservation of the large investment of capital in the building and its equipment.

Contracted services or skilled employees

The larger the plant is and the more elaborate the equipment is, the higher the qualifications must be of the person responsible for this department. The question is whether to hire a highly skilled person who can perform the tasks or assign them to staff members or to establish contracts with local contractors to handle most of the major repairs and maintenance and have a less skilled employee on hand for the smaller day-to-day needs. The question must be one decided by the administrator and the owner or board. Variables to be considered would include (1) size of the facility; (2) age of the facility; (3) type and degree of sophistication of the mechanical, electrical, heating, plumbing, and air conditioning systems; (4) availability of local service contractors; and (5) availability of a qualified maintenance man.

Some equipment items definitely call for specialized service provided by a reliable contractor who is skilled in his specialty. For example, a firm capable of providing elevator system service should be contracted to supply this service. Reliable companies should be contracted to provide major electrical and plumbing repairs or services. City and state codes require specific methods of installation and modifications of these systems. Repair of heating systems, especially high-pressure steam systems, and of central air conditioning units requires specialized knowledge.

When it is necessary to call an outside contractor for assistance, the engineer should inform the administrator. Established contracts for elevator maintenance, for example, will not require further administrative action; a roof repair (excluding emergency repair), however, is a service that the administrator will want to discuss with the board and for which he will want to seek bids. The latter holds true for painting of the exterior of the building, tuck-pointing, gutter repair, major carpentry work, and the like.

Usually, the routine day-to-day needs can be met without calling the outside contractor for service if the maintenance man has a good general knowledge of electrical, plumbing, and heating plant operation along with a knack for carpentry repairs.

The chief engineer

Following is a job description of a skilled maintenance man for a large residential complex. It illustrates the talents required for this important department head.

JOB DESCRIPTION OF CHIEF ENGINEER

Title: Chief engineer.
Days: Monday to Friday; subject to call on weekends.
Hours: 8:00 A.M. to 4:30 P.M.; subject to call or overtime when necessary.
Work area: Interior and exterior of building.

Major duties: Under the direct supervision of the administrator, the chief engineer has the following responsibilities:

1. Operates and maintains the boiler, heating and air conditioning systems, domestic water systems, refrigeration systems, pumps, motors, fans, electrical systems, and emergency electrical generator. Sees that each system is functioning properly and that preventive maintenance, routine servicing, and seasonal repair and changes are carried out.
2. Plans and conducts a complete preventive maintenance system, including lubrication,

changing and cleaning of filters, replacing of worn parts, and oversight of outside contractors providing similar services on certain specialized equipment and systems.

3. Makes minor building and equipment repairs, changes, and additions; supervises work of outside contractor.
4. Orders repair parts, supplies, water-treatment chemicals, and fuel.
5. Paints and redecorates rooms as requested by administrator.
6. Reads meters of fuel supply, water supply, and electrical supply and recommends methods to administrator for conservation of these utilities. Checks utility bills when received.
7. Repairs plumbing and fixtures when necessary. Contacts contractor for major problems.

The areas of responsibility that should be assigned to this person are as follows: (1) electrical power and lighting systems; (2) plumbing system; (3) heating and air conditioning systems; (4) power plant supervision; (5) pneumatic controls; (6) air-handling equipment (ventilation and exhaust systems); (7) broken glass replacement (note that large-plate replacement should be contracted, since it is a dangerous procedure that must be professionally handled); (8) preventive maintenance program; (9) repair to equipment and building; (10) supervision of outside contractors and service contractors; and (11) maintenance and cleaning of refrigeration units.

The administrator should make a policy that no structural changes are to be made within the building without his written consent. Usually changes such as this will require approval of the board of directors as well as municipal and state inspecting agencies. Likewise, changes in the function of a room or a corridor or other portion of the building should be done only with administrative permission. For example, the permanent closure of a doorway should never be allowed without proper approvals.

The administrator should give sufficient purchasing authority to the engineer so that he can readily obtain repair and replacement parts. However, a dollar limitation should be given. If a large piece of equipment stops working, the engineer should report this to the administrator to get his approval for replacement, since this may involve a larger expenditure of money that would require board approval.

The engineer should make sure that he has a sufficient supply of minor repair supplies and parts on hand for the day-to-day needs. He should have such items as fuses, wire, washers, gaskets, filters, nuts and bolts, small motors, electrical supplies, nails, screws, lubricants, indicator lights, belts, refrigerant gas, copper tubing, galvanized pipe and elbows, putty, sealants, small electrical elements, valves, sheet metal, plywood, and small plumbing repair items.

It is usually the policy that the maintenance man supplies his own small hand tools. However, the home should provide expensive tools such as large pipe wrenches, sewer "snakes," chain hoists, ladders, die sets, and welding and torch equipment.

Preventive maintenance program

Along with keeping up with the necessary repairs of equipment and the building, the maintenance man must be responsible for a preventive maintenance program for all the mechanical and electrical equipment of the home. Just as an automobile needs a regularly scheduled program of maintenance (oil change, lubrication, tune-up, seasonal changeover), so does the equipment of the home. Almost every mechanical device installed in the home is provided with a service manual by the manufacturer, which indicates the care required to keep the machine in good operating order. This care is preventive maintenance.

Equipment file. A list of major mechanical equipment, such as motors, pumps, air-handling units, and refrigeration units, should be prepared on file cards, with a separate card for each item of equipment. The purpose of this card file is to provide a record of special data necessary for the maintenance, repair, or replacement of equipment. Actually this should be done when the building is new and all the service manuals are available as well as the salesmen or installers. The card should include such data as (1) name of item; (2) location and tag number, which is used for identification of the item listed on the card; (3) serial number or model numbers; (4) name of manufacturer and address; (5) name of installer and address; (6) length of guarantee or warranty; (7) notation about where to obtain parts or service for item; (8) type and frequency of maintenance required, such as oiling, greasing, and filter change; and (9) other necessary data, such as voltage required (single phase or three phase), direction of rotation of pumps, capacities, pounds of pressure, safety ranges of gauges, and general operating instructions when required.

Mechanical equipment maintenance manual file. All service manuals should be filed in the chief engineer's office for future reference. The file can be identified either by the equipment item name or by the tag number used on the card file system. Warranty cards and guarantees can be placed in this file also. Diagrams used in installing or servicing the equipment also can be included in this file.

Mechanical equipment service log. The equipment file mentioned previously can be adapted with signal tags that indicate frequency of maintenance attention. Weekly the engineer can check this file to see what preventive maintenance should be carried out and then can compose a schedule for the week's service work at that time. When the servicing is done, he can make a notation of this in the mechanical equipment service log. This provides a written record of the servicing and can be used if necessary to document proper care of equipment if failure occurs during the warranty period. It is also a record of work done that the administrator will want to inspect from time to time to be sure that the preventive maintenance program is working.

Emergency lighting systems. Most homes now have some sort of emergency lighting system for use in power failures. It may be battery operated. Actually, a generator powered by gasoline, diesel, or natural gas is preferred. The equipment should be installed so that it comes on automatically at the onset of a power failure. The maintenance man must check this equipment regularly and make immediate repairs if it does not function properly. If an electrical generator with automatic switching gear is provided, he should run it at least weekly, testing both the generator and the switching mechanism, putting a load on the equipment. Proper preventive maintenance is mandatory with this piece of equipment.

Color coding of piping and conduit systems. All pipes should be banded at regular intervals with color codes indicating their function. In the modern power plant, dozens of pipes and conduits crisscross each other, moving liquids, steam, or electrical energy from one piece of equipment to another, through pumps, valves, electrical panels, storage tanks, and pressure chambers. Suddenly they mysteriously leave the power plant either singly or in small groups to reappear in various places within the building in pipe chases, electrical panels, access panels, or mechanical equipment substations. Bands of colored tape coded to indicate the purpose of the pipes and conduits aid in repairing in the future.

Building plans and diagrams of systems. Safe storage of these valuable documents must be provided. Although the engineer will need to refer to them frequently, they must be protected. Hanging them from racks is a better method than storing them rolled. A master set of the architectural, structural, mechanical, electrical, and framing plans of the entire building with a set of the original specifications should be stored in a safe place elsewhere. Frequently, a contractor makes changes in the plans as a building progresses. These "as built" changes should be indicated on the engineer's set at least.

Schedules for valves and controls. The engineer should make a master list showing the location and tag numbers of all shut-off valves within the building. Nothing can prove to be more unnerving than to have a pipe freeze and break and not to be able to remember the location of the shut-off valve.

The electrical panels should be numbered to correspond with the electrical plans. Each control in each panel should be identified.

Diagrams of underground supply systems. The engineer should indicate on the plans where underground services enter and leave the building. He should note water lines, gas lines, underground electrical conduits, sewer lines, and telephone service lines.

List of emergency service contractors. The engineer together with the administrator should develop a list of emergency telephone numbers for both day and night of contractors who can be called for major mechanical, electrical, water, or sewer service. This list should be reviewed regularly. A copy of this should be available to the person in charge of the facility in the absence of the administrator.

Water treatment. Hard water that is not properly treated with chemicals can quickly ruin a heating or air conditioning system. The water treatment equipment should receive professional service from a reliable chemical supplier. Periodic checks should be made of the water system and of the tubes in the boilers and air conditioning equipment to determine if scale is building up.

Seasonal changeover. As seasons change, the needs of the building naturally change. During the winter, time should be set aside for thorough inspection, cleaning, and preventive maintenance of the air conditioning systems. Frequently such service is performed by the facility staff. If the equipment is highly technical, however, a service firm should be engaged for this maintenance. As summer approaches, the same procedure should be done for the heating systems.

Care should be taken to drain outside pools, water lines, and water towers when cold weather arrives again.

Breakdown of major equipment

Regardless of how careful the preventive maintenance program is, eventually a major equipment item will break down, such as an elevator, a dishwasher, a heating plant, an air conditioning unit, or an electrical system. The engineer must have instructions to notify the administrator immediately when a breakdown occurs, so that the administrator may make emergency plans if necessary for the protection of the residents.

Requisitions for work—work order

In the small facility usually no formal method of requisitioning repair is necessary or practical. Verbal requests given to the maintenance man or the administrator are usually sufficient. Requisition or work order procedure is necessary in the larger and complexly organized home. The work order is a written request for service or repairs of equipment sent through channels for approval and scheduling. In emergencies, verbal requests for service should be accepted, but a written request should follow the report.

The written record is necessary for control purposes. Also, it serves as a cost-accounting mechanism. Approval of work orders by the department head or the administrator allows for control so that proper appraisal of the request is given. A work order to remove a door in a corridor is likely to be vetoed by the administrator or department head because of the specific need for the door for fire safety.

Moreover, repeated orders to repair a certain piece of equipment will focus the attention of the administrator or the department head on the possible need to replace the machine rather than to suffer continued repair costs and lost time while it is out of service.

Cost-accounting features of the work order is of interest to the accountant, who spreads indirect cost or overhead to the revenue-producing departments.

For minor repairs another method is practical. The head of each department, such as nursing station, business office, kitchen, and housekeeping office, keeps a notebook in which needed minor repairs are noted. The maintenance man makes weekly rounds with a special cart well stocked with repair and replacement parts. As he arrives at each station, he examines the book; makes the necessary repairs; and initials the request, indicating that he has done the work. This system worked successfully in a large midwestern hospital; however, daily rounds were necessary to keep up with the work load.

GROUNDS MAINTENANCE

Grounds care may be included as a subsection of the housekeeping department or the mechanical maintenance department. The responsibility of this function can be easily given to either department. The strength of the department heads and the size of the exterior grounds together with the extent of development of gardens and the amount of formal and ornamental shrubbery may help the administrator to decide who should have the responsibility.

Sometimes it is more economical to contract for this service. This might be prudent if there are a lot of plants that require technical care. On the other hand, simple grass cutting and occasional trimming can be done by part-time summer employees.

Daily attention must be given year round, however, to the exterior appearance of the plant. The grounds must always be well groomed and free of trash, debris, and hazards. Walks should be swept regularly.

Someone must be given the responsibility of inspecting the grounds daily and correcting unkempt conditions. Hazardous conditions should be corrected immediately whenever possible. Broken steps, loose railings, and uneven or pocked walks should be barricaded until repair can be completed. Excavations occasionally necessary for the repair of underground lines should be blocked off and lighted at night.

Tree trimming should be left to contractors unless an experienced person is on the staff. Improper trimming can damage the trees and can be a dangerous operation if done by inexperienced labor.

Exterior water lines, underground sprinkler systems, and fountains must be drained if the climate requires this procedure.

Attention should be given to the appearance of outdoor signs. They should be kept in good repair and in good appearance. Parking lot lines, center road lines, and direction-of-travel indicators painted on the roads also should be kept in peak appearance.

Exterior lighting systems are important for adequate security as well as for enhancement of the appearance of the building. All parking lots and walkways should be well lighted. Good lighting should be provided at all exits, too. Exterior lighting is necessary for the safety of personnel and helps to keep vandalism to a minimum.

Homes that are located in areas where there are cold winters should have procedures established for clearing walks and drives of snow and ice. Since there must always be access to the facility in case of emergency, during storms snow must be removed from main drives and walks as it accumulates. Therefore, a procedure must be set up for calling in personnel for special night or weekend duty in areas where there are heavy snow or ice storms. Mechanized snow-removal equipment should be owned by homes in such locations. Chemicals for melting of ice should be stocked prior to the season. Care should be taken in selecting such chemicals, since some can damage concrete walks. Salt is inexpensive and is quite useful in most cases. However, it can be tracked into the home by visitors and employees, causing damage to entry floors if they are not properly protected or cleared quickly. Other commercially available chemicals can be used, although they usually are more expensive. In areas where there are extremely heavy amounts of snow, some thought may be given, in the original construction, to the use of a snow-melting system that is built into the walks at the main entrances. A separately controlled system of steam or hot water pipes can be installed below the surface of the walks. This can be turned on by staff on duty to help to delay accumulation until the snow-removal staff arrives.[5]

In residential facilities, if there is available land, residents should be allowed to develop individual or joint-project gardens. The heavy work, such as plowing, discing, or other ground preparation, should be done by staff. The resident can then take over using his green thumb to the best of his ability. Frequently, harvest time can provide the home's kitchen with lettuce, cabbage, carrots, tomatoes, potatoes, and melons that can be served with special flair. Perhaps a sign stating, "Grown with loving care by Mr. _____" could be displayed when such an item is on the menu. Often the residents may want to invite other residents for special parties in their own apartments to serve their home-grown vegetables, using their own special recipes and techniques.

A convenient water supply near the garden area should be provided.

Residents can be encouraged to develop flower gardens near their apartments in homes with ground-level cottages. The heavy work of preparing the soil should be done by the staff, but the day-to-day care can be a great pleasure to the resident himself.

Residents who are interested in helping with the home's formal gardens should be allowed to participate, but should be given some special guidelines. The guidelines should be specific, since the care of some plants—roses, for example—requires special knowledge. Certain residents who wish to volunteer for assisting in the care of the formal gardens should be given instructions and some supervision by the home's gardener.

Every facility, regardless of its level of care, should have an area developed for a formal garden of some type. This, of course, is an expense item that may well be difficult to justify if costs of care are high and reimbursement (public or private) levels are restricted. Formal gardens, though, will enrich the life of most of the patients or residents. If the design of the facility allows for freedom of the ambulatory confused patients to enter an inner courtyard garden on a warm, sunny day and for the staff to assist the nonambulatory patients to go there also, these patients can benefit from this delightful experience. It should be noted, however, that attention should be given to limitation of such activity on extremely hot or humid days to avoid overexposure to the sun.

Good landscaping, in general, wherever possible greatly enhances the home's appearance to the general public and certainly adds to the patients' happiness. In large cities where ground is expensive, landscaping may be limited because of the size of the available land. Where land is available, trees, shrubs, and evergreens properly placed make the home more attractive. The patients can enjoy a view from their windows if they are looking out on a tree-shaded lawn.

BUILDING MAINTENANCE
Building exterior

All buildings need periodic maintenance. Postponing or ignoring these needs merely compounds the problem and leads to higher repair costs.

Regular inspections of the building exterior should be made personally by the administrator. He should look for the deterioration of painted surfaces, loose masonry, and deteriorated tuck-pointing material. Roof inspections should be made after the winter season has passed.

Usually the major maintenance of the building exterior should be done by contractors.

It is wise for the administrator to call for a semiannual meeting with the physical plant committee of the board of directors for the purpose of making an inspection of the exterior of the building jointly. This certainly should be done at least annually prior to the preparations of the facility budget.

Careful inspections should be made frequently in newly constructed plants. The inspector should watch for roof leaks; water absorption through brick walls that have not been properly waterproofed; settling of the foundation that creates cracks in plaster or masonry walls; erosion of backfills of earth at the foundation base that have not been properly tamped; leaks in the foundation walls in the basement areas; and premature deterioration of walks, drives, and parking lots. These are but a few of the many problems that may be found in a newly built home.

When a home is built, often there is haste in final work to meet a predetermined opening date. The pressure from the owner on the contractor to complete the job may contribute to lack of proper attention to final details. This should be anticipated and guarded against.

A new home may have landscaping problems. Frequently, a home is opened with the contractor still finishing part of the building. There may be unsightly construction debris resting on unsodded, muddy grounds. Landscaping may not have been done. The home's image may suffer. As quickly as possible, the ground should be seeded or sodded with grass, shrubs and trees planted, and the construction materials and equipment removed. A winter opening delays planting, of course, and hopefully the public will be understanding; but proper and suitable grounds cleanup should be done to show that, at least, there is a plan to offer a delightful environment as soon as the spring planting season arrives.

The maintenance of the exterior and interior of the older building may require high expenditures annually. There is a current trend of phasing out older plants through increasingly tighter and higher federal guidelines and the adoption of the requirements of the National Fire Protection Association (NFPA) in these guidelines. Owners of older buildings should seriously consider the costs of new construction versus the continuing costs of upkeep of an obsolete plant that may well soon be ruled unsafe for patient care as standards are raised further.

Building interior

In constructing a home, the owner should have his builder plan for ease of interior maintenance. Original costs may well be higher as a result, but ongoing annual maintenance costs could be lowered with intelligent building planned with this in mind.

First of all, local, state, and national codes specify the requirements for the interior finish of walls, ceilings, and floors. The Life Safety Code of the NFPA specifies the allowable "flame spread" characteristic for interior surfaces for nursing homes, residential-custodial care homes, and homes for the aged.[6] State and local codes, too, spell out certain requirements.

A hard plaster finish is recommended for most areas used by patients or residents.[5] It should be smooth finish rather than sand or rough-grained finish. The use of a good quality paint in the original application results in less frequent repainting. Wallpaper, which should meet NFPA specifications, can add to the pleasant atmosphere if good color coordination is used. Wallpaper surfaces should be limited to walls not subject to being struck by carts, vacuum cleaners, or other portable equipment. Metal corner covers can help to protect walls of corridors. If funds permit, more durable wall finishes can be used to save maintenance; heavy synthetic fabric materials that meet NFPA specifications should be considered. Exposed interior brick walls need no maintenance and, if done decoratively, can provide years of carefree service in a residential type of facility.

In bathrooms, utility rooms, and toilet rooms, walls with ceramic tile on wainscot to high levels are most practical. These areas are constantly exposed to high humidity, water, and soil and need to be cleaned frequently with strong detergents.

Although asphalt tile is probably the most economical floor finish,[5] other types of tile such as vinyl or rubber are more easily maintained and are more comfortable. Quarry tile floors are most practical in kitchens. Carpeted floors are becoming popular for use in corridors, lounges, offices, lobbies, and waiting areas. In my experience, carpets are the least expensive type of floor finish to maintain when used in areas other than patients' rooms.

There is much controversy over carpets in nursing homes and residential homes. Tests have been done to determine the safety qualifications of such surfaces. The latest edition of the Life Safety Code has a tentative interim amendment concerning floor finishes. It recommends that authorities having jurisdiction over fire safety standards of the local area (usually the state or city fire marshal's office) request test information on any floor finish material whose fire characteristics are unknown.[6] Severe danger can be created by the smoke from the combustion of some types of carpets and carpet pads.

LAUNDRY AND LINEN SERVICE

Generally speaking, it is better for homes providing nursing care to have their own laundry systems. Residential facilities that do not have nursing care may find contracting for linen service less expensive. However, there are many variables to be considered in deciding whether or not the home should do its own laundry. A small nursing home, one with 60 beds or less, probably could contract service more cheaply than doing the laundry itself. A 200-room retirement apartment complex for well senior citizens could likewise probably contract linen with less expense than operating a laundry. Volume is one of the major variables to be considered.

In the retirement complex, linen is changed once weekly, except when there are unusual needs. With proper scheduling of changes, only one fifth of the home's linens need to be changed each day. If there are 200 beds, approximately 80 bed sheets, 40 pillowcases, 80 large bath towels, 80 hand towels, 80 washcloths, and 40 bath mats are needed each day. Depending on local rental rates, this amount of linen can be rented for less than $8,000 annually.

The cost of operating a laundry includes the amortization of original equipment expense; cost of providing space; cost of investment in linen inventory and of replacement; cost of utilities, such as electricity, gas, and water; cost of washing supplies; cost of routine maintenance and repairs to equipment; and the cost of salaries of laundry workers. These costs far exceed the rental costs in this type of facility.

Coin-operated washers and dryers can be located conveniently throughout the facility for the personal linen needs of the residents, and the home can arrange to have a local dry cleaner pick up the residents' articles and bill them directly for their dry cleaning needs. Small nursing and personal care homes also may find it cheaper to contract for linen service.

Cost of equipment, space, and utilities

Recently I discussed linen service with a group of administrators operating several different types of homes. Most of the homes provided nursing care and residential care combined. The administrators advanced several thoughts about cost of equipment, space, and utilities.

First of all, space is needed. How much space is needed depends, of course, on the volume of linens and the method of finishing. Today, no-iron linens can be used in most instances; thus the problem of the space and cost of a mangle is eliminated. However, if the home is to do patients' linens, ironing boards and mending room space must be considered.

The equipment itself involves a minimum investment of several thousand dollars, plus there are costs of installation. The cost of utilities must be considered: water will be a big expense factor in some areas; the cost of energy to run the equipment, heat the water, and dry the clothes may be a major item in other areas.

The servicing of the equipment, too, must be considered. The breakdown of equipment that puts machinery out of service for several days until repair parts arrive should be anticipated. Such breakdowns, especially in older plants, can be a serious problem that the administrator must face at some point. Standby equipment can be available, but this adds further to the capital expenditure.

If the laundry is located in the basement, the cost of an elevator or dumb waiters may have to be added. Proper ventilation is essential for the comfort of the personnel. Noise, heat, and vibration of the machinery require that the laundry be located away from the patient areas.

Hidden costs are often forgotten in the original consideration of the problems. There are the overhead costs of possibly higher workmen's compensation rates, since laundries, as do kitchens, often have high accident rates. The possibility of a higher employee turnover rate for the laundry employees may affect the home's unemployment insurance costs. These and other employee benefits such as Social Security contributions; vacation, sick leave, and holiday benefits; plus special individual benefits that the home may also provide its employees, such as participation in part of the health insurance package, retirement benefits or pension plans, and other special courtesies, must be considered.

There are equally strong arguments for homes, especially personal care and nursing homes, to have their own laundry. Most important is the matter of control: of quality, supplies, costs, inventory, and life of the linen.

One home changed from its own laundry to a contract service because the age of the home's original equipment presented constant breakdown problems. Another home made the change because the board of directors thought the service could be done cheaper by an outside firm. The administrators of these homes mentioned that they soon had quality and supply problems. The incidence of bed sores increased in one home shortly after switching; it was found that the commercially prepared linen had a harsh chemical residue remaining in the materials that caused these bed sores. The infection rate also increased. Strikes at the commercial laundry; poor delivery schedules; poor quality of finished products; and badly worn, tattered, and stained linens with many mends also were reported as discouraging factors by the second administrator. Both administrators mentioned that frequently the linens they received were not put into service but merely returned unused because of the poor condition. This often left the home short of adequate supply.

The consensus of the group of administrators was that if it is economically feasible, it is better for the home to do its own linen. It is primarily a matter of volume. One administrator who controlled a 900-bed operation that included a hospital, reported that his linen costs were approximately 3 cents a pound. An administrator of a much smaller home mentioned that his costs were about 8 cents a pound. These figures are for 1969.

A home should also consider approaching a local hospital that operates a laundry to see it it would be interested in doing the facility laundry on a contract basis. A hospital also is concerned with quality and infection control and might be anxious to run its large laundry a few extra hours a week to help lower costs when the equipment normally would not be in use.

It is difficult to determine at what point it becomes cheaper for the home to do the laundry itself. Generally speaking, however, a nursing home or personal care home with 100 beds or more finds it more economical to do its own linen. It encounters problems, but it has better control, better quality, and probably less expense. A home that size probably has a laundry to do patients' personal linen. It is not unusual for the patients' family to take over this responsibility in many homes. Often, however, there is no one to do this chore and the problem falls on the home.

Personal linen needs of patients and residents

In the retirement residence facility for well aged people, provision of coin-operated machines and contact with a local dry cleaning–laundry service usually meet the needs. It is that simple. The home staff does not need to get involved unless there is a problem.

In the nursing home or personal care home it is a far different matter, since this type of home is often responsible for personal laundry. When someone's dress is lost, all the personnel from the administrator to the laundry supervisor, including the director of nursing, the consulting dietitian, the cooks and kitchen personnel, the activity director, all the maids and the housekeeper, the entire nursing staff, the janitors, the grounds keeper, the contracting exterminator, the mailman, the patient's daughter, the patient's physician, and the patient's cousin Maude 300 miles away, hear about the "tragedy." To the uninitiated reader—one who has not taken on the job of administrator of a nursing home—this may seem quite far fetched and perhaps humorous. Those who have experienced this know that I may have omitted some who also might hear of the incident.

There are ways to help to avoid the loss of personal laundry. First, all items brought into the home on arrival should be marked permanently with a label or with an indelible pen. To help in identification, the patient's name or a code number can be used. This should be the responsibility of the relatives, but often the home must see that it is done. The family should be asked to make sure that all new items brought to the home are marked properly first. The home should discourage patients from bringing large amounts of clothing; they should have only enough for proper supply while the soiled items are being laundered. Expensive dresses and items requiring dry cleaning should be sent home with relatives, too, unless there are satisfactory reasons not to, and the relatives should assume the responsibility for the care of these items.

Second, a clothing list should be completed when the patient first arrives. The list should be complete and should be filed with the patient's records. One fallacy of this concept is that the home usually cannot control what the relatives subsequently bring in or later remove.

Third, the administrator should impress on his staff the importance of helping to avoid the mix-up or loss of residents' personal linen. Careful attention to detail will help. If all are concerned and are trying to be helpful, loss can be minimized. Hopefully, theft will not occur, but it is a possibility, and all personnel should be warned of the seriousness of such action.

Fourth, the method of collecting patients' linen for laundering is important. One administrator told of the use of single bags for each patient's linen, marked with a special code identifying that particular patient. The linen is washed along with the bag, and then it is finished, ironed, folded, and returned. The items folded are returned in the bag; the items ironed are returned on hangers with the bag. Although this method is not foolproof, it can reduce errors.

Proper laundry techniques

All the potential economies that can be achieved by the home's own laundry can be lost by improper laundry techniques. Although sending the home's linen out for processing is no guarantee, either, of proper technique, a well-controlled laundry operation is necessary to realize the maximum in savings. Probably the greatest loss in the washing process occurs because of the improper use of washing chemicals. Through poor control of the amounts of detergents, sours, bleaches, and additives, severe loss of tensile strength of fabrics occurs. With good practices, average linen life is greatly increased. With improper or careless methods, linens may have a short life and soon end up as rags.

If the administrator does not know anything about laundry techniques, as a start, he can talk with laundry equipment salesmen, linen salesmen, and supplies salesmen. He should listen to representatives of several different companies to learn as much as possible before making final decisions about equipment, linen materials, and washing supplies. Several companies supply literature and handbooks offering excellent instructional opportunities for the uninitiated. Also, the American Hotel and Motel Association has a fine publication entitled *The No-iron Laundry Manual* available at modest cost.[7] It is a highly valuable document for the home operator.

An example of a handbook provided by a supplier is *Your Guide to Martex Presslin 303 Sheets and Pillowcases* prepared by WestPoint Pepperell. This manual discusses a specially developed, patented process that modifies the fibers of the no-iron linen (a blend of Dacron and cotton) so that the material can be washed using proved sanitizing techniques long employed by hospitals (high water temperatures, chlorine bleach, and sour) without damage to the material and with no-iron results.[8]

The administrator must understand several basic techniques in order to oversee his laundry operations: He must first understand the capabilities and limitations of the equipment. This is essential before investment in equipment is made. The proper size washer must be selected. If warranted, two or three washers should be considered. A second washer, even though not always needed, can act as a standby for breakdowns or can double productivity of the employees. Besides seeking advice from more than one supplier of equipment, the administrator should, if possible, visit other homes, hospitals, or motels in the area that do their own linen. Large hospital types of machines are not necessary in most cases. Hospitals have much greater linen demands than do nursing homes because of their requirement of linen for special needs, such as surgery, obstetrical care, x-ray, central supply, and nursery, not found in nursing homes.

The type of linen purchased by the home is a factor determining the type of equipment and number of personnel needed. No-iron linen is a God-send for the home. No longer is it necessary to run linens through a hot mangle for a good finish. The specific manufactured product Martex Presslin 303 material illustrates the newest concepts. It was developed by WestPoint Pepperell. With this new material, ordinary hospital type of washing techniques can be used to assure bacteria kill, and sours can be added at the end to remove any alkaline substances that might tend to prove harmful to a patient's skin if left as a residue.[8]

No-iron linen is definitely the type to use in the home's laundry program. Research done by WestPoint Pepperell shows that the average life of a 180-count cotton sheet is about 100 commercial washings. Just a few years ago, the very best sheet was the 180-count percale. The no-iron product Martex type 180 303 Dacron/cotton blend has been tested and shown usuable after 350 similar washings. As shown by this research, the life of the Martex type 180 303 no-iron sheet is more than three times that of the previously best available all-cotton product. Although the original cost per dozen is somewhat higher for the Martex sheet, there is a proved savings in attrition and in personnel finishing time.[8]

Methods of washing linen. Another aspect of the laundry that the administrator should know is the washing formulas for the linens and the washing supplies needed. A suggested guideline formula for Martex linens is found in the WestPoint Pepperell booklet, as follows:[8]

This formula is an outline. Alterations may, and should, be made at the discretion of the Laundry Manager based on his requirements, experience and equipment and the supplies he used. The Laundry Manager will doubtless have a formula which he uses for cleaning cotton sheets to his satisfaction. By all means, use that formula, altering the supplies as necessary.

OPERATION	[WATER] LEVEL	TEMPERATURE	TIME
1 Flush	High	90° F.	5 minutes
2 Break	Low	160°–170° F.	10-15 minutes
3-5 Suds	Low	160°–170° F.	5-10 minutes
4 Flush	High	150° F.	3 minutes
5 Bleach	Low	150° F.	5-8 minutes
(antichlor—as necessary)			
6 Rinse	High	135° F.	3 minutes
7 Rinse	High	120° F.	3 minutes
8 Rinse	High	105° F.	3 minutes
9 Rinse	High	90° F.	3 minutes
10 Sour	Low	90° F.	5 minutes

Typical supplies per 100 lbs.

Break—nonionic detergent	8-12 oz.	Heavily soiled loads
Sodium metasilicate	10-20 oz.	may require the
Caustic	0-4 oz.	higher amount of
Sodium tripolyphosphate	4-6 oz.	supplies.
Brightner	0-.5 oz.	

Suds—½ break supplies
Bleach—1-2 quarts 1% sodium hypochlorite
Sour—Ammonium silicofluoride 1 oz. *or*
    acetic acid to pH 5.5.–6.0

Some of the terms used in this formula may need to be defined. The term *break* refers to the initial contact of the soiled linen to a high concentration of detergent products with a high pH (very alkaline). Its shocking action breaks loose the soils in the fibers and floats them free into the wash solution. *Suds* is a lesser concentration, usually of the same alkaline products. This action continues to remove the embedded soil from the material fibers and deposit it in the wash solution. As the break and suds cycles are dumped, the greatest amount of the soil is removed. This removal action is continued by the following *flushing* cycle. The use of the highly alkaline solutions in these cycles begins the bacteria-killing process. The high temperature of both cycles also contributes to the killing action on most bacteria.

The term *bleach* is self-explanatory. It should be noted, however, that the proper concentration of a chlorine bleach is a most effective bacteria-killing agent.

Antichlor is used to remove any residue of chlorine that might remain. It is important to make sure that no chlorine residue is in the finished product.

Sours, which are on the acid side of the pH scale, are added at the final cycle to remove the last traces of alkaline material in order to bring the product to a natural state, or a balance between alkalinity and acidity. *Softeners* may be added along with the sour to increase the quality of the finished product.

After the linens are washed, excessive water must be removed by mechanical extraction. Depending on the equipment, either the water is extracted in the same machine, or the linens are manually removed and placed in a centrifuge. In extracting water from linens of special blends, it is important to see that the temperature after washing is reduced to at least 100° F. or lower before the extraction process is begun. Extraction of water at higher temperatures could possibly harm the Dacron filaments.[8]

The next step is tumble drying. The tumbler must not be overloaded. There must be sufficient space for the linen to tumble and flex during this step. When the sheets are dry to the touch, the heat should be cut off, but the tumbling action must be continued until the sheets are cooled to 100° F. or lower. Stopping the tumbling action before the sheets cool to the lower temperature produces a finished product of poorer quality.[8]

At this point, the no-iron sheets are ready for folding and returning.

Quality of finished product. I believe that the finished product must have the following qualities for optimal patient use. It must be (1) sanitary; (2) free from chemical irritants; (3) soft and smooth; (4) white and with no stains; and (5) in good condition, with minimal visible repairs.

The washing formula shown on p. 84 produces a sanitary product free from chemical irritants if handled correctly, and sheets of the Dacron/cotton combination have a gentle finish that is less irritating to the patient. Most stubborn stains may be removed from this type of product with some spot cleaning or presoaking methods. The laundry supplies salesman or the linen company representative can provide assistance if the laundry manager encounters difficulties with stains.

There have been some questions raised about the sanitary qualities of the finished product of no-iron linens that cannot withstand a high temperature and chlorine bleach wash formula. This is why I was pleased to find a no-iron sheet that can be washed under conditions that will produce effective sanitation. The WestPoint Pepperell Dacron/cotton sheet is such a product, and it can be washed just as an all-cotton sheet, with high temperatures, bleaches, or any other sanitizing or germicidal agent that the laundry manager would ordinarily use. The material may even be autoclaved if necessary.[8]

Handling of finished product. All the care the laundry manager has put toward supplying a sanitary product with a good appearance can be defeated if the product is not handled properly after leaving the laundry. Delivery to the linen storage or distribution area must be done in carts used only for clean linen. The carts may be lined with paper. They should at least be covered. Clean linen should never be placed in carts used for collection of soiled linen. Color codes on the carts can help identify their purpose: for example, the use of a red stripe for soiled linen and a green stripe for clean linen is a convenient method of identification. Storage space for linen should be clean and free of moisture. For control purposes, it should be locked.

Linen distribution systems must be individually devised according to the needs and staffing of the homes. Linen distribution can be assigned to either the nursing service department or the housekeeping department or can be the responsibility of the laundry. In a residential complex, usually the housekeeping service should supervise this function, since there is a minimal change of linen (weekly) that will be performed by maids. In a combination facility such as a home for the aged that offers various levels of care, residential settings through nursing care, the responsibility may best be divided as follows: housekeeping overseeing the residential areas and nursing overseeing patient care areas, with the laundry responsible for delivery to two or more storage points.

Emphasis should be placed on keeping the linen clean throughout the delivery-storage-delivery-application series regardless of who has the responsibility. For example, maids and nursing aides should be shown how to keep the fresh linen clean while transporting it and while changing a patient's or resident's bedclothes.

Handling of soiled linen. It is essential that safe and sanitary techniques be used throughout this process. It begins with removal of linen from the bed. Linen should be folded inward, with the top sheet and pillowcases in the center, making a bundle. The attendant should not lift the bundle so that it touches the uniform. It should be placed in the collection cart at once and not placed on the floor or chair.

Linen stained with fecal matter, blood, and the like should be taken to the hopper in the soiled-linen utility room and rinsed free of debris. It should then be placed in a plastic bag and put in the soiled-linen cart.

Although canvas carts for soiled linen are usually less expensive, carts made of fiber glass or a light-weight plastic are ideal. Either fiber glass or plastic is easily cleaned with disinfectants. If a canvas truck is used, the liner should be removed regularly and put through a wash cycle.

It is unusual for a nursing home to have much *contaminated* linen—linen that has been in contact with patients with a contagious disease or infection. Usually such patients are transferred to hospitals that are equipped to care for them. However, there may be a period of time when isolation techniques are necessary while the patients are awaiting transfer. In these cases, special techniques are necessary for *all* departmental personnel coming in contact with the patient. These procedures will involve the nursing, housekeeping, dietary, and of course, laundry departments.

Contaminated linens should be placed in a specially marked bag, and the laundry must follow specific methods, keeping the linens separate until they have undergone the complete wash cycle. A special cycle should be developed for this purpose. The manager should consult his products supplier about modifying the cycle for contaminated materials. There are bags available that will decompose in the wash cycle so that once placed in the bag, the linen will not have to be touched until the wash cycle is complete. When using such a bag, the manager should consult with the manufacturer for any special changes necessary in the cycle.

Control of linen

Although elaborate systems are set up to prevent the theft or embezzlement of cash, frequently protection of other assets in the form of supplies is neglected. Unfortunately, employee pilfering has become a major hidden expense in many businesses. The long-term care profession is not immune to this problem. Office supplies; foodstuffs; and housekeeping supplies, such as paper goods, light bulbs, soaps, and linen, are frequently targets of theft.

Although it is impossible to develop a foolproof system, a tight linen control program can be used to minimize loss. Depending on the general linen program and the staffing of the home, the system should be under the individual or joint responsibility of the housekeeper, nursing director, and laundry manager. When linen is transferred from one department to another, an accounting should be made. Likewise, the housekeeper or nursing supervisor should issue a specific amount of linen to a maid or aide, sufficient for the assigned needs.

One method that is popular in hospitals is the pack system. Packs are made up by the laundry personnel for specific needs. In the nursing home there might be several types: a pack for bedfast patients that contains a complete change of linen, including two bed sheets, a draw sheet, a pillowcase, bath towel, and washcloth; a pack for incontinent patients that contains a complete change of linen plus a diaper and a patient gown; and a pack for ambulatory patients that contains two sheets, a pillowcase, towel, and washcloth but none of the other items. Under this system, daily requisitions are sent to the laundry for a specific number of each type of pack by patient name. The linen is delivered at the end of the working day for the following day's use.

When this system is used, an allowance must be made for special needs that occur between deliveries. A linen standard for loose extra linen can be developed by experience for each nursing unit. Therefore, if extra linens are necessary between deliveries of packs, they are there. This extra supply is inventoried daily and refilled to the standard. This supply must be kept locked and under the control of the person in charge of the unit.

Whatever system is used, it is important that the home have something that will work efficiently to the satisfaction of the nursing department, the housekeeping department, and the laundry. It is logical, then, that the administrator should have these three department heads jointly develop the specific details.

In the residential home, control is more easily maintained. Generally, the home's administrator assigns linen control to the housekeeper, who in turn, issues to each maid the exact amount of linen that she will need for her daily tasks. The housekeeper keeps the supply of linen under direct supervision in a locked room or closet.

Linen inventory. The inventory of linen is a tedious task, but one that should be done at least quarterly. There are various problems to be overcome, depending on the type of home.

A major purpose of the inventory is control. It is necessary that the housekeeper or laundry manager be the only person who is designated to approve the removal of linen from service that is unfit for use. A record is kept of the linen that is converted to rags so that when the inventory is taken, this normal loss can be taken into account. If the inventory shows a large loss, the distribution system should be reviewed. The mysterious disappearance of, say, four dozen sheets, means a dollar loss to the home of $200, more or less.

Another need for the quarterly inventory is to anticipate the need to order new linen. Depending on the type of linen and the methods of purchasing, it is necessary to be able to anticipate the needs of the home well in advance. With a reliable and regular count, the person doing the purchasing of the linen can have enough statistical data to know when to take advantage of special linen buys offered by suppliers.

FOOD SERVICE

It is assumed, for the purpose of discussion in this section, that the home owner has determined not to contract with an outside firm for this service. He has elected to have the home administrator establish a food service department that has a department head directly under the administrator's or assistant administrator's control. This person may be a food service manager or, in the smaller facility, the head cook.

It is also assumed that the home provides a minimum of three meals for each resident or patient each day, the cost of which is included in the monthly rate.

It should be pointed out, however, that both these assumptions are rather arbitrary. There are retirement facilities that do not provide any food service and those that provide it on an optional, or pay-as-you-go, basis. There are some that include only one or two meals a day in the monthly rate, usually lunch and/or supper.

It is my opinion that at the minimum, two meals a day should be included in the monthly rate of a residential retirement facility. Ideally, all three should be included to ensure that the resident has an adequate dietary program. If the cost of the meals is included in the rate, the resident is more likely to have a well-balanced diet. If the meals are optional or not available, there may be a tendency for the resident to omit meals in order to cut costs. Moreover, if the resident has to leave the building to eat or to purchase food to prepare his meals, he may be limited by inclement weather or distance to the shopping areas. One of the benefits that can add to the success of a retirement facility is the relief provided by food prepared on the premises by the staff. Facilities should be provided for cooking, however, in the resident's apartment if the agency sponsoring the project can afford the original expense. This option of cooking an occasional meal within his own "private home" will allow the resident sufficient freedom to escape from the boredom of the institutional routine that will inevitably come in even the best retirement residential programs.

No matter how well the food service program is planned, there are always complaints. Some of these complaints may be superficial, concerning the food, its preparation, the variety of the menu, or the service. Quite often, however, they are really the result of monotony of eating with the same people, at the same table, in the same room, at the same time, discussing the same things day in and day out.

Eating is an activity that is usually an enjoyable experience and that people like to share with one another. However, there is always need for change. Thus a kitchen is a desirable feature in each apartment in a retirement facility so that a resident can prepare a meal now and then alone or for a special group. It is a normal continuation of a previous life style. Of course, in a nursing home or personal care home, this cannot be done.

People complain of poor food service for other reasons than monotony. The older person may have other very legitimate reasons to complain about the food no matter how well it is prepared or how choice the selection is. One of these reasons is poorly fitting dentures that make even the most tender cuts of meat difficult to chew. Quite often there is a definite loss of taste or of ability to smell the savory odors of excellently prepared food, as a result of the normal aging process. Restricted diets, too, play a definite role in the loss of enjoyment of eating. Salt-free food simply will not satisfy a person used to gourmet cooking or even good old-fashioned home cooking. Bland diets or low-calorie diets also add to displeasure at mealtime. If because of an ulcer, a resident is restricted by his physician from coffee, which he has enjoyed day after day for 40 or 50 years or longer, he may not be happy at mealtime no matter what is served. Also, certain medication regimens may alter the taste of food somewhat.

The administrator must be prepared to listen to complaints about food service, since he will get them. If the complaints are legitimate, he must discuss them with his food service supervisor or department head. He must keep in mind, however, the possibility that the problem is really not with the food or its preparation, but is with the patient himself.

Consulting dietitian. Usually a home is not able to afford a registered dietitian to manage the food service department. Furthermore, some argue that the management of the food service department is not the proper function of a dietitian. Many administrators prefer to employ a food service manager rather than a dietitian to oversee the department. This is my preference. However, it is mandatory that a registered dietitian provide ongoing *consultative service* to the food manager and the administrator.

Once a month, at the minimum, a registered dietitian should visit the home for at least a full day. One of his many duties should be to review complaints. He should talk with the complaining residents and then evaluate the complaint with the administrator and the food manager. The role of the consulting dietitian should be merely advisory; he should not direct the activities of the department. He should advise the food manager and the administrator, using his expertise in nutritional science; act as a liaison when necessary between the resident's or patient's physician and the home when special dietary problems or requirements are not met by standard special diets; instruct the resident or patient in his special dietary needs when necessary; inspect the department in all its areas and functions, making recommendations for changes when necessary; review the menus to make sure that they are adequate in quantity and nutritionally in balance and offer suggestions to help reduce monotony; review the standard recipes and observe the preparation of the food products, giving advice when necessary; assist the food manager with purchasing and with writing specifications for quality of foodstuffs; give advice about the safe use of leftovers; conduct in-service training sessions for the food service personnel; and interview the patients or residents to determine their attitude toward the food service. These are several suggested duties of the consulting dietitian. Depending on the strengths or weaknesses of the food manager, this list can be expanded or reduced accordingly. In general, however, at the minimum, the dietitian must be consulted whenever special nutritional programs are required, and he must approve the menu and recipe program.

The administrator can have a major problem on his hands if the relationship between the consulting dietitian and the food service manager is not positive. Each must clearly understand each other's role and responsibilities. The administrator must remember that the food manager is the one primarily responsible for the performance of the department. He should, before introducing a consulting dietitian into his organization, discuss the idea with the food manager. The administrator should make it clear that the food manager is definitely still in charge. He should be aware that the introduction of the consultant into the home might well be considered by the manager as a threat to his job. The manager might think of the sonsultant as a spy. The administrator should carefully discuss the role of the consultant with the manager prior to seeking the service of the consultant. He should ask the manager to assist him in developing the job description for the consultant. The administrator can suggest areas in which he feels the manager needs assistance and note the reaction of the manager. Hopefully, the two can develop a job description that complements and expands the talents of the food manager.

Considering that a good relationship has been developed, the administrator should allow time to meet jointly with the consultant and the food manager each time the consultant visits. The consultant should be expected to render a written report directly to the administrator after the visit. A copy of the report should be given to the food manager.

In facilities providing health service, the dietary consultant should also meet with the chief nurse and the food manager during the day at the home. The purpose of this meeting is to explore nutritional problems noted by the nurses and to help to solve interdepartmental problems that do not require the intervention of the administrator. The consultant should be allowed to see patients' or residents' medical files and should be encouraged to write notes in the records whenever notes are needed. He should be encouraged to participate in the development of the patient care plan.

In a retirement facility providing no on-site nursing care, a typical consultant's day might be as follows:

8:00 A.M.   Arrives at facility and meets with food manager to plan day's activities.
8:30   Observes manager and assists him when requested in placing food orders with suppliers. This may involve cutting open sample cans of supplies brought in by salesmen.
9:30   Inspects food storage areas. Checks temperatures on refrigeration and freezer equipment.
10:30   Observes preparation of noon meal.
             Reviews menu for day and observes the way cooks follow recipe guidelines.
11:30   Reviews menus for next 30 days and makes necessary suggestions.
12:00 noon   Observes serving of noon meal. Samples food. Walks through dining room and casually chats with residents, noting their comments.
1:00 P.M.   Observes waste return and cleanup procedure.
1:30   Meets with nurse and food manager (if on-site health service is offered).
2:30   Meets with residents or patients who are in need of consultation.
4:00   Meets with administrator and food manager for review of day's activities.
4:30   Departs from facility.

The consultant's schedule should be flexible. If the dietitian believes that he is not needed during the purchasing process and that prior inspections of the food storage areas have been satisfactory, he may prefer to spend most of his day carrying out one particular function, such as interviewing residents. He should be allowed the freedom to make this decision, and the food manager should also be allowed to suggest the concentration in a certain area in which he may be having a particular problem. The dietitian should occasionally come later in the day so that he can observe the evening meal preparation and service.

In facilities offering health care, federal guidelines require a minimal amount of dietary consultation—at least monthly. It is my opinion that more frequent consultation is necessary and that the dietitian's arrangement with the facility should allow for regular consultation via the telephone between visits when dietary questions arise. New residents or patients admitted between visits may require special dietary advice and contact between the dietitian and the physician in certain specific instances. The arrangement the facility has with the consulting dietitian should allow for this assistance in between visits.

One may argue that a consulting dietitian is an expense that a retirement facility housing only "healthy" aged people does not need. If costs are a factor, the argument is strengthened. I believe, however, that this is a valuable service for well aged people and the facility is likely to save money in the long run with the services of a food consultant. Certainly the health status of the residents is better protected by good nutritional supervision by a qualified dietitian.

Organization of the department

Management function

Management techniques. The head of the food service department is a manager, as is the administrator. Therefore, he employs the same techniques of management that any manager utilizes. He plans, directs, organizes, controls, and staffs the department. He gets the work done through the use of specialized employees with certain skills, trades, or training. He gets them to work as a team to produce, as a single unit, the food service needs of the organization. This requires a great deal of people-management ability. He often has temperamental personnel who, although highly skilled, provide the manager with frequent disciplinary or group morale problems. This department often has a higher rate of turnover than other departments. Accident rates are usually higher, too. The personnel do not have the comforts that most of the staff have who work in air-conditioned areas during the summer.

There is no doubt that the food manager's job is difficult. Often people have remarked to me that they would not want to be the administrator of a retirement complex for anything in the world. (Well, frankly, at times, I can see their point.) However, this is exactly the way I feel about the food manager's job! The workday is long and the days off are often infrequent. The complaints can be deflating, and the personnel conflicts, confounding.

Nevertheless, there is an increasing number of professional food managers who are well paid and well qualified. There is a demand for good food managers, not only in the retirement and long-term care field, but also in the hospital field. A good food manager, of course, has long been in high demand in the commercial restaurant business.

Administrators expect food managers also to perform the following functions besides the management techniques.

Menu planning. The food manager should develop a cycle menu, in consultation with the dietitian, that is well balanced, provides variety, uses foods in season, and is within the cost per day projected for the food service operation.

Purchasing. The food manager should purchase from reliable purveyors foodstuffs and supplies that meet the standards set by the administrator or owner and that, when it is appropriate, are government inspected and graded according to the home's standards.

The food manager must maintain ethical relationships with suppliers. There are often temptations to purchase certain items at questionable prices or in greater-than-needed quantity in return for "premiums" that a company offers to send directly to the manager's home. These premiums may be transistor radios, television sets, or similar items. Everyone who is in a position to act as purchaser for an agency sooner or later is confronted with such an offer. In the long run, the home really pays the cost of these items. The food manager must carefully guard against this practice and politely refuse the offer.

In purchasing, the food manager must be certain of the safety of the product. He should refuse items received that do not meet specifications. When he deals with a reputable dealer, the dealer usually gladly replaces them at no cost. Less reliable suppliers may be reluctant to cooperate. It is also a dangerous practice to buy salvage items or damaged or dented cans.

Careful inspection of the items received should be made prior to their acceptance. It is necessary to have a large scale to verify weights of items priced by weight. Produce should be carefully examined. For example, the manager should inspect more than just the top several heads of lettuce in a crate. The consistent or inconsistent quality of items received soon lets the manager know which suppliers are being fair and delivering goods that are of the quality specified and in proper condition for consumption. An excellent discussion of purchasing practices and standards can be found in a book entitled *Nursing Home Menu Planning—Food Purchasing Management.*[9] It very clearly describes the various grades and qualities of canned goods, meats, poultry, fish, eggs, and the like. It also offers a valuable discussion on menu planning and a set of menus for an entire year with recipe references and a section devoted to special diets. It is an excellent resource for the food manager, head cook, and administrator. There are many other good reference books that should be included in the food manager's library.

Control of costs and keeping of records. Another function of the food manager is the controlling of costs and keeping of cost and statistical records. The use of efficient purchasing practices that incorporate the set standards of quality is the first step in cost control. However, the manager must take other steps as well.

Poor food-production techniques can contribute to unnecessarily high costs. Foods poorly prepared are usually not consumed and end up in the garbage. The manager should frequently inspect the returned trays or plates in the dishwashing room for unusual amounts of uneaten food. He should frequently sample the food as it is served to be sure of its taste quality and its temperature. Cold vegetables, no matter how well prepared, will usually be returned. Meat should be cooked properly so that shrinkage of it is minimized. The manager should make sure that during preparation of vegetables and fruits, the cooks take care to trim them properly, but with minimal waste.

The correct use of leftovers will contribute greatly to lower food costs. The manager must be certain that the product is safe to use and that it is stored correctly. Nothing that has been served to a resident or patient can be saved, of course. Products that have been prepared but not served should be refrigerated immediately and worked into the following day's menu or frozen for future use. Leftover meats and vegetables can be used in a variety of ways that are tasteful and nutritious. The manager should be very cautious about leftovers, making sure that they are safe to use. Often the manager controls the use of leftovers himself or delegates the control to the chief cook. It is important for the manager to be cautious about the use of leftovers, but he must remember that this unused food represents part of his inventory and thus part of his food cost.

Efficient scheduling of personnel must be done. The manager should see that weekly work schedules are well planned to avoid overstaffing and to prevent overtime. Job assignments should include work for employees during the slack periods of time during the day. Mealtimes and coffee breaks of the employees should be well supervised. Busboys, waitresses, and dishwashing room men should have general cleaning assignments to do when their main jobs are completed.

For cost comparison, meal cost per resident or patient per day should be prepared monthly. A daily *meal count* must be maintained on an accurate and consistent basis. For example, in a retirement facility for well aged people, it must be determined whether it is a statistical meal if a resident requests only a bowl of soup for lunch or if an employee who brings the rest of his lunch purchases a salad or dessert. After the guidelines are established, it is important to be consistent.

The meal count is very important. By dividing the dietary costs by this count, the manager can arrive at the cost per resident or patient per day. This can be further broken down to show the cost per day of *raw food*, the payroll, supplies, and miscellaneous items.

In a nursing home that does not provide any meal service for the employees, the problem is somewhat simpler. The manager merely uses the monthly patient-day figure for the divisor. In the retirement facility, however, where residents may or may not show up at every meal, a meal-count system is mandatory.

The administrator should make sure that the food manager uses the agreed formula in reporting the meal count. Meal counts can be inflated by counting employee coffee breaks or minor purchases of food such as desserts, milk, salads, or other items that do not fully constitute a meal. An inflated meal count will make the food manager look good on paper because he reports a lower cost per meal.

Inventory control. The inventory of foodstuffs and supplies is an important area of management control. The food manager should attempt to turn over his inventory quickly unless he has made a large-volume purchase. Rotation of stock, with the oldest item being used first, is necessary too.

The manager should take a physical inventory count at least monthly. Orders are based on future menu demands and present inventory levels. For some items, it is necessary to do this more frequently. Produce, fresh meats, dairy products, bakery goods, and similar perishables are used within a short period of time, and inventory control is needed on a daily basis. Canned foods, dry packaged goods, and frozen foods and meats, however, may be on hand for several weeks or longer; therefore a monthly inventory count will suffice.

Dating of the items in storage is important. In this way, the manager can determine the age of the product and use the oldest item first. Boxes or tags on packages can be marked with the date quickly with a marking pen when the items are first placed in storage.

Environmental sanitation and food-handling techniques. The food manager must be expertly qualified in food and environmental sanitation. He must understand and apply all the necessary safeguards to see that the kitchen is clean; that the employees are free from communicable disease, wear clean uniforms, and use proper personal cleanliness techniques; and that the food is prepared, handled, stored, and served with safe, sanitary methods. The raw food product must be safe for consumption and correctly prepared. Proper temperature controls must be maintained after the product has been prepared. Hot foods must be kept hot (140° F.) after preparation and constantly during the serving time. Since foods may lose flavor after prolonged periods, it is essential that good timing be maintained during the serving period. Cold foods, likewise, must be kept cold until served.

The food manager must understand the great dangers inherent in not following these simple basic rules. If these principles are not scrupulously followed, the home is in danger of a serious, perhaps deadly epidemic of food poisoning.

General cleaning of all utensils, working services, storage areas, floors, ovens, sinks and other similar items must be carried out constantly throughout the day. The kitchen should be left in immaculate condition at the end of the day, with all garbage and trash removed.

Proper sanitary techniques must be employed in cleaning dishes, trays, and silverware. There are approved methods of washing dishes by hand. Small homes may well utilize these techniques. The large facility needs an automatic dishwasher that can handle large quantities of plates, cups, silverware, glasses, trays, and miscellaneous patient service items. The dishwasher should include a wash cycle with a rinse with a minimum water temperature of 180° F. Proper supplies that are automatically dispensed must be used. There are several very reliable detergent supply companies that can provide excellent technical advice along this line.

Pot and pan washing, likewise, must be done with approved methods. A two-compartment sink with a water agitator can be helpful. Correct usage of supplies and high water temperatures is necessary. Nothing should be dried with towels. All items should be either dried automatically or allowed to air dry.

Insect and rodent control requires cooperation from the staff and the engagement of contract exterminator services. All doors to the exterior and windows that can be opened must have screening that is kept in good repair. Cooperation from the staff is necessary to see that the doors are never propped open or kept open for prolonged periods of time. Even during the receiving of goods, care must be taken to keep the doors open as little as possible. A fly control fan is quite helpful; it is a strong, downdraft fan that sends a blast of air across the threshold of the doorway and inhibits the insects from entering. Local or state health regulations should be checked before this type of equipment is installed.

I highly recommend professional extermination service on a regular monthly basis. For only a few dollars a month, depending on location and size of the home, an exterminator can keep this problem to a minimum. The use of sprays and chemical agents to kill vermin in the kitchen areas requires the skill of a professional so that the utensils, foodstuffs, and equipment are not contaminated.

Storage of foodstuffs and supplies. Items should never be stored directly on the floor. Air space should be left between stacks and rows of boxes. Shelving or wooden skids should be utilized in bulk storage areas. Although expensive, heavy stainless steel wire shelving is a good long-term investment. It is sturdy and easily cleaned.

Storage of foodstuffs or supplies in basement areas often is practical, since the cost per cubic foot of construction of a basement is somewhat less.

Careful inspection of the storage area should be make regularly for signs of vermin and for signs of dampness. In certain areas with known high-water problems, back-pressure gates should be installed in the floor drains. This will prevent drain or sewage water from being forced back up through the drain openings by pressure of high water or a stopped-up system. Stored materials should never be placed under exposed drainpipes serving systems on upper floors. Other pipes that collect condensation should be wrapped.

Adequate lighting is essential. Storage heights should be limited for safety. The accumulation of trash should not be allowed. Cleaning supplies, poisons, and chemicals must not be stored in the same area as the foodstuffs.

Stock in storage longest should be drawn out first. Boxes should be dated and used accordingly.

The storage areas, freezers, and refrigerators should be locked at night. Remote storage areas should be kept locked at all times.

Food preparation function

Cooking. Recently there has been a big swing to the use of *convenience foods.* Convenience foods are precooked and/or frozen items ranging from entrees, vegetables, and desserts to the complete many-course types of dinners served on airplanes.

There are several major companies producing these products. Among the largest of these companies are Litton Industries, Stouffer's frozen food unit, Armour and Company, Swift and Company, Sara Lee, and the Marriott Corporation.[10] The use of these foods seems to be the answer in some institutions and restaurants to the problems of increasing costs of labor and the difficulty in finding skilled personnel. To a certain extent, this approach has been successful. A few hospitals have utilized this method totally and have found it workable.

So far, however, with certain exceptions, it still seems more practical for the home to do the majority of the cooking with its own staff. Convenience foods are still too costly for most homes. Moreover, since the residents of the home are fairly stable, they would soon tire of the still rather limited line of entrees. I recently spoke with an official of a large food service program that operates in several states in the Midwest and South. He pointed out that meat loaf and other ground-meat products cannot be satisfactorily precooked and frozen. Moreover, he is not a believer in convenience foods, preferring to do the food production with cooks at each individual unit.

A supply of precooked frozen dinners in the home's freezer might be used for an emergency backup in the event of a temporary severe personnel shortage or some other serious problems, however.

Although some food managers predict that within a few years convenience foods will be the major method of institutional and restaurant food service, the mainstay of the home today continues to be the on-site cook.

Even though the cook prepares the food in the home, he relies more and more on frozen raw vegetables, fish, and meat products. The deep-freeze area of a home's kitchen should be planned so that it can be expanded with little difficulty. Modular units are commercially available. As the knowledge of freezing of foods continues to increase, more and more items will become available, and quantity buying in this area will be advantageous.

Cooking for older people can be a very confounding problem. Many have restricted diets that require special attention. Others cannot tolerate spices. The complaint of many in homes that the food is tasteless comes from the problem that the cooks are limited in the amount of seasoning they can use.

Standard recipes must be developed for almost every item on the menu. The home's food manager should see that the home has a reliable set of recipes. These can be obtained commercially. The home's consulting dietitian should review these recipes. The cooks should be required to follow them without alteration unless the manager approves a test of a recipe that is an old favorite of one of the cooks. If the test is successful and the dietitian approves the change, the recipe can be added to the menu.

For control, it is essential that the cook follow the preplanned menu for the day. Cycle menu planning is the job of the manager and the consulting dietitian. The manager buys in anticipation of the menu. Changes made by the cook without authorization can cause many problems for the home's food manager.

Baking. Bakery goods, breads, pastries, cakes, pies, cookies, and puddings, are necessary items on the menu. In some special individual dietary situations, these items are to be avoided. In general, however, they are necessary items and form a significant part of the budget. The home may find it cheaper to buy all its bakery goods, or it may be able to employ a baker who can produce many of these items. If the home has a large freezer, certain items can be prepared in large quantities and frozen for future needs. A large quantity of pie shells can be made and frozen at one time, for example, and used as necessary for later meals.

Many nursing homes need to serve nourishments to their patients. Nourishments are usually made by reducing foods to a liquid state in a blender. Since there is usually no cooking of these products, a heat sterilization process is not present. Careful attention must be given to the preparation of these items to keep them as bacteria free as possible. They should be refrigerated until used.[11]

Serving function

Table service. Even in skilled nursing homes, patients should be encouraged to come whenever possible to a central dining room for their meals. With the exception of the breakfast meal, only bedfast patients should be served meals in their rooms. There are exceptions, of course. Generally speaking, community dining is a part of the social rehabilitation program needed for the invalid elderly person.

Waitress service provides excellent portion control, but when selective menus are offered, it is sometimes slower. Of course, in the nursing home environment waitress service is the only method possible.

Cafeteria or buffet service. In the retirement facility for well aged people, buffet, or cafeteria, style service is possible. Portion control is more difficult with this method, since a person can ask the line server for another slice of meat or two different entrees. Another disadvantage is the temptation of the residents to touch or handle the food and not take it. This occurs if part of the line has self-service items such as desserts, salads, bread, butter, lunch meats, and the like.

Meal tray service. In a retirement facility offering food service, some method should be developed for the delivery of trays to apartments of residents suffering from minor, temporary illness. There is a question of whether this should be the task of the dietary personnel or the health office personnel or both. My experience has been that usually the tray can be taken by a dietary worker who has instructions only to deliver and set up the tray. If the resident requires assistance in getting up, the health office should see that he is prepared prior to the serving time or should send someone with the dietary worker. Occasionally, when a resident returns from the hospital, there is a period of time when he continues to convalesce in his apartment. Temporary tray service is necessary during this period also.

Portion control. The size of the portion of meat, of the scoop of ice cream, and of the serving of vegetables should be rather precise and equally accurate. A cook or line server should know that he can serve a certain number of portions from a roast of beef and a certain number of individual servings from a gallon of ice cream, depending on the size of the scoop and the number of scoops served. This is one of the very important aspects of cost control. Although no patient or resident should leave the table hungry, waste or extravagancy of serving should be avoided.

Employee meals policy. The individual home must make its own policy about employees' meals. Some homes offer a meal at no cost to their dietary employees. Other homes provide one free meal to every employee. This practice is quite costly and, in view of the rising costs of care, is one employee benefit that may soon be abolished. Many homes allow the employee to purchase a meal at cost.

An employees' dining area should be planned for the home. Employees who bring their lunch should have a refrigerator available to them for safe storage. Since this is a highlight in the employees' day, the area should be conducive to comfortable, informal dining. It is not a good practice to allow the employees to leave the premises for meals. They should be encouraged to remain in the building.

The lunch hour, usually limited to a half hour, should be controlled. Employees should not be allowed to stretch this period beyond the period allotted.

Cleaning function

Trays, dishes, silverware, and utensils. The task of cleaning these items usually begins with a scraping of garbage and a prerinse done by hand, preferably over a large, electric garbage disposal unit. The operator should be trained to watch for silverware so that it is not lost in this process. A piece of metal dropped into the disposal can easily damage the equipment. Silverware lost in the garbage because of carelessness of the employee can account for a high replacement cost.

Cleaning of equipment and work area. Cleaning of the equipment used in the kitchen requires the help of all the kitchen personnel. Cooks, although they may not be happy with the idea, should be trained to do some washing of their equipment as they proceed with their working day. The baker, too, should cooperate. Although they should not be expected to actually do the washing of the pots and pans, except in a small home, they should be expected to keep their work area clean as they work. Since the kitchen usually has one of the highest accident rates, care should be taken to keep the floor free of debris, grease, and liquids throughout the day.

At the end of the day, all the stoves and ovens should be scrubbed clean; all tables should be left clean and dry; all utensils should be washed, dried, and stored in their proper places; all sinks should be wiped dry; and the floor should be given a thorough mopping. Trash and other wastes should be removed to storage or pickup bins and not left in the area. The kitchen and dining room, at the end of the day, should be immaculate, ready for the following day's work.

Periodically (at least weekly) the hoods and grease filters in the exhaust systems must be cleaned with a degreaser. If this is neglected, grease may quite possibly be the source of a fire in the kitchen.

At least twice a year the walls should be washed and, depending on the finish, painted as necessary. Chipping or cracked paint or plaster should be attended to without delay.

Disposal of wastes. Waste products from the kitchen often have a value for a salvage or scavenger company. Grease, for example, may bring a small return if saved in containers provided by the scavenger company. Although garbage used to have value, laws relating to its use now make it more practical to dispose of it mechanically through a disposal system whenever possible.

Other wastes are large cans and cardboard boxes, bones, coffee grounds, paper goods, and trimmings of foods too tough for mechanical disposal. These should be disposed of in large Dumpster containers if this service is available.

By all means, waste products must be removed from the kitchen area by the end of the day.

General considerations

The administrator should consider installing a separate locking system for the kitchen area. The kitchen should be secured in order to protect the storage of foodstuffs. All refrigerators and freezers should be locked at the end of the day.

However, the main key ring carried by the charge nurse or supervisor should include a key to the kitchen for emergency needs. If she needs to enter the area after it has been locked, she should leave a note for the manager stating her business in the kitchen.

The kitchen should be secured at the end of the day by a responsible kitchen employee. This person should see that all the electrical and gas appliances are turned off and that the locking of all storage areas has been completed correctly.

The administrator should be interested mainly in seeing that his food department produces with regularity, products that are constantly of good quality, satisfy the nutritional needs of his charges, are prepared within the budgetary allowance set out at the onset of the fiscal year, and are prepared within the guidelines of the state or local health and licensing authority, and that the results satisfy the patients or residents psychological and social needs, including the palatability of the finished product.

FIRE SAFETY

At 3:30 A.M. an administrator receives a telephone call: "Come quickly! Your nursing home is on fire!" What a horrible event this must be for the administrator to experience. What a terror it must be for the helpless, elderly, or infirm patients to be surrounded by smoke or flames, waiting for help. What a tragedy fire is to the patients' families who trusted you to care for their mothers and fathers. The staff on duty will never forget the sudden urgency, the screams, the sirens, the firemen, and the ambulances, as they personally witness the horror before them.

Recently I was allowed to go through a nursing home that had experienced a devastating fire several days earlier. As a result of the fire, 10 persons died and more than 30 were hospitalized. The smell of charred wood, the sight of burned bed linen, the smoke-blackened walls, a melted television set, a few pitiful personal belongings twisted out of shape by the intense heat will never be forgotten. This home was not constructed to meet the current standards set forth by the Life Safety Code of the National Fire Protection Association (NFPA). It therefore was not licensed for and did not have patients who were classed as requiring skilled nursing care. Nevertheless, patients died.

Fire safety construction standards

The 1970 edition of the Life Safety Code calls for sprinkler systems in all hospitals, nursing homes, and residential and/or custodial or personal care facilities, except those of fire-resistive or protected noncombustible construction that are not more than one story.[6]

The code also warns that the recommendation of early-warning detection devices and automatic sprinkler systems in all new and existing homes regardless of construction may possibly be added to the code. An NFPA committee has been assigned to study this to determine whether or not it should be part of the requirements of the 1973 edition of the Code.[6]

Fire-resistive construction, sprinkler systems, and early-warning detection devices are certainly necessary for protection of residents and patients. However, these are not absolute guarantees of fire safety. Building contents; finishes of floors, ceilings, and walls; draperies; and accumulation of flammable materials can create killing fires or smoke. In selecting interior finishes, the administrator must review code requirements, too; unless local or state codes are more stringent, he would be wise to follow the NFPA Life Safety Code recommendation. Flame-spread ratings are specified for homes in this code. The local or state fire marshal can provide assistance by explaining the meaning of these ratings. The same precautions must be followed in selecting carpeting. In a tentative, interim amendment, the NFPA recommends that local authorities request test information on the material before it is approved.[6]

Fire evacuation planning and training of personnel

A building of fire-resistive construction with all of the fire safety devices still can have killing fires. The administrator must consider not only the construction and the added safety devices, but also the following very important ingredients for fire safety: a good fire evacuation plan rehearsed regularly by all personnel, adequate staffing of fire-alert personnel for all shifts, and good housekeeping and maintenance techniques and practices.

Several recent nursing home fires have had tragic results because of failure of personnel to respond adequately. Therefore, training of all staff members should be a regular feature of the home's fire safety program. If a staff member knows what to do on discovering a fire and performs in an intelligent, cool, efficient manner, lives will be saved. The mere closing of the door after a patient was removed from a burning room could have prevented the spread of smoke and fire that subsequently killed over 30 people in a midwestern nursing home recently.[12]

Adequate 24-hour staffing is mandatory in all facilities. Administrators of homes providing care must take into consideration that sedated patients may be quite difficult to arouse from sleep and may be confused. Frequently the major loss-of-life fire has occurred on the third shift. This is traditionally the shift with the least personnel on duty. Elaborate well-rehearsed fire programs are of no value if the training of the third shift personnel is overlooked or if there simply are not enough hands to provide the essential first line of fire defense until the firemen arrive.

The administrator should occasionally visit the home unannounced on the third shift. If he arrives at the home at 2:00 or 3:00 A.M. once in a while, the conscientious administrator should soon learn of the difficulties and dangers that might be encountered if a fire were to break out at that time.

During the periodic fire training sessions, special attention should be given to night-duty personnel. Sessions should be held on this shift so that the instructor can adapt his training to the special night-shift environment and staffing.

Fire prevention is everyone's job. All personnel should be instructed to be on the alert constantly for fire hazards. Electrical wiring and equipment should be inspected regularly. Fuse systems should be checked often to ensure that proper fuses are correctly installed. Trash and refuse should never be allowed to accumulate. Wastepaper and empty cardboard and wooden cases should be removed from the building daily.

Hazardous and highly flammable liquids and gases should be stored in segregated areas in accordance with section 6-5 of the Life Safety Code. Safety cans must be used for the storage of small amounts of flammable liquids that are necessary for daily use within the building. Glass jars should not be used for this purpose in any case.

Perhaps the best way to begin to design a fire evacuation plan for the home is to invite representatives of the local fire department to the home for a conference. The state fire marshal, too, could be involved. The home administrator should develop a good relationship with the local fire department personnel, listening to their recommendations and welcoming their inspections.

The fire plan should have at least two sections: one covering the immediate responsibilities of the person discovering the fire and a second describing the specific duties of the several departmental groups. Each departmental group section should begin: "If the fire is in your area, do the following: . . . ." Then there should be a second set of instructions reading: "If the fire is not in your area, do the following: . . . ."

Fire authorities and administrators have suggested several basic steps that should be taken when a fire is discovered.[6,13,14] Ideally, they should be done simultaneously. However, a staff member should use judgment about which to do first in a particular situation if he is the only one on hand at the scene of the fire. Protection of life is paramount; therefore, calling the fire department and removing patients or personnel from immediate danger should be done first. Next, sounding the alarm by pulling the lever on the firebox should be done quickly. Isolation of the fire is likewise essential and must be done quickly. It may be the first step if, for example, the fire is in an unoccupied area and a door to the area can be closed.

Notification of the fire department must be accomplished at once. In several recent nursing home and retirement home fires, this was not done immediately and tragedy was the result. Ideally, the home's fire detection and alarm system should be connected directly to the fire department dispatcher. The NFPA Life Safety Code requires that the system be designed to transmit the alarm according to local regulations.[6] The fire plan must provide for a backup of this system with a telephone call by a staff member to the fire department. If the home's alarm system is not connected to the fire department, the fire plan should point this out and include telephoning the fire department as the first step.

Certainly, removal of people from immediate danger, notification of the fire department, sounding of the alarm, and isolation of the fire must be accomplished first. However, the plan must not end with these four steps. Attempting to extinguish the fire should have high priority in the plan. Immediate action by a properly trained staff member may eliminate the need for taking any of the four steps in many situations. For example, an aide who notices a small fire in a wastebasket may extinguish it simply by smothering it, by pouring water on it, or by using a fire extinguisher. This prompt action may be the most logical first step and may end the problem before the fire becomes dangerous.

Since what is to be done first is a matter of judgment on the part of the staff members present, it is essential that staff be trained and knowledgeable so that their judgments are based on predetermined logical methods. Good staff training helps to control panic and gives employees and patients confidence at the critical moment of discovery.

Evacuation of patients or residents must be part of the fire plan. The staff should practice the safe and proper methods of lifting and carrying patients and dragging them on blankets, as both individual and team efforts. These techniques should be practiced regularly and incorporated into in-service programs for new personnel.

Evacuation routes must be preplanned and made a part of the written plan. Assembly points should be established so that an accounting can be made to determine whether or not all patients and personnel are out of the area affected.

The nursing department or, in a residential setting, the administrator's staff should develop a list of residents or patients who would require special personal assistance in an evacuation. This list should be updated regularly and kept available for all shifts. An example of a person who should be included in such a list is an ambulatory resident in a retirement home setting who does quite well with an artificial leg and is able to come and go with ease when wearing his appliance and thus is considered eligible for a residential type of living accommodation but who would, however, probably require special assistance in a fire emergency. Confused nursing home patients and bedfast patients would likewise require special individual assistance. I learned recently that one particular nursing home administrator uses color-coded name tags on patients' doors for the purpose of identifying those who need assistance.

Special precautions should be taken by the staff to make sure that patients or residents, once safely evacuated, do not return to the fire scene. A confused patient or a resident anxious to obtain some forgotten article might suddenly bolt back into the buildlng without warning. The staff should be warned of this possibility.

The proper use of fire extinguishers must be stressed in the personnel training sessions. Quick action with these units can extinguish or hold the fire until the fire department arrives. Frequently, untrained personnel fear these devices and do not understand their specific use and operation. The noise from a carbon dioxide extinguisher may frighten one who has never operated it. The loud whoosh can be frightening the first time it is heard.

Extinguishers must be inspected and tested annually. This inspection time is a good time during which to call a general training session to let the personnel operate a few units. While the service company is on the premises, the units that have been operated can be refilled and immediately put back into service.

If the building is equipped with standpipes and fire hoses, fire department personnel should be consulted to provide proper training to staff in their operation. This is especially necessary if the hoses are under high pressure from a pump. Special grips by two or more people may be required to control the hose. By all means, the staff should understand how to use the hoses properly if the fire department believes that they can be used by the staff with safety.

Automatic alarm devices and early-warning signal equipment, such as heat detectors, rate-of-rise detectors, smoke detectors, carbon monoxide detectors, and ionization detection systems, must be periodically checked. Some of these units have electronic components that can fail. Without regular testing, the systems may be inoperative at the time of need. Personnel should be instructed in the manual operation of pull stations.

The fire plan must also incorporate a notification of the fire department. This is called for in the Life Safety Code, which requires that arrangements be made to wire the automatic and manual fire alarm systems so that they send a signal directly to the fire department. If the local fire department does not allow this, a commercial alarm system company might provide service. In all cases, however, the plan should call for a secondary backup call by personnel on duty by telephone to the fire department. Since an automatic alarm system can fail, it should never be the only method employed.

Smoking by patients and residents is often a problem. In the controlled environment of the nursing or personal care home, regulations governing smoking, limiting its practice to certain safe areas, should be designed and enforced. In the retirement complex, where residents maintain independent living, this is difficult to legislate. Resident handbooks should include instructions about safe disposal of cigarette ashes. Residents should be warned not to smoke in bed.

Special fire hazards can exist in independent living quarters. The handbook should alert residents to fire safety practices. Residents should be reminded not to allow unsafe conditions to exist within their apartments. Administrators of facilities providing maid service should warn the housekeeping staff to be alert for these hazards and to report any to the supervisor, who should take action.

Where residents are allowed to furnish their own apartments, the administrator should oversee this practice to guard against potentially hazardous items. Electric equipment that is the property of the residents should be checked to make sure that proper grounding is maintained and that it is in good repair. Draperies and carpets supplied by the residents should likewise be fireproof and subject to administrative approval.

The following resident evacuation plan is an example of a plan designed for a typical retirement residence with a health service. These are all ambulatory residents, living in an apartment-type, independent living residential complex. These instructions are developed therefore for residents who are able to evacuate the building themselves. A separate fire plan has been developed for the staff. It is included after the section on resident evacuation.

RESIDENT EVACUATION PLAN
TYPICAL RETIREMENT RESIDENCE WITH A HEALTH SERVICE

To all residents:

Please familiarize yourself with these fire safety regulations. Never try to fight a fire by yourself, no matter how small you think it might be. An alarm must be turned in and help summoned.

Turning in the alarm

If you see a fire, it is essential that you report it at once. You may report it by doing any of the following things:

1. Pull down the lever on the red fire alarm box located conveniently in all the corridors.
2. Dial operator and report, in a clear calm voice, the location of the fire.
3. Use the emergency intercom system in your bedroom to report the location of the fire.

Evacuation of your apartment

If the fire is in your apartment, evacuate your apartment at once. *Close the door behind you.* Do not reenter the apartment under any circumstances. After you have left your apartment, you should be sure to pull down the lever on one of the fire alarm boxes, if you have not already done so. You may then evacuate the area in the most convenient manner. Please do not run. In the high-rise building, *never* use the elevators to evacuate; use only the two fire escapes located on either end of the building. Report to the assembly area assigned to you. (The assembly points for all sections of the retirement residence are listed at the end of these regulations.)

If you hear the fire alarm bell ringing and the fire is not in your apartment, the most practical thing to do is to first feel your apartment door to make sure that it is not hot. If the door is cool, leave your apartment, closing the door behind you, and report to your assembly area to await further instructions. If there is light smoke in the corridor, place a wet cloth over your nose and mouth and proceed to your assembly area. If the door is hot or if the corridor is filled with smoke and evacuation through the corridor seems impossible, close the door. Residents on the ground floor should exit through their patio doors or apartment windows and residents in the high-rise building should go to their windows and await assistance from the fire department. If smoke enters the apartment under the door, place some sheets under the door so that the smoke cannot enter.

The buildings are constructed so that it is unlikely for fire to spread from one apartment to another as long as the doors are kept closed. The greatest danger from fires in the buildings arises from the smoke and gases created by the fire.

In the event of a disaster, such as a tornado, earthquake, explosion, or falling aircraft, in which the building or any apartments are damaged, the residents are to evacuate the apartments of the affected building and report to the assembly points.

Assembly points

The purpose of the assembly point is to assist the staff and the fire department in accounting for the residents. It is therefore necessary for you to go to the assembly point assigned to you if you do evacuate your apartment.

The assembly point for apartments 1 through 64 (all high-rise building apartments) is the main floor of the high-rise building. An alternate to that assembly point is the laundry/utility room areas by apartment 114 and apartment 150.

The assembly point for apartments 65 through 70 and 142 through 150 is the lounge in the high-rise building.

The assembly point for apartments 71 through 76 and 88 through 90 is the chapel.
The assembly point for apartments 77 through 85 is the lounge in the high-rise building.
The assembly point for apartments 91 through 96 is the lounge in the high-rise building.
The assembly point for apartments 102 and 103 is the lounge in the high-rise building.
The assembly point for apartments 98 through 101 is the main lobby, front entrance.
The assembly point for apartments 104 through 117 is the lounge in the high-rise building.
The assembly point for apartments 118 through 141 is the lounge in the high-rise building.

The assembly points are necessary for a quick counting by personnel to determine who is not yet there. This will be valuable information for the fire department personnel when they arrive. They can be told who is missing and thus can concentrate lifesaving measures toward specific areas. The residents themselves can assist in this count, since they would know which of their neighbors have not yet reported.

To fully implement such a plan, the fire department personnel should have a diagram or floor plan of the complex. Moreover, they should be familiar with the design of the building through firsthand contact during the development of the evacuation plan and in subsequent visits. This is why it is so important that the home administrator invite the local fire department personnel to the home at frequent intervals. Each time the department personnel come to the home, they will become more familiar with the floor plan, evacuation points, and assembly areas.

Instructions also must be given to the staff. The following instructions have been developed for a typical retirement residence and are presented as a suggested guide.

PERSONNEL FIRE AND DISASTER PLAN
TYPICAL RETIREMENT RESIDENCE WITH A HEALTH SERVICE

GENERAL INSTRUCTIONS TO ALL PERSONNEL

Refer also to individual department fire emergency plan.
If you discover a fire:
1. Turn in fire alarm by pulling lever on alarm box in the corridor.
   The fire alarm system in the retirement residence is a local alarm system. This means that it will sound the alarm only in the building where the alarm is turned in and will

notify the telephone operator which zone the fire is in. The telephone operator will place the call to the fire department and then alert the other staff members by use of the public address system.

It is imperative that you turn in the alarm as soon as possible, no matter how small you may think the fire is.

    a. Know where all alarm boxes are located in your work area.

    b. The fire alarm is a very loud bell.

2. Rescue anyone in immediate danger and close all doors.

    a. Keep calm and avoid panic.

    b. Extinguish fire on burning clothing, and remove the person from the fire area.

3. Confine the fire. Close all doors and windows and keep them closed.

    a. The fire doors will close automatically when the lever on the alarm box is pulled.

    b. Close all other doors and windows.

    c. Shut off *all* ventilation systems.

4. All necessary personnel will be notified by the telephone operator.

    Do not shout "fire"; be calm.

5. Fight fire using equipment as explained later.

6. During a fire alert, all personnel should refrain from unnecessary phones calls so that the lines will be free for important calls.

7. Personnel who have not been assigned specific duties during a fire alert should remain in their work area. If they are needed, they will be notified over the public address system.

Fire extinguishers

How to use fire extinguishers:

1. Water (silver container).

    a. Use on paper, wood, furniture, cloth, and rubbish.

    b. Remove seal, aim nozzle at base of fire, and press handle to operate.

    c. *Do not use* on flammable liquids or electrical fires.

2. Carbon dioxide (red container).

    a. Use on flammable liquids and electrical fires.

    b. Remove seal and press handle to operate.

3. Fire hose.

    a. Use on five-story building only.

    b. This is best for all large fires *except electrical.*

Precautions:

1. The water pressure on the fire hose in the five-story building will be low until the fire department has connected their pump to the connection on the outside of the building. Be prepared for an increase in pressure when this occurs.

2. Do not overestimate the life of water or carbon dioxide extinguishers. They do not operate for longer than a brief period of time.

3. Realizing the above problem, do not let the fire work you into a corner; *leave an escape route.*

4. *Do not use water on an electrical, grease, or oil fire.*

5. Always make every effort to keep calm, and close all doors and windows to keep fire and smoke from spreading.

6. Electrical fires may be controlled somewhat by carbon dioxide extinguishers. However, the current must be turned off before the fire can be put out completely. *Do not use water.*

Removal of residents and visitors

Residents should leave the building when the fire alarm rings. Personnel should assist them. Study the resident evacuation plan for details.

1. In nice weather, the residents in the cottage units should leave through their apartment patios.

2. During inclement weather, they should be guided to their assembly point through the corridors if they are not filled with smoke.

3. Residents and visitors on the second floor to the roof of the five-story building should be directed to the fire escape farthest from the fire. Use of the elevator should be avoided.
4. If the fire is difficult to control and the person in charge deems it necessary, the fire alarm should be sounded in the neighboring fire zone by pulling the lever on a fire alarm box in that zone and that zone also should be evacuated.
5. The residents will not be able to move as fast as you may think is necessary, so you must at all times be careful not to run into them. The more excited you appear, the more worried they will be. The more calm and orderly you appear, the less worried they will be. *Keep calm.* Remember that fear and panic can cause as much damage and loss of life as the fire itself.

Mobilization of personnel

You will be notified of the location of the fire over the public address system by the code name Mr. Rife. For example, "Mr. Rife, report to zone 6" or "Mr. Rife, please report to apartment 140." The fire alarm will sound only in the area that is affected. When a fire alarm is sounded, the administrator, nurse, housekeeping supervisor, all maintenance personnel, janitors, chauffeurs, and gardeners should report to the scene of the fire. All other personnel should remain in their work area, unless otherwise notified.

The buildings are divided into sixteen separate fire zones. It is imperative that each employee become familiar with all the buildings and the location of each fire zone so that he knows the shortest route to the fire when an alarm is sounded. The personnel who are to report to the scene of the fire should also familiarize themselves with the location of all fire extinguishers, since everyone, except the nurse and the housekeeping supervisor, should report to the fire with an extinguisher.

The nurse and assistant should report to the scene of the fire with the necessary equipment to administer first aid if needed.

The housekeeping supervisor's primary objective will be to help the residents leave the affected areas and to make them as comfortable as possible in a community area outside the fire zone.

The high-rise building is zone 5. The different floors of this building are designated as follows:
5–0 Basement—resident storage
5–1 First floor—lounge area and hobby rooms
5–2 Second floor
5–3 Third floor
5–4 Fourth floor
5–5 Fifth floor
5–6 Roof—solarium

DEPARTMENTAL INSTRUCTIONS
Switchboard operator

Follow general instructions also.
1. As soon as the annunciator bell sounds, signalling a fire, stop the bell by pushing the alarm silence button on the annunciator panel. Then notify the fire department. In reporting a fire, be calm and talk slowly and distinctly. Give full name: Best Homes, Inc. Give the exact location of the fire and, if possible, the apartment number and the fire zone and, if known, information about what is burning.
2. Notify personnel. Using the paging system, announce the location of the fire by giving the code name Mr. Rife and the zone number; for example, "Mr. Rife, please report to zone 6." If you know the exact location of the fire within the zone, include it; for example, "Mr. Rife, please report to zone 6, apartment 140" or "Mr. Rife, please report to zone 9, kitchen." In making these announcements, always *keep calm.*
   a. Notify personnel by two-way radio pagers. After you have notified the personnel by use of the intercom, use the two-way radio as follows: Press the microphone switch on. Push the red buttons, starting at the top and going to the bottom; for example,

1-3-6-9. Then push them again, starting with 9 and going back to the top; for example, 9-6-3-1. Repeat this procedure two times. You must keep the microphone switch on at all times while you are doing this. By doing the above procedure, you will contact all the pocket paging units and walkie-talkie units. Next, still keeping your microphone switch depressed, give the same instructions that you gave over the intercom system. After you have given the message over the radio two times, sign off and clear.

    b. After 4:00 P.M. on weekdays and all day on Saturdays and Sundays, notify the dietary department by phone, and give them all the details. The dietary department will take the place of the housekeeping and maintenance department on weekends and after 4:00 P.M. on weekdays.

3. During the day notify the administrator and assistant administrator. At night and on weekends notify the following people at their homes in the order listed, giving them all the necessary information, such as zone number and apartment number or area within the zone: administrator, maintenance engineer and assistant, assistant administrator, and chaplain.
4. Remain at the switchboard to give and receive instructions.
5. If switchboard current is affected or if the fire is in the switchboard area, use the pay telephone in the hall. Be sure to take the resident emergency file with you if you must leave the switchboard area.
6. Incoming calls may be answered after all the procedures previously listed have been taken care of. However, every effort should be made to keep all the telephone lines as free as possible so that if it is necessary to make a call in regard to the fire, lines will be available. If there is an incoming call to any of the personnel who are at the scene of the fire, simply take a number and have that person return the call later.
7. Announce "all clear" when instructed to do so.

Since the fire alarm system is a local system, the telephone operator plays the most important part in the total fire protection plan. The fire department will not respond until it has been telephoned by the operator. It is very important that the operator remain at her post and keep as calm as possible.

Although these guidelines are set down for your help, always remember to use your own good judgment when necessary. It is impossible for us, in setting up these guidelines, to foresee all the questions that may arise during a fire or emergency, and that is why you must use your own judgment in these circumstances.

Always remember that the telephone operator plays the most important part in the fire and emergency safety plan; therefore, always keep calm and alert.

Nursing office staff

If the fire is in your area:
Follow general instructions.

If the fire is in another area of the residence:
Proceed to the fire area with the nursing first-aid kit and resuscitator. There are two sets of these items: one is kept in the nursing office, and the other is kept in the nursing cabinet in the lounge in the high-rise building. Help remove the residents and visitors from the fire area and make them as comfortable as possible. Apply first aid if needed.

If an order is received to evacuate the fire zone, be sure that all residents are accounted for by a roll call.

After the all clear signal is given, a roll call of all residents within the fire zone must be conducted.

Maintenance department

If the fire is in your area:
Follow general instructions.

If the fire is in another area of the residence:
1. Go to the location of the fire, and take along a fire extinguisher.
2. Rescue anyone in immediate danger.
    a. Keep calm and avoid panic.
    b. Extinguish fire on burning clothing, and remove person from the fire area.
3. Confine the fire. Close doors and windows in the fire area.
4. Turn off the utilities, such as gas, electricity, and water, and cooling and heating systems in the fire area.
5. Fight the fire, using the equipment explained in the general instructions.
6. It is the responsibility of the maintenance department to know the location of all the fire alarms and fire-fighting equipment in the residence.
7. In the absence of the administrator or his assistant, the maintenance man on duty should act as fire marshal until the fire department arrives. If possible, one person should be sent to the main road to show the fire department which fire lane to use.
Note: Exit signs must be on at all times and must never be left with burned-out bulbs.

Housekeeping department

If the fire is in your area:
Follow general instructions.

If the fire is in another area of the residence:
1. Housekeeping supervisor should proceed to fire area and help to remove residents and visitors from the fire area and make them as comfortable as possible. Obtain blankets and other items to protect residents and visitors while they are outside. *Keep calm.* Close all doors.
2. Maids not in the immediate fire zone should stay in their assigned area unless instructed otherwise. Keep the residents in your area calm and out of the hallways. *Do not* let them go to the fire zone; ask them to stay in their apartments. Maids working in the fire zone should assist the housekeeping supervisor.
3. Janitors should report to the fire area with an extinguisher and follow the instructions of the fire director or maintenance man on duty.
Note: Never block fire doors, residents' apartment doors, or building exit doors with your carts.

Food service personnel

If the fire is in your area:
Follow general instructions.

If the fire is in another area of the residence:
Remain in your work area and await instructions over the public address system or from your supervisor.

After 4:00 P.M. on weekdays and all day on Saturdays and Sundays all dietary personnel should answer the fire alarm. You will be alerted by the public address system. You will also be notified by telephone. Always keep in mind that after 4:00 P.M. on weekdays and all day on Saturdays and Sundays you will be taking the part of the maintenance department and the housekeeping staff; therefore, it is important that you know the fire procedures for the residence. Always remember: *keep calm; avoid panic.*

Summary. The resident evacuation plan and the personnel fire and disaster plan presented in the chapter are for specific circumstances and building conditions. Each physical plant requires certain adaptations for its peculiar needs. To merely copy these plans would be foolhardy. They are successful plans for a retirement residence but *not* for all facilities. They are presented merely to provoke thought and criticism and to stimulate the reader to develop a better plan for his own home.

Plans often look good on paper. To find their weaknesses and flaws, they must be tested regularly through drills or dry runs. They must also be reviewed at least annually and updated and revised when necessary. Training programs must be held regularly so that the staff members understand the words written on paper. Drills, although time consuming and even boring to personnel, must be held. Documentation of the drills and their results is an excellent method of showing concern for fire safety to insurance company inspectors and other interested individuals.

The administrator must seek consultation and assistance in the development of the fire plans from the local fire department personnel. These people are vitally concerned with the well-being of the residents. They can lend invaluable assistance during the planning phase of the fire safety program. The local fire department should receive copies of the completed fire safety plans. They should also have on hand a set of building plans or schematic layouts of the campus if several buildings are involved.

Staff training is of paramount importance, especially for those serving from 11:00 P.M. to 7:00 A.M. This training should be repetitive so that newcomers as well as old-timers are constantly reminded of their specific duties.

An adequate staffing pattern is most essential, too, for the safety of patients or residents in view of fire dangers. The administrator must be sure that all shifts have sufficient, well-trained, and alert personnel on duty at all times.

BUILDING SECURITY
Keeping patients from wandering

Keeping patients from wandering away from a nursing home requires constant vigilance on the part of the staff and some basic building and grounds safety designs and appliances. Ordinarily, fire exit doors cannot be locked. Only under special conditions can this be done, and these conditions rarely are permitted in nursing homes. Since these unlocked doors are a known "escape" route, efforts must be made to supervise these doors. One approved method is the use of electric buzzers and indicator lights that are activated when the door is opened. The signal terminals should be located at the nursing stations.

A second way to add protection is to fence off part of the yard, leaving sufficient space for evacuation in case of fire, so that the patient cannot go too far from the protection of the home in the time it takes to check the door-open signal. This fencing is not always practical, however, especially if the home is located in a city where open land is at a premium. In the construction of the home, the location of exit doors are fixed by local, state, and national codes. If the nursing station, however, can be located so that there is a clear view of the majority of these exits, part of this problem will be better controlled.

Remote television monitors are successfully used in many homes to watch distant doors. These devices, now relatively inexpensive, can be mounted on the corridor wall near the ceiling to scan the exits.

A watchful, concerned staff is the best controlling feature a home administrator can utilize for resident safety. This consideration should be a part of the indoctrination of the new employee and should be made a part of the ongoing in-service training program. A list of the patients who wander should be kept at the nursing station. Every home should make sure that these patients have plastic identification bracelets that identify the patient and the home. Other personnel, too, should be enlisted to help watch and should be aware of these special patients' surveillance needs.

If a patient is successful in leaving unattended, the administrator should never hesitate to request the aid of the police department in locating the patient. If the weather is bad, it is urgent that the patient be located as quickly as possible. The patient's relatives should be notified, too, so they can be on the alert. Often, patients have sufficient ability to return to their old neighborhood or to go to a relative's or friend's home. The relatives may be able to offer suggestions about where to begin the search.

It is not uncommon for patients to walk away unnoticed, and most of the time, their absence is discovered at once and they are found quickly. However, I recall that once, while administering a nursing care facility, I received a telephone call from the office of a local bus company. The bus company officials told me that one of my charges was sitting in the terminal, waiting peacefully as he watched the busy travelers come and go. The old gentleman had left the home and had taken a local bus that stopped near the nursing home to the downtown terminal. He had done this for years prior to his coming to the home. Although he could not recall his name or where he lived, he did know where he was and was not the least bit disturbed. Needless to say, I was disturbed but relieved to go to the terminal to rescue this contented patient and return him safely home.

Unfortunately, not all patient disappearances end as happily as that. Sometimes the lost patient is injured or killed. Vigilance must be the watchword.

A patient who continually attempts to escape or wander away may have to be discharged from the home and sent to another facility better equipped to handle him.

Security against intruders and undesirable visitors

Every residential and health care facility must control the entrance areas to the buildings. This is a cardinal rule in the larger cities where the home may be located in a high crime area. In many instances, all entrance doors must be kept locked to the outside, and all who enter must be screened. Although this is burdensome and often brings criticism from visitors, it is frequently necessary. In some areas, guards are required to be on duty to screen those entering.

Several years ago, I was employed as assistant administrator of a large hospital in a metropolitan area. There were several doors that were always open to the public during the day. This was necessary because of the location of parking lots and sidewalk entrances. It soon became apparent that this was an uncontrollable, dangerous practice. At first we discovered that offices were entered while employees were on coffee breaks or at lunch. Desks were jammed open, and cash, purses, and business machines were stolen. Once someone unknown entered a remote area and pulled the lever on a fire alarm box. Soon after this we were forced to lock all the doors except those to the emergency room and front entrance.

It might well be the policy of a retirement residence to keep all entrance doors locked at all times from the oustide. Residents should constantly be cautioned about admitting strangers. Volunteers should sit at a desk in the front lobby at the main door. Every visitor, even if known to be a relative, should be referred to a staff member, who should contact the resident to see if he wishes to allow the visitor to come to his apartment. At the times when no volunteer is on duty, a telephone mounted outside the front door could be used for screening. This particular system can be improved with the addition of closed-circuit television surveillance and an electrically operated lock release.

In a retirement home, the staff should exercise control over who enters the building. A resident may not wish to see the person calling on him and should be offered the courtesy of a telephone call from a staff person to see if it is convenient to let the visitor proceed. Without such controls, strangers could enter under false pretences and could roam the building looking for an opportunity for theft, vandalism, or a worse offense.

Control over visitors should also be maintained in nursing care facilities. Keeping all but the main entrance locked from the outside is a wise practice. Building designs dictate the practicability of this. If at all possible, however, a reception area is ideal. Visitors who are known to be relatives or friends should, of course, be admitted with a cheerful greeting. Strangers should be questioned.

The administrator should see that his staff is alert for strange people. It is a good practice for a staff member to drop by a patient's room when a new person appears to visit. A tactful question or two will enable the staff member to determine whether or not the visitor is welcome and the patient is safe. If, after the encounter, the staff member is uncertain of the visitor's identity or purpose in the home, he should be encouraged to alert the head nurse or other responsible person to help further. The majority of the patients' families and friends will appreciate such vigilance.

There have been cases in which strangers have entered hospitals unnoticed by the staff, posing as physicians to unsuspecting patients who have submitted, on request of the stranger, to physical examinations. Such incidents should not be allowed to happen.

Guard service, although costly, is necessary in most facilities in metropolitan areas. Even if the residence is located in a rural setting, a guard should be on patrol from late afternoon, with a second shift, until the morning. Radio contact from the switchboard should be maintained constantly throughout both shifts.

Radio communication is a necessary tool in many retirement residences because of their rambling layout. Key staff people should carry pocket paging units, and the night-shift personnel should carry small walkie-talkies. Many homes may find this a good security adjunct. Although the original investment in transmission and receiving equipment is high, radio communication provides added security and the convenience of locating key personnel quickly.

At a retirement residence, the radio service can be extended to the several vehicles used for transportation of residents to the city for shopping and for physicians' appointments. Much valuable driver time and unnecessary mileage can be saved if the switchboard operator acts as dispatcher and coordinator of the drivers.

NOTES

1. Principles of inspection control in health facilities, U. S. Public Health Service, Health Services and Mental Health Administration, publication no. 930-C-21, March 1971, Superintendent of Documents, U. S. Government Printing Office, Washington, D. C.
2. The care and cleaning of housekeeping equipment and the storage room in health facilities, U. S. Public Health Service, Health Services and Mental Health Administration, publication no. 930-C-20, March 1971, Superintendent of Documents, U. S. Government Printing Office, Washington, D. C.
3. Zoffer, Pat: Humanizing the institutional environment, The Executive Housekeeper **17**(6):88-90, 1970.
4. Finney, H. A., and Miller, Herbert E.: Principles of accounting, ed. 6, Englewood Cliffs, N. J., 1963, Prentice-Hall Inc.
5. Mathiasen, Geneva, and Noakes, Edward A., editors: Planning homes for the aged, New York, 1959, F. W. Dodge Corp.
6. Life safety code, an American national standard, 1970 edition, no. 10-2341, National Fire Protection Association, 60 Batterymarch St., Boston, Mass. 02110.
7. The no-iron laundry manual, 1970, American Hotel and Motel Association, 888 Seventh Ave., New York, N. Y. 10019.
8. Your guide to Martex Presslin 303 sheets and pillowcases, WestPoint Pepperell, 111 W. 40th St., New York, N. Y. 10018.
9. Zaccarelli, Brother Herman E., and Maggiore, Josephine: Nursing home menu

planning—food purchasing management, Chicago, 1972, Institutions/Volume Feeding Magazine. Distributed by Canners Books, 89 Franklin St., Boston, Mass. 02110.

10. Presto, John A.: The vanishing chef: restaurants serve more frozen dishes, The Wall Street Journal, March 18, 1970.
11. Lane, Mary Margaret: Bacterial hazards and how to avoid them, Nursing Homes, vol. 19, no. 3, 1970.
12. Downey, George W.: Expert says homes need drills, detectors, and sprinklers, Modern Nursing Home 28(4):47-52, 1972.
13. Quinan, Dan J.: Sounding the alarm, Nursing Homes 20(3):38, 1971.
14. Sister Suzanne: To make written fire procedure effective, keep it simple and sensible, Modern Nursing Home 28(4):54-57, 1972.

Chapter five

HEALTH SERVICES

Less than 5% of the aged people in the United States require institutional type of care; therefore, 95% live in their own homes, with relatives, or in apartment type of retirement complexes, ever growing in number, for well aged people. It is becoming apparent that many of this 95% live in less-than-adequate housing with poverty-level means. Many, too, are in need of care but are too independent or are not able to seek or accept it. Others are not aware of special federal, state, and local assistance available to them in their home setting.

Project FIND (friendless, isolated, needy, disabled), funded originally by the Office of Economic Opportunity and conceived, developed, and administered by the National Council on the Aging, began with an in-depth search for noninstitutionalized elderly people with unmet physical, economic, and emotional needs. The council issued the documentary *The Golden Years—a Tarnished Myth*, known as the Project FIND Report.[1] This was the first major step in learning of the problems of the 95% of aged people who are not institutionalized. The report is required reading for every student of gerontology. It explodes the concept that the majority of older people are self-sufficient, not needing care.

From an economic approach alone, the report shows that in 1968, 75% of people 65 years of age and older had incomes of less than $2,500 annually. The median family income was $3,928 annually, and the median individual annual income was $1,480. In 1969 the Office of Economic Opportunity defined the poverty line for an individual as $1,600 annually or, with an adjustment in the index for rural living, as $1,100.[1]

This report states that within this poor and near-poor aged population, there are substantial health care needs that are not being met. Recognizing this fact as a major problem in this country, many leaders in the field of care of aged people recommend expansion of the concepts of home health care. More outreach services established as local community-based services are needed. These agencies, often administered through the existing local visiting nurses' association, can be designed to provide homemaker services, home health services, transportation services, nutritional services, social services, and many other necessary programs for aged people who still live in their own homes.

The administrators or managers of housing projects for aged people must be aware of the local community resources available to the residents that can possibly prevent or forestall institutionalization. If these services are brought to the elderly resident in the housing unit, he may be able to continue to live in this apartment setting longer and with safety. Even though dependent on the home or community-based agency for some supportive services, the resident can still live in the housing facility, delaying the often-feared institutionalization.

The concept of home health services is not new. It has been a basic approach in the care of residents in homes for aged people. Residents come to these facilities by choice to spend their final years. Usually they enter as well aged people and on an independent living basis. As care needs are determined, these needs are met by the several services of the home, and the resident continues in the independent living environment with this assistance. The emphasis is on meeting the total needs of the resident, with special attention being given to the social components of care. Nursing care needs are often met with an infirmary section of the home. These nursing care needs may only be temporary, and the resident may return subsequently to his independent living status.

Homes for aged people are traditionally nonprofit institutions. They are usually sponsored by religious or fraternal groups who responded to an unmet community need. Often dependent on declining charitable donations, many homes for aged people are finding it increasingly difficult to offer needed social and religious programming. Recognition of these problems must be given by the federal government so that fiscal policies can be changed to assist in meeting these deficits.

Physical, emotional, and other needs of elderly people

I will now examine the concepts of the aged in terms of their physical, emotional, and other supportive needs.

In 1971 I attended a conference on long-term care sponsored by the American Medical Association in Chicago. Dr. Jack Kleh, Associate Clinical Professor at the George Washington University School of Medicine in Washington, D. C., was one of the main speakers of the day. His paper "The Physician's Role" (in management of the patient in the long-term care facility) placed in clear perspective the various degrees of need of aged people who have chronic disease or disability. Kleh first published this material in 1963, long before Medicare was on the scene.[2] It is very relevant today and should help the student understand the reasons for the need for many levels of care for the aged.

I. *Preventive care*
    Despite chronic illness the patient is ambulatory and able to carry out the activities of daily living. He is capable of making judgments necessary to function in society and requires no personal supervision in following his prescribed medical care program.
    This patient requires a continuing program of secondary disability prevention through disease detection and control, and the use of restorative services to achieve and maintain maximal functional competence. This should be based on periodic evaluation and utilization of any broad range of medical, paramedical and related nonmedical services necessary usually on an out-patient basis.
II. *Comprehensive care*
    This patient is ambulatory and able to perform the activities of daily living although he may fail to do so without direction. He is unable to coordinate the factors in the usually extensive multidisciplinary care regimen or even maintain control of medication, dietary habits and prescribed activities.

He requires coordinated interdisciplinary management by a professional team to utilize effectively a range of services in stemming a trend toward increasing disability and the need for institutional care.

III. *Custodial care*

This patient is usually ambulatory, has impaired judgment and is incapable of accepting responsibility. He cannot carry out the activities of daily living satisfactorily without direction and supervision. He may be mentally incompetent.

He needs a protective environment with constant supervision or other forms of activity restriction. He requires supervision in personal care. While he may remain at home in the right setting, he usually requires the services of a long-term care facility.

IV. *Personal care*

This patient may be ambulatory or able to transfer himself in a wheelchair. He is definitely restricted in the activities of daily living.

He almost invariably needs assistance in bathing and frequently requires help in dressing, feeding and other personal-care activities as well. Under general graduate-nurse supervision, direct care for this patient can be carried out by practical nurses and nursing assistants.

V. *Skilled nursing care*

This patient usually is either bedridden or wheelchair-fast with inability for self-transference.

He requires direct professional care in addition to other services and almost invariably should be in a facility for long-term care.

VI. *Extended nursing care*

This patient is usually bedridden, either acutely ill or unable to carry out even minimal functions.

He requires more than usual or intensive professional nursing care in addition to a broad range of medical and paramedical services.[2]

According to Kleh's criteria, people in category I can easily live independently and are suitable applicants for a retirement community. However, they require medical supervision through periodic visits to their physician's office. A retirement residence with a health office can assist the resident and his physician in the early detection of medical problems. The service can be geared to close follow-up of borderline residents who, through good surveillance, can be prevented or delayed from needing a higher degree of health care. The health office staff can make sure that the resident sees his physician regularly and that preventive measures and regimens prescribed by the physician are followed. If the facility provides a food service, special diets can be given if ordered by the resident's physician.

The health office staff usually cannot require the resident to cooperate without some sort of rules, regulations, or agreements that are entered into mutually prior to admission. Even then, the resident is still free to disagree with prescribed care, and unless the problem is of sufficient magnitude to cause the administrator to request the resident to cooperate or leave, the facility has little choice but to advise the resident that he is not following his physician's orders and record the fact of the resident's negative response.

Persons in categories II and III require supervision. Under proper circumstances, these people can remain in their own home. This would require good supervision, especially for those in category III. In many cases this supervision is provided by a wife, husband, or other relative in the resident's own home. Often, especially among the poor and those living in rural areas, there is no supervision, and medical and personal care needs go unmet. Project FIND reported several case histories that illustrated this fact.[1] Frequently the aged person lives with his children. Depending on family finances and the presence or lack of acceptance of the aged person, the need for institutional care is either prolonged or hastened.

Persons in the other three categories described by Kleh require institutional care. The following chart illustrates the continuum of care and how Kleh's categories adapt to the several levels.

RETIREMENT COMPLEX FOR WELL AGED PEOPLE (1)	PERSONAL CARE HOME (2)	INTERMEDIATE CARE HOME (3)	EXTENDED CARE FACIL- ITY AND/OR SKILLED NURSING HOME (4)	HOSPITAL (5)
Minimal health care needs; health service may not be for- mally or- ganized	Personal care needs	Minimal nurs- ing care and high degree of personal care needs	High degree of nursing care needs and personal care needs	Intensive health care needs
Category I	Categories II and III	Categories III and IV	Categories V and VI	Category VI (during acute phase)

Frequently these health needs are not constant. Patients can drift from one level of need to a higher one and then return to the lower level again. It has been my experience that a resident can need extended care, skilled care, or personal care for a while and have his health status improve to the point where he can return to independent living again. This drifting can occur repeatedly. With good super-vision from the patient's physician and a well-coordinated health office in a retire-ment facility, frequently a resident can be returned to his apartment environ-ment.

Range of health care services

The degree of health service offered in each facility is a basic decision to be made by the owner. It ranges from no health service in some facilities to complete life care, including hospital, skilled nursing, and personal care, in other facilities. Many retirement complexes must depend on the local community hospitals and nursing homes to provide medical and nursing care. Some have a health office with a nurse on duty to assist with emergency needs and the general oversight of the health of the residents.

Although some retirement residences with health services offer contracts for lifetime care to their residents, usually the residents must be fully ambulatory and able to care for themselves when they enter. When hospital care becomes necessary, the resident must leave the residence to go to one of the facilities in the local area. If the facility is a typical home for the aged, the resident can receive on-site nursing and personal care often under the same roof. Many homes for the aged provide needed care on a monthly-charge basis, although a good number offer the lifetime-care contract.

The primary function of the residence is to provide retirement living in an inde-pendent apartment type of setting for active, well aged people. However, most such facilities, known as homes for the aged, also provide on-site nursing and personal care sections.

Some people have valid arguments for keeping well aged people isolated from those who are ill, who need personal care, or who are nonambulatory. Others believe that a mixture of such people is good. I prefer a multiple type of complex separated by buildings with connecting covered corridors or by floors so that the well aged people can enjoy an active, independent life with retirees of similar capabilities, but with a section for on-campus nursing and personal care beds. When independent living is no longer a possibility for the individual resident, he is moved to the care units, depending on his needs. However, he remains at the same location; thus his friends, both staff and residents, are nearby, and he is still in his home and a part of the community.

The spectrum of health care of elderly people in homes is broad. It can exist in various degrees in different types of homes.

A home for the aged usually embraces the first three to four categories illustrated in the chart on p. 114. A nursing home usually offers intermediate care and/or skilled care (categories 3 and 4). Extended care facilities may be separate facilities but usually are separate self-contained units of a hospital or nursing home.

A retirement residence usually limits its care to only the first degree on the scale and may not offer any formally organized health care.

Most nursing home patients need skilled care for a relatively short period of time, usually reaching a plateau in their chronic or terminal illness where a minimal degree of skilled care is necessary but a great deal of personal care is required.

HEALTH OFFICE IN THE RETIREMENT RESIDENCE
General considerations

The residents in a retirement home need at the maximum the first category of care described by Kleh. Many have not yet reached this first level of need, having no chronic or disabling disease. For the most part, they may be described as well aged people. Most of them could live completely independent lives and choose the community type of living simply for the security, convenience, and comfort it offers them. They live in their own homes within a protective environment not unlike a walled city. They come and go at will but with the knowledge that once home within the "city gates," they have a certain degree of protection and assistance for emergency needs. Such a residence may provide three nutritionally balanced meals daily. The residents may be able to attend church; go to social and entertainment functions; receive weekly housekeeping service; receive beauty shop services; purchase notions, cards, and miscellaneous convenience items from a small shop; and use free or public transportation service to a nearby small community or to a larger city. They may also have grounds that provide safe areas for daily walks.

This type of residence may have a home health service not unlike a visiting nurse. The nursing office should be under the supervision of a registered nurse who is under the direct supervision of the administrator. The facility should have a medical director who provides necessary consultation to the administrator, the nurse, and other facility personnel. He should also be available for emergencies and be on call for medical decisions when the resident's personal physician cannot be reached. Licensed personnel should be on duty or on call 24 hours.

Prior to acceptance, each resident should furnish the residence with an extensive medical history and results of physical examination. The examination may be done by the resident's personal physician at his own expense, or the facility may choose to have its own physician conduct the examination. This form should be reviewed by the administrator, the chief nurse, and the home's medical director. The director should give the final approval or rejection of the resident on the basis of these medical findings.

Once the person is accepted, this form, coupled with a form to record such vital facts as names and addresses of relatives, persons to act in the event of death or serious illness, and similarly important data, should become the basis for the resident's health chart.

Shortly after the person is received as a resident, the nurse should interview him to determine his preference for medical care. Each resident should have his own physician, who must have an office in the nearby community and local hospital privileges. The home should maintain a roster of specialists in internal medicine and in family practice. The resident should assist in selecting a physician during the interview. If the resident is from the neighboring community, this would not be done, since he would already be established with a local physician.

After the physician has been selected, the nurse should make an appointment for the resident. On the first visit, the health chart should be sent along with the resident so that the newly selected physician can review the admission history and results of physical examination. If special diets or other orders are needed, the physician can note such on the order sheet sent with the resident if the home provides this service.

Thereafter, the orders are usually taken over the telephone by the nurse, who should send a telephone order confirmation slip to the physician by mail. Frequently the order sheet is sent on subsequent visits, depending on the resident's particular need. Residents who need nursing or personal care, of course, should not be allowed to remain in the home.

All appointments with the resident's physicians should be made by the nursing office unless the resident objects, preferring to do this on his own. Residents should be discouraged from this practice, however.

Each visit to the physician should be recorded in the resident's chart. When he returns from each visit, the resident should be asked to report the physician's comments to the nurse on duty. Significant items should be noted in the daily log and subsequently recorded in the patient's record.

The daily log is a large permanently bound, ruled book. The nurses on duty should write specific comments in the book that are pertinent to residents' special problems. When a resident has a minor illness, for example, this is noted and the physician's orders are written in the book. Other items that might be recorded are blood pressure if requested by the resident's physician, prescribed vitamin injections, accidents and first aid, future physician appointments, and similar matters. The log is given to the administrator each morning for review. The log books are kept permanently, as are the residents' health charts.

Weekly, the nurse, the medical director, and the administrator hold a conference to discuss the home's health service progress and to review certain residents' medical problems. These three people, along with the resident's personal physician, decide when a resident is no longer capable of living in the independent environment of the residence and must be transferred to a nursing home.

Most residents' physicians will give written permission for the medical director to temporarily treat the residents if they are not available. The medical director, who may be on duty at the home on a full-time or part-time basis, can provide emergency, lifesaving care when it is needed. This could be an invaluable service to the resident. At other times, the resident may be rushed to the hospital for emergency care by his own physician or the physician on duty at the hospital.

As a home health service, the nursing office coordinates the outpatient care of the resident under the direction of his personal physician. This may involve arranging for x-ray films, laboratory tests, or physical therapy treatments at the local hospital; calling for prescriptions; requesting the consulting dietitian to counsel the resident on medically prescribed diets; arranging for dental and podiatry care; assisting the resident with obtaining special services such as hearing aid care; and ordering special appliances such as support garments.

When a resident is hospitalized with an illness, the health office should maintain liaison with the patient's relatives if they do not live in the area. The nurse should contact the physician and the hospital regularly for reports to keep the relatives informed as needed. Together with the administrator, the nurse should visit the patient weekly, or more frequently if he is critically ill or undergoing surgery. Likewise, they should visit the patient who is in a nursing home. They should talk with the home or hospital staff as well as the patient on these visits. As the resident recovers and plans are made for his return to the residence, the nurse should coordinate the return with the resident's physician and the nursing home or hospital staff so that all will be well. When the resident returns, a standard transfer sheet should be requested and be made a part of the resident's chart.

The health office staff should perform a preventive health service regularly. Residents should be encouraged to discuss their general health status. Many residents are monitored with weekly weight checks, blood pressure checks, observations for edema, checks of urine for sugar, and the like. Residents should be encouraged to see their physician as often as needed, but at the minimum, they should have a physical examination annually. If in the meantime the nurse notes that a resident has a special problem, she should request that he allow her to make an appointment for him with his physician. The resident usually is quite cooperative if the nurse suggests this.

The health office has the responsibility of accounting for every resident every day. To do this, the nurse must have the cooperation of all of the staff members and must be informed in writing of the absence of residents overnight or longer.

Each resident apartment should be equipped with two call systems: an intercom located in the bedroom and an emergency buzzer located in the bathroom. Both should terminate at the switchboard, which should be staffed on a 24-hour basis, seven days a week. When either is activated, the switchboard operator should immediately contact the nurse by telephone or pocket page to dispatch her to the resident's quarters. Emergency kits, resuscitators, and oxygen should be located in the health office.

When patients are sent to the hospital, a staff member should go along also if at all possible. In the health office an envelope for each resident should be kept on file with sufficient data printed on it for preparation of the hospital admission forms. There should also be a place on the envelope for recording previous hospital admission dates. Inside the envelope should be kept a photocopy of the resident's Medicare card and photocopies of cards for other insurance policies that the resident maintains. This envelope should be taken by the staff member who accompanies the resident to the hospital.

Although it is not the best practice for a resident to be sent to the hospital with just the ambulance attendant, it happens occasionally if the resident is sent during the second or third shift. In all cases of hospital admission, the administrator should be notified. If the resident goes unaccompanied, the administrator should go to the hospital from his home to meet the ambulance. If the administrator is not available, his assistant or the nurse should go. Together, the administrator and his assistant should schedule their out-of-town activities so that one or the other is always at hand.

Job descriptions

Following are examples of descriptions of jobs in the health office at a retirement residence. The material represents one approach to providing a health service to well aged people living in a retirement center. This facility by choice staffs the health office 24 hours a day with licensed personnel and nurse's aides. This is done because of the large size of the facility and the intent of the facility's governing board to give 24-hour emergency assistance to the residents.

JOB DESCRIPTION OF CHIEF NURSE

Title: Chief nurse
Days: Schedules herself for weekdays, 5 days a week.
Work area: Retirement residence; local hospitals and nursing homes for visits.
Supervision: Under the direct supervision of the administrator, the chief nurse has the following responsibilities.

Major duties:

1. Schedules the hours of all nursing personnel and makes out time cards.
2. Supervises nurses' work and assigns special tasks to individual nurses as necessary.
3. Meets with administrator daily and with the medical director and Administrator weekly to discuss special problems of health care for the residents. Reviews special problems concerning residents' health care with administrator whenever necessary.
4. Assists medical director in reviewing prospective residents' medical histories and physical examination forms.
5. Interviews new residents to determine their preference for physician assignment and assigns them to a local physician of their choice or recommends one from the list of physicians if they do not have a preference.
6. Supervises the entire health needs of all residents, overseeing their general well-being. Maintains contact with residents' physicians for specific problems not assignable to subordinates.
7. Advises administrator on health safety and sanitary problems noted within the facility.
8. Maintains liaison with families of residents when indicated by residents' physical or mental status.
9. Attends weekly meetings of department heads and dispenses information concerning employees to her staff.
10. Meets with dietary department weekly and consulting dietitian monthly to discuss special dietary problems of residents.
11. Places log book on administrator's desk each morning, and reviews contents with him daily.
12. Arranges orientation period and explains job descriptions to each new employee, assigning to them also the reading of the procedure manual. Conducts in-service training sessions.
13. Prepares annual budget for the nursing department with the assistance of the business office and administrator. Orders supplies as necessary.
14. Oversees the employee health service and new employee health screening. Arranges for yearly tuberculin test with local tuberculosis association for all employees.
15. Interviews and hires all nursing personnel. Disciplines and terminate when necessary.
16. Visits residents in hospitals and nursing homes and contacts them by phone when practical.
17. Checks that residents see their physicians at regular intervals.
18. Supervises filing of the original physician's telephone orders in residents' charts when they are returned by the physicians, and destroy the carbon copy.
19. Prepares list of residents who require special assistance in the event of an emergency according to the following procedure:
    a. Regularly prepares and posts in the health office on the bulletin board and in each emergency nurse kit, a list of those residents who may need assistance in the case of a fire or similar emergency requiring evacuation of the building.
    b. Checks this list weekly and revises all copies, as necessary.
20. Performs the duties of a staff nurse as necessary.

JOB DESCRIPTION OF STAFF NURSE

Title: Staff nurse

Days: As assigned by supervisor.

Hours: Day (7:00 A.M. to 3:30 P.M.)—Licensed practical nurse

Evening (3:00 P.M. to 11:30 P.M.)—Registered nurse

Night (11:00 P.M. to 7:00 A.M.)—Licensed practical nurse

Supervisor: Chief nurse

Work area: Retirement residence—entire area.

Major duties: Under the direct supervision of the chief nurse and the indirect supervision of the administrator, the staff nurse is responsible for the day-to-day health needs and well-being of the residents.

1. Reviews log book at beginning of each shift.
2. Accounts for each resident each day. The census is recorded individually in the special log.
3. Makes physicians' appointments according to policy and schedules transportation with chief housekeeper. Sees resident on return from physician for diagnosis or new orders.
4. Applies first aid procedures to residents or staff for minor injuries and completes accident reports.
5. Responds in emergencies to residents' needs according to procedure for medical emergency.
6. Calls a resident's physician when necessary and keeps him informed of any unusual change in resident's condition, using telephone order procedure.
7. Calls for ambulance for transportation to the hospital in emergency, using procedure for medical emergency.
8. Applies emergency procedures, such as giving oxygen or using resuscitator, when necessary.
9. Responds to fire emergency according to fire plan for nursing personnel and goes to location of fire with special equipment.
10. Contacts resident's relatives in the event of an emergency and keeps them informed of the progress of resident as long as deemed necessary.
11. Maintains records about special details concerning residents in log book and residents' medical charts.
12. Visits residents in apartments when minor illness prevents them from coming to dining room and follows procedure regarding resident meal service in rooms.
13. Assists resident's physician if he comes to the residence to visit patient.
14. Delivers appointment slips and bills to appropriate offices.
15. Knows location of fire alarms and other equipment and knows building zones and apartment numbers in case of fire.
16. Contacts food service manager to arrange for special dietary needs of residents. Sends meal tray list of sick residents to dietary department each meal. Readies residents to receive trays according to procedure for tray service.
17. Reports daily occurrences to nurse coming on at end of shift.
18. In absence of the administrator and his assistant, the nurse on duty during the day is the senior officer in charge of the building, and the responsibility for the welfare of the residents and building security rests with her until she is able to reach the assistant or the administrator. The evening nurse and the night nurse are senior officers in charge of the building.
19. Relieves switchboard operator when necessary. (Aide does this on evening shift.)
20. Checks remote areas of building for fire and security watch on night shift.
21. Carries radio pager for voice communication with switchboard on day and evening shifts. Carries walkie-talkie during night shift.
22. Carries keys at all times. Keeps all cabinets locked unless in use.
23. Records in the nurse's notes in individual residents' charts, visits to physicians and other pertinent information written in the log book. (Night nurse completes work not charted by nurses on day shift.)

JOB DESCRIPTION OF NURSE'S AIDE

Title: Nurse's aide

Purpose of job: To relieve nurse of nonnursing functions.

Major duties:
1. Works under direct supervision of the licensed nurses.
2. Carries out only those functions that are assigned to her by nurse on duty.
3. Reports residents' complaints or requests to nurse.

Functions:
1. Checks temperatures.
2. Assists residents who are recovering from hospital or nursing home stays in going to and from dining room, if necessary.
3. Relieves switchboard operator.
4. Runs errands for health office; accompanies residents in ambulance when necessary.
5. Keeps health office in order.
6. Writes out appointment slips (only those that physicians have given residents for next visit).
7. Performs other duties as assigned by nurse on duty.

Qualifications:
1. Graduate of nursing assistant training program.
2. Good personality and kindness; ability to work with older persons.

Medical and nursing health office policies and procedures

Residents' health files. A health file should be set up for each resident. This file should be kept in the health office. It is composed of the following forms:
1. Admission history and physical examination results.
2. Physician's order sheet.
3. Nurse's notes. These are a record of residents' complaints and their visits to the physician. Any serious illness or accidents are also noted. If the resident's physician requests, records are kept of blood pressure, temperature, pulse, and respiration during minor illness. Frequent notation of the patient's progress are made until he recovers from current minor illness.
4. Medication permission form. In this form the physician gives his permission for resident to administer his own medications. The form is signed by the physician on the resident's first visit.
5. Resident's consent form. This is signed by the resident to allow the chart to be sent to his new physician at the time of his first visit to the physician.
6. Transfer sheets. These are requested from the hospital or nursing home when the patient returns from the facility.
7. Accident report.
8. Laboratory and x-ray reports.
9. Confidential form. This lists name and address of next of kin, individuals to be notified in case of serious illness or death, name of person to take action, the executor of the estate, and any final arrangements that the resident may have preplanned.

These records are strictly confidential. Only the personal physician and the retirement residence medical director, nurses, and administrator and his assistant should have access to these files. No exception to this regulation should be made without approval by the administrator. No one else, including the resident, his relatives, attorneys, insurance agents, and other parties, should view the records unless authorized by the administrator of the residence. Any request to see the files should be referred to the administrator.

The residents' health files are the property of the residence. They should never be removed from the premises unless authorization is given by the administrator. The health records should never be destroyed. When a resident dies, goes to live elsewhere, is permanently hospitalized, or for another reason leaves the residence on a permanent basis, the health chart should be closed by the nurse and sent to the administrator's office for review and filing.

Residents' physician visits. Residents who, in the opinion of the medical director, the chief nurse, or personal physician, require some oversight should be seen by their personal physician at least every 90 days. Residents in good health also should see their physician at least once a year. The usual frequency of visits, however, is every 90 days. In some instances, visits every 30 days or oftener may be indicated. The nurses should ask physicians to make note of this need for frequency of visit. These residents are those who are close to needing personal or nursing care but are still capable of independent living at a residence. They must be observed closely. When necessary, the chief nurse should advise the administrator, after consulting with the medical director and the resident's personal physician, that the resident is not able to remain in the independent living environment.

At the time of each visit, the nursing office should send a copy of the physician's order form along with the patient for the physician to complete. The form should be returned to the nursing office at the end of the visit. The physician's orders should be transcribed in the log book and the form placed in the resident's chart.

Medical emergency. The nurse should proceed as follows in the event of a medical emergency:
1. Contact the medical director if he is on duty at the residence and request his assistance. Follow his directions. If he is not on duty, proceed to 2.
2. Contact the switchboard. Ask the operator to call an ambulance and to notify the chaplain and the administrator or his assistant.
3. While awaiting the ambulance, call resident's physician. Advise him of the resident's condition and tell him that you are sending the resident to the hospital emergency room.
4. After the ambulance leaves, immediately call the hospital emergency room to give details of the patient's illness and to advise them that the patient is on the way. Be sure to give them the name of the patient's physician.
5. As soon as time permits, call the relatives and tell them about the situation; *please do not delay in doing this.* Tell relatives that a second call will be made when the patient's condition is known.
6. On every hospital admission, send vital statistics with staff member accompanying resident. If resident is not accompanied by staff member, call hospital admitting office to give them resident's vital statistics as soon as possible.
7. Call hospital again about one hour after admission to learn of condition. Keep relatives posted as necessary.

Apparent death. The nurse should proceed as follows in the event of an apparent death:
1. Call the medical director, who will ascertain whether the resident is indeed dead.
2. After calling the medical director, notify the switchboard operator and ask her to call the appropriate clergyman and the administrator.
3. Then call the resident's physician and follow his instructions. Question the physician about the need to call the coroner.
4. Quickly check the confidential statistics file located in the resident's medical chart for specific orders about the undertaker and funeral arrangements.
5. Then immediately contact the relatives to notify them of the death. Acquaint

them with the confidential file data to see if they agree with the resident's indicated wishes.

6. Call the undertaker, after the physician and relatives have given their permission.

Medications. Occasionally a physician may request that the licensed nurses temporarily administer the resident's medication. If this is done, specific procedure should be followed:

1. Medications should be dispensed only by the licensed nursing personnel and on specific orders of the resident's physician.
2. All medications should be given on hours ordered. The resident should take the medicine while the nurse is present.
3. No resident should take medication from the medication tray himself. The nurse should do this.
4. The medication tray should be kept in the medicine room and the door locked if the nurse must leave the office.
5. Medication cards should be made for all medications dispensed by nurses.
6. Medications should be dispensed by the nurse who sets up the medication tray.
7. The medicine cabinet should be locked at all times when it is not in use. The nurse should carry the keys with her.
8. Medications should not be "borrowed" from one resident for another.
9. Medications should be dispensed only from individual prescriptions ordered by the resident's personal physician, prepared by a local pharmacy, and delivered or picked up for the individual resident's use. Medications should not be transferred from the original container to another except when a single dose is administered in a medicine cup. Medications with labels that become defaced, damaged, or soiled should be returned to the dispensing pharmacy for relabeling.
10. All doses of medications dispensed should be charted in the resident's health record.
11. Reactions to medications should be reported immediately to the resident's personal physician, and the reaction should be recorded.
12. Medications should not be stocked in bulk.

Special diets. Some guidelines are as follows:

1. When a resident has a special diet ordered by his physician, the nurse should send a special diet request to the food manager. A copy should be filed in the resident's health folder.
2. The food manager should instruct the dietary personnel in the proper methods to follow in each case.
3. No changes in special diets should be made without approval of the health office after written orders are received from the resident's physician. All changes should be in writing.
4. The consulting dietitian should be called by the nurse for assistance in helping the resident to understand and adjust to his special diet.

Meal service to residents in their rooms. Residents, when temporarily indisposed for minor illness, may be served meals in their rooms. The responsibility for this service should rest jointly with the nursing department and the dietary department.

1. On learning that a resident needs tray service, the nurse should contact the food supervisor to arrange for this service.
2. The nurse on duty should instruct the dietary department about the proper diet for residents having trays delivered to their rooms. The dietary supervisor should make sure that the trays are delivered in good order.

3. The food supervisor should arrange to have the dishes picked up no longer than two hours after delivery of the tray.
4. Residents' meals should be ordered only by the nurse. If the food department personnel receive a request for a room tray from anyone other than the nurse, they should contact the nurse, who should see the resident at once to learn of the problem and then should order the tray.
5. The health office personnel should deliver the trays.

Evening and weekend administration duty. In the absence of the administrator and the assistant administrator, the nurse on duty should be the acting administrator. Problems that cannot be handled by the employees on duty in any department should be referred to the nurse.

Visitors entering building after daytime hours. The security of the building depends on the proper screening of persons desiring entry to the building after normal daytime working hours. Of course, the residents' visitors and employees coming on duty should be allowed to enter. The residents' visitors should be announced to the residents over a communication system or telephone before they are allowed to enter the apartment area. All other persons desiring entry to the building should state their purpose, and the nurse in charge should use her judgment about admitting the person. Visitors desiring to inspect the residence for possible occupancy of an apartment or just out of curiosity should be politely told that it is not possible at that hour.

Receiving telephone orders from physicians. The following guidelines should be used:
1. It is preferable that physicians give new prescriptions directly to the pharmacist. They should be encouraged to do this; either they should call the pharmacist, or the nurse should ask the pharmacist to call him.
2. If for some reason this is not done and the physician gives the nurse the order over the telephone, the physician's telephone order form should be used.
3. If changes in medication orders are received from physicians for medications already on hand, the physician's telephone order form should be used.
4. For any other telephone orders received from physicians, the physician's telephone order form should be used.
5. Telephone orders should be taken only by a registered nurse or licensed practical nurse. The nurse should sign the order form.
6. The order should then be transcribed in the nurse's daily log.
7. A carbon copy of the physician's telephone order form should be filed while awaiting the signature.
8. The original of the form should be mailed to the physician's office for his signature. The nurse taking the order should be responsible for this procedure:
   a. Attach the request for signature to original of physician's telephone order.
   b. Address envelope to physician.
   c. Enclose physician's telephone order form (original copy) together with a self-addressed, stamped return envelope.
   d. Seal and take to business office for mailing.
9. The chief nurse should have the responsibility of controlling the return of the original forms.
   a. The carbon copy of the form should remain in the file awaiting signature.
   b. When the original form is returned, the chief nurse should remove the copy from the file and destroy it.
   c. The chief nurse should daily review the copies remaining in the file for the purpose of controlling the return of the originals. She should contact the physician's office if the original is not returned within 72 hours of the taking of the order.

10. The originals, when returned, should be attached to the resident's health chart beginning at the top with the first order and continuing below with subsequent orders.

• • •

These policies and procedures suit the needs of a certain retirement residence. They are not necessarily totally adaptable for every residence. An administrator must consider state and local regulations before planning the facility and writing the policies. During this time, he must determine the extent of the health office responsibilities. Local licensing regulations may require more details or prohibit certain practices.

In general, the purpose of a residence's health service should be to attempt to keep the resident functioning independently for as long a time as possible. I firmly believe that people tend to live, respond, and react to the level of their environment. I have seen many incapacitated elderly people with strong determination, fight to regain a higher level of self-help. With a lot of encouragement, good medical and nursing care, and this strong will to recover, many elderly people can indeed prolong the time when the need for institutional care becomes a reality.

NURSING DEPARTMENT IN THE NURSING HOME OR HOME FOR THE AGED

Patients who require only supervision, personal care, and assistance with the activities of daily living usually can be well cared for in a home offering only part-time professional nursing. The nurse, much as in a retirement home, offers the professional guidance and oversight of the health care given the patient.

As the patient's needs for professional nursing care increase, however, a more complex service is necessary. Homes offering nursing care must have an organized nursing service department headed by a registered nurse with the title of director of nurses. Depending on the size and the degree of sophistication or level of care, other licensed nursing personnel will be required in varying numbers.

Federal guidelines establish direction for this organization. For example, the federal requirements for skilled nursing homes are that the director of nursing must be a full-time employee on duty during the day shift, devoting her duties solely to supervision of the department. She is expected by these requirements to develop standards, policies, and procedures for the nursing service department, and she must be held responsible for making sure that these standards are met by her staff. She must be qualified by education and training and have experience as a supervisor. It is preferred that this experience and education be in geriatric nursing and that she have knowledge of restorative nursing techniques. Familiarity with psychiatric nursing concepts is helpful also.[3]

The director of nursing sets the tone of the patient care in the facility. She must be a leader and a teacher. She must be skilled in management techniques and understand the principles of employee motivation in order to build a good patient care system. As the manager of the team that works the closest with the patient, she must be sympathetic and understanding about the needs of these patients. She must be available to meet with the relatives to help them understand the specific problems as they develop with their loved ones. She must oversee all the patients in the home, being certain that they are receiving the proper care.

Patient care plan

One of the basic tools the director of nurses can use to outline the care needs of her patients is the patient care plan. This is an individual program for each patient

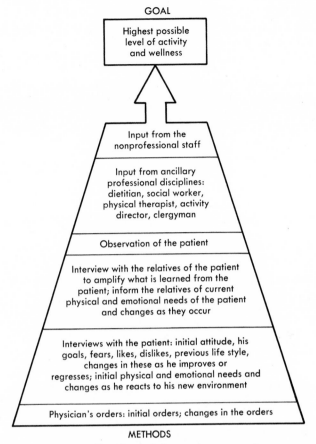

GOAL

Highest possible
level of activity
and wellness

Input from the
nonprofessional staff

Input from ancillary
professional disciplines:
dietitian, social worker,
physical therapist, activity
director, clergyman

Observation of the patient

Interview with the relatives of the patient
to amplify what is learned from the
patient; inform the relatives of current
physical and emotional needs of the patient
and changes as they occur

Interviews with the patient: initial attitude, his
goals, fears, likes, dislikes, previous life style,
changes in these as he improves or
regresses; initial physical and emotional needs and
changes as he reacts to his new environment

Physician's orders: initial orders; changes in the orders

METHODS

Fig. 19. Building of the patient care plan.

that begins with the orders of his physician and is designed to meet the needs of the patient, with one of the goals being to restore him, whenever possible, to the highest level of wellness and activity. Although the patient's individual care plan begins and revolves around the written orders of his physician, the director of nurses includes other personnel and disciplines in designing and updating the plan. She gets assistance in the amplification of the individual care plan from the activity director, consulting dietitian, the food manager, the social service worker, the physical therapist, and the ancillary nursing service personnel. Building of the patient care plan can be diagrammed as in Fig. 19.

The initial care plan should be developed when the patient is admitted to the home with as much data as is available. It should be revised and updated as soon as more knowledge is gleaned. The care plan should never be regarded as static but should be revised and modified as the patient's needs change.[4]

The structure of the care plan varies with the individual training and background of the director of nurses. In general, the plan should include, at the minimum, the following data:

1. Identification of the patient. Name, age, physician's name, primary diagnosis, religion, and room and bed numbers should be included.
2. Safety precautions. Notations should be made concerning limitations for ambulation; need for assistance; need for special devices such as canes, braces,

prostheses, walkers, and wheelchairs; transfer problems; vision and hearing problems; need to be watched for wandering; potential belligerence; and need for safety devices such as geriatric chairs.

3. Mental status. Notations should be made about the patient's status of orientation to time and place and about the goals established to improve disorientation.
4. Individual preferences. Likes and dislikes of foods, activity preferences, sleeping habits, daily-routine preferences, and religious practices should be noted. Goals should be established if patient expresses negative attitudes.
5. Restorative goals. These goals should be highlighted here as outlined in the physician's orders. These goals should be further expanded by other professionals such as the physical therapist, psychologist, psychiatrist, and speech therapist.
6. Patient teaching and retraining. Closely allied to the restorative goals, this section covers teaching the patient to live with new physical disabilities. Teaching colostomy care, diabetic routines, ambulation and transfer techniques, and use of artificial limbs is included here, together with the goals established.
7. Family relations. This section can be a helpful addition if notes are made about how to help the family understand the behavior and needs, both physical and psychological, of the patient as they are currently manifested and as they change. Also, the patient's attitude toward his family should be noted if significant.

Each care plan should be individually tailored and reviewed regularly. The director of nurses should see that the goals set are realistic and attainable. As the goal is reached, a new goal should be established with the intent being constantly to help the patient to increase his ability to perform the activities of daily living as independently as possible.

The frequency of review of these plans depends on the individual patient. However, at the minimum, they should be reviewed every 30 days. Regulations require a review of the patient's medications at the minimum of once a month with the attending physician.[3] This is a good time for a review of the care plan. Changes in patient's needs that occur in between medication reviews require further revisions.

Nursing responsibilities

In their book *Nursing Care Planning*, Little and Carnevali make the observation that the nursing home nurse has to rely much more on her own observations and judgments than the nurse in the environment of the hospital, where the physician is on the scene daily.[4] Weeks may go by between the physician's visits to the patient. The nurse must therefore be much more alert to changes in patient care needs. Since these changes may occur swiftly and be disguised by the multiplicity of symptoms and complaints of the chronically ill person, the nurse must learn to recognize abstruse physical or emotional variations in individual patients. She must be able to determine the significance of symptoms and separate the serious problems from minor difficulties. The serious problems, of course, should be reported to the physician for his orders; there is no question about that. However, the difficulties that seem minor may or may not be minor. It takes a discerning professional nurse to detect the difference. The administrator must keep this in mind when selecting his director of nursing, and the director likewise must be cognizant of this when selecting her charge nurses.

The charge nurse is responsible for a nursing unit during one eight-hour shift. The federal guidelines broaden this definition to include a person who is in charge of nursing activities at times when the director of nursing is not on duty. Ideally, however, each nursing unit should have one charge nurse on each shift. This is not required in the intermediate care facility. It is my personal belief that any facility offering any degree of nursing care should have at least one professional nurse on duty at all times.

The director of nurses delegates to the charge nurses the responsibilities for the care of the patients on their individual nursing units. It is the charge nurse who does the charting, passes medication, contacts the individual physicians, and gives the nursing treatments to the patients. The charge nurse may be either a registered nurse or a licensed practical nurse who is a graduate of a state-approved school of practical nursing.

Nursing care is defined by the individual state's nursing practice acts. It includes such things as the recording of nurse's notes and other data in the patients' charts; administration of medications as prescribed by the individual patients' physicians; giving of treatments such as catheterizations, irrigations, and enemas; application of bandages and dressings; observation of patients, including their vital signs, such as temperature, pulse, respirations, and blood pressure; supervision of personal care given by ancillary nursing personnel; utilization of restorative nursing techniques; patient training and retraining; giving of care to patients' skin; administering of oxygen; and the teaching of other nursing personnel. This does not mean that the registered nurse or licensed practical nurse has the authority or ability to prescribe therapeutic medication or corrective measures or to make medical diagnosis. The latter is the distinct field of the physician.

Nursing service master plan book

In organizing a nursing service department, the administrator must make sure that the director of nursing has clearly outlined and established, in writing, the lines of administrative supervision and responsibilities of all the supervisory nurses, the charge nurses, and the auxiliary nursing personnel. This organizational material should be compiled in a master plan book for the nursing service department. It should include an organizational chart indicating lines of supervisory authority, descriptions of the typical job categories, patient care policies, and written instructions for carrying out, in detail, patient care procedures.

Typical nursing personnel job descriptions. Job descriptions vary according to the philosophy and needs of the facility. Following are a job description for a director of nursing who has the responsibility of supervising a facility providing intermediate nursing care and a job description for a charge nurse in the same facility. This particular home in which these descriptions are used, by decision of the board of directors, has a charge nurse on each nursing unit on each shift, seven days a week. This staffing pattern exceeds the federal guidelines but is typical of the philosophy of many nonprofit homes for aged people and proprietary nursing homes that desire to provide a higher standard of care.

JOB DESCRIPTION OF DIRECTOR OF NURSING

Title: Director of nursing.
Days: As scheduled (a minimum of 40 hours, 5 days per week).
Hours: As scheduled by administrator.
Work area: Entire nursing care section of the home.

Major duties: Under the direct supervision of the administrator, the director of nursing service is responsible for the entire nursing service department, including all three shifts.

1. Assigns and directs the duties and activities of the nursing care personnel.
2. Plans and keeps up to date a patient care plan for each patient based on their individual needs, in accordance with the stated policy.

3. Recommends to the administrator the numbers and levels of nursing personnel to be employed.
4. Interviews and hires all nursing service personnel.
5. Verifies references, registrations, and licenses and keeps personnel records on all nursing service staff (duplicate copies of all such records are kept in the personnel file in the business office).
6. Participates in planning and budgeting for nursing service needs.
7. Develops and carries on an active in-service training program for all nursing service personnel.
8. Develops and maintains nursing service objectives and goals for the nursing care of the patients.
9. Assists the administrator in developing written job descriptions and updates such job descriptions for all nursing service personnel.
10. Coordinates nursing service activities with all other departments of the home.
11. Participates in the development, implementation, modification, and updating of all patient care policies in connection with quarterly meetings of the medical advisory committee.
12. Brings to the attention of the administrator, patient care problems that require his assistance.
13. Participates with the administrator in the screening of prospective patients.
14. Reviews the time cards for all nursing service personnel and signs each time card at the close of the pay period.
15. Delegates the immediate supervision of all patients to the charge nurses on duty on each shift.
16. Checks daily with the charge nurses on the shifts on which she is on duty and is available after hours for calls from charge nurses if necessary.
17. Reviews the general conditions of all patients in the home daily with the charge nurses.
18. Keeps the administrator regularly informed of the condition of seriously or critically ill patients.

Job specifications:

1. Current registration as a registered nurse, licensed to practice in the state.
2. Knowledge and training in restorative nursing.
3. Preparation, training, and skills in management and principles of supervision.
4. Genuine interest in geriatric nursing.
5. Ability to use initiative and good judgment in determining the needs of patients under her care.
6. Ability to manage properly the department of nursing service in order to maintain good quality nursing care.
7. Ability to maintain good working relationships with all staff members under her supervision and with all other staffs and departmental supervisors of the nursing home.

JOB DESCRIPTION OF CHARGE NURSE

Title: Charge nurse.
Days: As scheduled by director of nursing.
Hours: As scheduled by director of nursing. Shifts are 7:00 A.M. to 3:30 P.M., 3:00 P.M. to 11:30 P.M., and 11:00 P.M. to 7:00 A.M.
Work area: The nursing station assigned.

Major duties: Under the direct supervision of the director of nursing and the indirect supervision of the administrator, the charge nurse is responsible for the total nursing care of the patients assigned to her unit during her tour of duty. She supervises and evaluates all work performance of the nursing service personnel assigned to her shift and to her unit. She coordinates the needs of her patients with all the other departments in the home providing services for these residents and seeks assistance from the director of nursing when necessary for this coordination.

1. Regularly visits each patient to ensure maximum care and to help alleviate any anxiety that may exist on the part of the patient.
2. Makes sure that her staff similarly visits each patient as often as possible.
3. Makes sure that all patients' calls are answered as promptly as possible by auxiliary nursing personnel.
4. Admits, transfers, and discharges all patients according to policy.
5. Contacts the attending physician for initial orders on each admission unless these orders accompany the patient in writing and are currently dated and signed by the attending physician.
6. Is directly responsible for the physical and mental care of all the patients in her charge as ordered by the attending physician.
7. Contacts the physician whenever necessary, according to the needs of the patient, and records and carries out his orders.
8. Is responsible for the oversight of the patients' medications, which includes seeing that refills are ordered as necessary and that all medications are handled in accordance with the written policy on medications.
9. Administers treatments, medications, and various procedures ordered by the physician that cannot be assigned to auxiliary personnel.
10. Makes sure that the patient is receiving the special diet as ordered by the physician if such is indicated. Any changes in diet are handled in accordance with written policies.
11. Assists the director of nursing in developing a patient care plan for each resident or patient.
12. Determines the amount of supervision necessary for each resident or patient under her care on her shift.
13. Assigns to auxiliary personnel all functions that can be normally carried out by them that do not require professional nursing. Such assignments are made at the beginning of each shift.
14. Makes sure that the relatives of all patients who visit are greeted and that any questions they may have about the care of the patient are answered to the best of her ability, in keeping with good nursing practice.
15. Meets daily with the director of nursing.
16. Reports all problems and incidents as soon as possible to the director of nursing. In the absence of the director, these are reported to the assistant director of nursing or, in the absence of both the director and the assistant, the administrator.
17. Assists the director of nursing with the ongoing in-service training for all nursing personnel.
18. Gives a report at the end of her shift to the charge nurse coming on duty and does not leave her station until properly relieved by the charge nurse assigned to come next.
19. Makes all necessary appointments for patients with physicians, dentists, and other specialists if the patient is to be taken to the physician's or specialist's office.
20. Arranges for hospitalization when so ordered by a physician.
21. Notifies the relatives of such need of hospitalization.
22. Does all major charting in the patient's chart.
23. Makes sure that, at the minimum, blood pressure, pulse rate, temperature, and weight are recorded weekly for each patient unless it is determined that they should be recorded more frequently or unless a physician orders that they be recorded more frequently.
24. Is responsible for the psychological, social, and spiritual needs of all of her patients. This includes calling a member of the clergy if requested by the patient or by his family.
25. Makes sure that auxiliary nursing personnel on each shift give personal hygiene to all the patients as necessary for their comfort and cleanliness.

26. Makes sure that the patients are presentable at all times, encouraging them to be dressed in street clothing, including shoes and socks, whenever their condition permits.

Job specifications:

1. Graduate of a state-approved school of nursing and currently registered as a registered nurse in the state, or a licensed practical nurse who is a graduate from a state-approved school of practical nursing and currently registered in the state.
2. Genuine interest in geriatric nursing and human empathy.
3. Leadership ability and ability to carry out the orders of her superiors and the orders of the physician.
4. Ability to make sure that the needs of the patients are met with dispatch, courtesy, and accuracy.
5. Ability to assume responsibility in a cool and efficient manner.

These job descriptions are merely suggested outlines. Each facility must develop descriptions individually tailored to suit its particular goals and to comply with the licensing requirements of the particular state in which the home is located.

Patient care policies. The nursing service master plan book should next include patient care policies. They are developed jointly by the administrator and the director of nursing, with professional assistance. This professional advice must come from an advisory physician or a medical advisory committee composed of physicians. The policies relating to medications should be developed with the additional assistance of a registered pharmacist. Other professionals may be included in consultation as necessary when these policies are developed. These persons, such as dentists, podiatrists, and physical therapists, can enhance the quality of the policies and provide insight into better methods of service to the patients. A detailed example of a set of patient care policies can be given, but it must be emphasized that these are policies for a specific home with certain goals set by its board. Moreover, requirements vary from state to state. Since each home has its own philosophy of patient care and is governed by local or state regulations, a pat set of policies cannot be given. Therefore, these are given merely as an illustration of one approach.

Patient care plan. A patient care plan should be developed in writing for each patient based on his individual needs, physician's orders, and his individual restoration potential. The primary responsibility for developing the patient care plan rests with the director of nursing. The director of nursing should seek assistance from the patient's individual physician, the charge nurses, other nursing personnel, and consultants when necessary. She should also seek advice and assistance from other departments of the facility, such as the activities department, the dietary department, and the administrative department. She should also seek advice from the patient's relatives when indicated.

In developing the initial care plan, the director of nursing and the charge nurse should follow the physician's orders and should seek additional assistance from the patient and his relatives concerning the patient's likes and dislikes for food, his sleeping habits, his general attitude toward coming to the home, his normal life habits, and his ideas about which activities he wishes to join. Much of this information frequently can be obtained from the patient himself and amplified with information gathered from his relatives.

The patient care plan should be begun initially when the patient is admitted. Since the initial patient care plan will need to be modified as the personnel get to know the patient better and as the patient adapts to the facility, the initial plan should be reviewed after the first week or ten days of the patient's stay. Changes in the care plan indicated by the patient's reaction to his environment or by specific orders of the physician should be made at this first review. Thereafter, the plan should be reviewed and modified at least monthly and changes made as necessary in keeping with the care needed as indicated by the patient's condition. The care plan should be changed more frequently if necessary.

Patient care plans should be written on cards and kept at the nurses' station. They should be available to all nursing personnel, to certain supervisory personnel from other departments, and to the patient's physician. All personnel in the home having contact with patients should be encouraged to be familiar with the patient care plan.

The patient care plan should include the goals of the physician toward the restoration of the patient and should encompass the home's concept toward restorative nursing. Limitations of activities of daily living should be stated with goals to improve these activities whenever they are deficient. Other restorative nursing techniques required to bring the patient to his maximum potential should be so indicated. The plan should state any limitations or contraindications that the physician may have given to participation in the activity programs of the home. Each section of the plan should end with goals and objectives that are desired for each particular patient.

Although it is the primary responsibility of the director of nursing to initiate the patient care plan, the charge nurse has definite responsibilities for input, and she should seek advice from all the auxiliary nursing personnel regularly when implementing the patient care plan, to see if modifications are necessary.

Admission of patient to facility. All patients admitted to the facility should have prior approval from the administrator and the director of nursing. Prior to admission, the administrator or the director of nursing should advise the charge nurse of the patient's expected arrival time and the room and bed to be assigned to the patient. Whenever possible, all required medical records should be on hand awaiting the patient's arrival.

The charge nurse is responsible for overseeing the admission of each new patient. She is responsible for contacting the attending physician for initial orders if they are not received prior to or when the patient arrives. These orders should be currently dated and signed. If the orders are dated prior to the patient's arrival and the patient's condition appears to indicate that additional orders or changes in the orders are necessary, the charge nurse should not hesitate to call the attending physician to seek additional orders. The charge nurse should make sure that all orders are recorded on the physician's order sheet. She should then direct the ward clerk to begin to prepare the patient's chart.

The charge nurse is responsible for making an admission note that includes the mode of admission; source of admission and party bringing resident; physician's admitting diagnosis; general mental and physical status of the patient; evaluation of the patient's vision, hearing, and teeth; patient's diet order; patient's level of activity in care of daily living needs; and his blood pressure, pulse rate, temperature, respiration rate, and weight. The note should also state the general condition of the patient determined by an examination of the patient's body to see if there are any abrasions, burns, bedsores, or bruises and by observation of the general condition of the skin of the patient. Any items should be noted. Bruises, bedsores, rashes, and the like should be described in detail, and the note should state which area of the body is involved.

Prior to making this note, the charge nurse should see to the well-being of the patient. She should assign to an aide the task of taking the patient to his room. The aide should assist the patient in unpacking his belongings and indicate to the patient where his belongings should be stored. The aide should assist the patient in storing the belongings in the proper drawers and closets. The aide should then orient the patient to his room, showing him his bathroom area and introducing him to his roommate. The aide should point out where the call light indicator is located and should point out any other details of the room of importance to the patient. If the patient is capable of taking a brief tour of the facility at the time and desires such a tour, the aide can then show him the location of the dining room and activity area that he will use. The aide should also point out other important items to the patient, such as the telephone, the drinking fountains, and the areas where the patient should not go. If the patient's condition does not warrant such a tour or if he does not desire it, the aide should see that he is comfortable and is seated in a chair or comfortably placed in his bed before leaving him.

After the aide has accomplished the above admission procedures, she should make sure that the patient is safe, has adjusted well to his new environment, and is comfortable. She should then report back to the charge nurse to indicate what has taken place.

It is essential that all new patients be visited several times during the first day, including evening and night shifts, in order to reassure the patient and to better evaluate the patient's reaction to his environment.

The charge nurse should see that the relatives are treated with courtesy and are involved in the orientation procedures by the aide. This should not be left to resident's relatives alone; the home must take the leadership in this orientation. It must be conducted by home personnel. The charge nurse should also take this opportunity to discuss the patient with the relatives to learn of any items that might be of assistance in helping the patient better adapt to his environment and in the development of the patient care plan.

Preparation of patient's chart. The charge nurse should delegate the responsibility of preparation of the patient's chart to the ward clerk. The patient's chart must contain, on admission, the following forms and data:

1. Completed identification sheet.
2. Hospital summary sheet or transfer sheet (if the patient has been admitted from a hospital or other nursing home). A hospital summary discharge sheet is preferred, along with the transfer sheet. A properly completed transfer sheet satisfies the requirements, but the hospital discharge summary amplifies the transfer sheet and can be obtained on request by the charge nurse or the director of nursing from the hospital on order of the attending physician with the consent of the patient.
3. Medical examination form containing complete medical history, physical findings, diagnosis, and restoration potential, signed by the physician attending the resident. Part of this form should be the physician's initial medical evaluation and physical examination.
4. Physician's order sheet. The initial orders may very well be written on the transfer sheet received from the hospital. If this is the case, the initial entry on the physician's order sheet should be a date and an explanation referring the reader to the transfer sheet. The physician's order must include orders for all medications, treatments (including restorative potentials and treatments desired), diet, activities and limitations of activity, and special procedures required for the safety and well-being of the resident. If the charge nurse believes that the initial orders on the transfer sheet are inadequate and do not cover all of these areas, she should contact the physician when the patient is admitted, to obtain a complete order covering what is lacking; this order should be noted on the physician's order sheet, and the telephone order procedure should be initiated.
5. Progress record and physician's initial recommendation for rehabilitation nursing, with goals stated for the particular patient. These records indicate the resident's initial condition and any changes that may occur in his condition

from time to time. Any changes should be recorded by appropriate staff members as they occur.

6. Nurse's notes. These are discussed later.
7. Medication sheet. This is used to record data about medications, including date given, time given, name of medicine or prescription number, dosage, and by whom administered. The administration of each dose of medicine should be recorded on this sheet.
8. Treatment sheet. This should be maintained for all patients and should include all special procedures performed for the safety and well-being of the resident.
9. Clothing and personal belongings record.
10. Special instructions from the resident or conservator of the resident pertaining to procedures that should be carried out in the event of death.
11. Incident reports. These are reports of any incidents or accidents that involve the resident or patient. They should include all medication errors and drug reactions. (A copy of this report should be sent to the administrator's office.)
12. Reports of social, dental, laboratory, and x-ray services and other special reports of consultants. These reports should be placed in the patient's chart as they are made.

If a patient is sent from the home to the office of a physician, dentist, psychiatrist, or the like, the physician's order sheet should be sent along with the patient; the practitioner should be asked to write orders, sign them, and date them. The sheet should be placed in the patient's chart and the orders carried out.

Records of business matters such as contracts with patients, personal money transactions that are maintained on behalf of the patient by the home, receipts of valuables of the patient, and similar business transactions should be kept in a separate administrative record that is kept in the business office. If the nurse is asked about any of these records by a patient or his relatives, she should refer the inquirer to the administrator.

Nurse's notes. It is the responsibility of the charge nurse to see that a nursing note is made at least weekly on each patient. This note should contain specific information such as significant responses to treatments, progress toward goals, appetite, general attitude, and medications given. A full written report should be made of any accident or incident involving a resident or patient, including errors and drug reactions. Other pertinent notes that should be included are anxieties and fears expressed by the patient, unusual reactions of the resident to relatives or friends visiting him, and requests for special assistance from outside sources such as clergy or social service.

These notes should be made only by the charge nurse or by the director of nursing. When it is necessary to make the notes more frequently, they should be made as required by the condition of the patient. If the condition of the patient requires that the notes be more complete than normal weekly notes, the director of nursing should be consulted for instructions and a special form should be utilized.

Since the charge nurse is responsible for the complete mental and physical care of all the patients in her unit, she should pay particular attention to the writing of complete nursing notes weekly. These notes should be detailed and specific. Although the evening and night charge nurses also may make necessary notes, it is preferred that the regular notes of *weekly evaluation* be made by the day charge nurse. There should be coordination and correlation between these weekly nursing notes and the patient care plan. The nurse should consult the patient care plan when making the weekly nursing notes and in the notes should evaluate the progress of the patient toward the goals of the plan. If satisfactory progress is being made toward the goals stated in the care plan, this should be noted. If satisfactory progress is not being made, the charge nurse should consult the director of nursing for possible consideration of revision of the plan or for suggestions about how to better meet the goals indicated by the plan.

If the charge nurse notes that the condition of the patient warrants closer supervision than the previous note indicated, she should record this and call it to the attention of all auxiliary nursing personnel and pass the information along to the charge nurse relieving her at the end of her shift.

If changes in the patient's condition warrant the physician's being called, the nurse's notes should indicate that this was done and the date the physician was called. Any visits by the physician or a consultant should be noted. If orders have been received from the physician, the nurse's note should so state and should indicate the date so that a cross-reference to the physician's sheet may be made.

The nursing notes should also include any appointments that have been made on behalf of the patient for visits to physicians, dentists, or other specialists that are made away from the home. Any special modes of transportation that have been arranged for the patient should be noted.

If the patient is discharged from the facility or is transferred from the facility, a note should be made indicating the circumstances of the transfer or discharge.

Physician's orders. The charge nurse should contact the physician when any change in the patient's condition indicates the need for a change in orders. She should record any change of orders on the physician's order sheet and should carry out the policy for verbal orders.

All orders for patient care, including medications, must be given by the physician in charge of the patient. All physician's orders must be signed. Telephone orders should be carried out; however, they must be countersigned within 72 hours. Physician's orders are also necessary for the discontinuation of medications, changes in diets, or changes in methods of treatments; they likewise must be in writing.

Nursing procedures and treatments such as enemas, irrigations, catheterizations, and applications of dressings or bandages should only be done on order of the patient's physician and under the supervision of the licensed nurse on duty.

Instructions and orders from physicians provide the basis for developing the complete plan of care to meet the needs of each individual patient. These orders must be clearly written and specific in order to be thoroughly understood. The nurse should not hesitate to question the physician if she does not understand his order completely. Any instruction from the physician to discontinue an order should show the date and time of the discontinuance and should also be signed by the physician. It must be emphasized that the nurse cannot carry out orders or changes in orders for medication, care, or treatment of the patient without first receiving directions from the resident's physician.

Changes of condition of patient. When a patient's condition changes, the physician should be contacted at once for orders. Likewise, the charge nurse should call this to the attention of the director of nursing as soon as possible.

If the patient's condition changes on a shift other than the day shift or when the director of nursing is not on duty, it should be the responsibility of the charge nurse to pass this information on to the next shift so that the director of nursing can be notified of the changes on her return to duty.

If a patient becomes critically ill or dies, the charge nurse should contact the director of nursing immediately. If death occurs after the normal working hours of the director of nursing, the administrator should be contacted as soon as possible. He should be contacted at any hour of the day or night. If he is not available, the director of nursing should be notified.

Laboratory tests, x-ray examinations, physical therapy, or other services not pro-

vided on premises of home. If a physician orders a laboratory test, the charge nurse should request that a technician from the laboratory providing the service to the home come to take the specimen from the patient and report the results both to the physician and to the home as soon as possible. If the physician desires an x-ray examination, the charge nurse should make the necessary arrangements. If the physician desires physical therapy, she should carry out the same procedures.

Review of physician's orders. The physician should be requested to visit his patient at least every month or as often as necessary to ensure good medical care for the patient.

The charge nurse should notify the physician of any accident, injury, or unusual change in the patient's condition as soon as possible. At the time of the accident, immediate first aid should be provided by the charge nurse. However, the physician's orders should be followed as soon as he is contacted.

At least once a month and oftener if indicated, the charge nurse should review with the physician, the patient's medication regimen. She should mention any problems to the physician that she believes are important. Any changes in medication should be indicated on the physician's order sheet and the policy for telephone orders followed if the orders are given via the phone.

It should be reemphasized that any time the physician's orders are changed, the charge nurse receiving such changes has the responsibility of pointing out these changes to the charge nurse relieving her on the next shift. Furthermore, all these orders must be in writing, and the charge nurse must follow the policy and procedure established for getting the physician's signature for changes in orders received verbally.

Any difficulty encountered with physician visits to the patient that are less frequent than the mandatory once a month should be reported to the director of nursing as soon as possible.

Nursing personnel staffing. During the day, there should be a licensed nurse on duty at each nursing care unit between the hours of 7:00 A.M. and 3:00 P.M. The same staffing pattern should be followed for the shifts from 3:00 to 11:00 P.M. and 11:00 P.M. to 7:00 A.M. This coverage should continue seven days a week. In addition to this, there should be a director of nursing on duty five days a week. On the days when the director of nursing is not on duty, a registered nurse designated as assistant director of nursing should assume the director's functions.

Similarly, auxiliary nursing personnel should be in sufficient numbers to assure safe, adequate, comfortable, pleasant, and reassuring care to the patients.

Accidents. In the event of a serious accident to a patient or to an employee, the administrator and the director of nursing should be notified immediately. First aid procedures should be carried out at once. If the accident involves a patient, the patient's physician should be notified. If the accident involves an employee, the employee should be taken to the emergency room of the nearest hospital of his choice. In every case of an accident involving an employee or a resident, accident report forms should be completed. A copy should be sent to the administrator's office if a patient is involved. If an employee is involved, the original form should be sent to the administrator.

Diets for patients. Each physician should indicate a diet for a patient. The physician should indicate whether it should be a regular diet or a special diet in every case.

On receiving orders for a diet or orders for change in diet, the charge nurse should notify the dietitian in writing of the diet order.

Telephone orders. It is desirable that all orders be written and signed by the physician before they are carried out. This is not practical, however, in most cases.

Therefore, the following telephone order policy should be observed: Telephone orders should be taken from the physician only by the charge nurse on duty. The order should immediately be written on the patient's clinical chart and a telephone order form prepared. All telephone orders should be countersigned by the physician within a 72-hour period. The charge nurse should have the responsibility for following this up to see that this practice is carried out correctly.

Taking patient to office of physician or specialist or to hospital. From time to time it may be necessary for an employee to take a patient to the office of a physician or dentist, to a hospital for outpatient physical therapy, or to a specialist for eye care, podiatry treatment, or similar services. Only certain personnel should be granted this authority. Whenever such a need is known by the charge nurse, she should contact the director of nursing and ask her to arrange for one of the authorized persons to take care of this problem.

Patient's death. When an apparent death occurs, the charge nurse on duty should notify the patient's physician immediately; she should follow his instructions. Next she should notify (1) the patient's relatives; (2) the director of nursing or her assistant if she is on duty; and (3) the administrator, who should be called at any time of day or night.

The charge nurse should determine from the family which funeral home should be notified. She should then contact the funeral home and have them make arrangements to pick up the body. The charge nurse may, at her discretion, move the body to the isolation room or an empty room if it is in the best interest of the patient's roommate to do so. The charge nurse should then direct the staff to prepare the body for the undertaker.

The funeral home taking the body should be asked to sign a form indicating receipt of the body. This form should be placed in the patient's chart.

If the patient owned glasses or false teeth, the charge nurse should see that these are sent along with the body when the undertaker arrives. A note must be placed in the chart indicating that this has been done. Rings or other items of jewelry and similar valuables that have been given to the home for safekeeping or that are at the patient's bedside should be held to be disposed of in accordance with the direction of the administrator.

The charge nurse on duty during the next day's shift should notify the housekeeper that the patient has died and should request that a terminal cleaning be given the unit.

Medical records of patients. Medical records of all patients should be kept confidential. Only the patient's personal physician; persons providing specific consultation to the patient; and certain specified personnel of the nursing home, including nursing personnel, the dietitian, the activities director, the administrator, and the director of nursing, should have access to the records. Certain other authorized people such as members of the departments of public health, public aid, and mental health also should have access to these records for inspection purposes.

There should be no exception to these regulations. No one else should see the patient's records without approval from the administrator and the patient or his conservator. If a nurse receives a request to see the patient's chart from a patient, a patient's relative, or any other unauthorized party, she should refer the party to the director of nursing or to the administrator.

It should be remembered that the medical records of all patients are the property of the nursing home. Medical records should never be removed from the premises without the administrator's approval. Medical records should likewise never be destroyed.

If an error is made in writing a note on the record, the error should be lined out so that it is legible. The word *error* should be written above the line and initialed by the writer, and the proper entry should then be made following the line.

Restorative nursing. Restorative nursing should be an ongoing policy in a nursing home. Restorative nursing should be practiced 24 hours a day, seven days a week, by all nursing and auxiliary personnel.

Procedures that require technical knowledge should be done only by qualified personnel on order of the physician. However, the general concept of encouraging patients to reach their maximum potential as indicated by the physician may be carried out by all nursing personnel.

1. Positioning and turning. All nursing personnel should encourage and assist patients in maintaining good body alignment while standing, sitting, or lying in bed, to keep pressure from bony structures of the body.
2. Exercises. Qualified nursing personnel should assist patients in maintaining active and passive range of motion of limbs and joints unless contraindications are given by a patient's physician.
3. Bowel and bladder retraining. All nursing personnel should encourage and assist incontinent patients in regaining their former bowel and bladder patterns through the use of the written procedures for this retraining.
4. Retraining in activities of daily living. All nursing personnel should help and train patients to regain the maximum level in the necessary activities of daily living.
5. Ambulation. All nursing personnel should help the patients to walk, with assistance when necessary, as much as can be tolerated each shift during their waking hours unless contraindicated by the orders of the physician.
6. Transfer activities. Nursing personnel should help patients to learn safe techniques in transferring from their beds to walkers or wheelchairs and from walkers or wheelchairs to toilet facilities and in other similar transfers.

The charge nurse should note the patient's reaction to and progress in these restorative techniques and chart the data in the weekly nursing notes.

If a physician wishes a patient to have physical therapy, he should write an order for this. After the patient has been evaluated by the therapist, the charge nurse should consult the therapist to see what activities the home's nursing personnel can carry on to complement the program that the therapist has established for the patient.

Personal care. The charge nurse should be responsible for the general oversight of the physical and personal care of her patients. She should make sure that each day auxiliary nursing personnel are assigned to care for personal hygiene needs of each of the patients, including body cleanliness, oral care after each meal and in the morning prior to breakfast, care of hair and nails, haircuts and shaves for the men as necessary, and beauty shop care for the women when needed. She should also make sure that the patients dress in clean clothing and in street clothing with shoes whenever the condition of the patient allows it. The charge nurse should have her personnel make every attempt to see that each patient is as neat and presentable as possible at all times.

The charge nurse should make sure that each patient receives at least one complete bath and hair wash weekly. In the interim, additional baths or partial baths should be carried out as necessary for satisfactory personal hygiene. The charge nurse should make sure that the auxiliary nursing personnel keep each patient's bed clean and dry, with fresh linens. When linens are soiled or become wet, they should be changed immediately.

Patients' personal possessions. A clothing record and personal property record should be maintained for each patient. When a patient is admitted to the home, a record of his personal possessions should be made. The patient's relatives should mark all clothing with laundry markers or name tags. If a patient's relatives are unable to do this, the home should provide assistance, making sure that it is done.

Provision should be made for safekeeping of valuables that are turned over to the home. If the nurse is given such valuables by the patient, she should contact the director of nursing or administrator immediately for instructions. She should not assume the responsibility of receiving these alone.

If the relatives are with the new patient on his arrival, they should be encouraged to let the patient have a little spending money, limited to $5.

Psychological and social needs of patients. It should be the philosophy of the home to provide a cheerful atmosphere for all patients. The charge nurse and all nursing personnel should be alert to the spiritual, social, and psychological needs of the patients. For example, the charge nurse should be sure that the patient is properly introduced to other patients in the home; she should make certain that the activity director promptly meets him and assists him in becoming involved in the activity program. The charge nurse should also assist in ensuring that the patient's spiritual needs are met, by contacting members of the clergy when requested to do so by a resident or his family. The charge nurse and nursing staff should encourage the patients to participate in all the home activities, including the recreational, spiritual, and cultural events that are provided on an ongoing basis.

The charge nurse should make sure that a friendly, homelike atmosphere is maintained and that the patients are treated with respect and courtesy at all times by all home personnel.

Relationship of patient's relatives to the home. The best way for the home to develop a good relationship with the patient's relatives is to begin to develop the relationship when the patient is admitted. It is important that the charge nurse make sure that the relatives and the patient are given prompt and courteous attention to their needs during the admission process.

The charge nurse should be alert to the fact that both the relatives and the patient may be very anxious and upset over this admission. She should do everything in her power to make them feel comfortable and to assure them that the patient will be well cared for.

The charge nurse should make an attempt to greet the patient's relatives each time they visit. This should be done on each shift. It is important for the charge nurse to maintain a liaison with relatives.

It is important for the relatives to understand in general terms the patient care plan that is designed for their particular relative. If they understand the home's aims and goals for the patient, they can accept them and cooperate with the home in obtaining these goals.

The charge nurse should discuss with the relatives the rehabilitation and restoration concept of patient care. She should point out that this includes the need to have the patient reach the maximum degree of independent activity. In discussing this program with the patient's relatives, the nurse should stress that during the day the nurses make every effort to have most of the patients dressed in street clothing, including shoes. Exceptions should be made for bedfast patients and patients with special bowel or bladder difficulties. The nurse should further point out that the home discourages the use of nightgowns and bathrobes during the day. The charge nurse should go into as much detail as she believes is necessary to emphasize the reasons for having the patient reach a higher degree of self-help if possible. If this is explained to the patient's relatives, they can better understand why the home personnel ask the patient to help himself as much as possible. Without understanding this concept, the relatives may misinterpret the home's aims and goals as attempts to cut down on staff or neglect patient needs. The total restoration program should be reviewed positively each time it is discussed with the relatives.

Sterilization of supplies and equipment. Although many of the items that require sterile techniques are disposable and are not used a second time, the home should maintain an autoclave for sterilization of certain materials. Sterilization of supplies and equipment in the autoclave should be done under the supervision of one of the charge nurses. Most of this sterilization work should be carried out on the night shift under the supervision of the night charge nurse.

Bedpans, urinals, washbasins, emesis basins, enema equipment, and similar nursing care utensils should be sanitized weekly. These items should be brought to the utility room where the sanitizing equipment is maintained. This procedure likewise should be done under the supervision of the charge nurse.

Nursing procedures. Specifics of nursing procedures should be developed next in the master plan book. These are the details of nursing and personal care techniques. Policies set the guidelines, and procedures tell how to carry out the guidelines.

Nursing procedures should be developed and put in writing by the director of nursing with assistance, when necessary, from the medical advisory physician. The physician should review and approve all nursing procedures when they are first developed. The procedures should be revised as necessary but definitely should be reviewed annually by both the director of nursing and the medical advisory physician.

Although the nursing procedures should be part of the master plan book, they should also be reproduced separately in loose-leaf style with sufficient copies available for use by the auxiliary nursing personnel. These procedures should be followed by the nursing staff in giving patient care and therefore should be readily available to all who are assigned to patient care. If they are kept in loose-leaf style, it is easy to insert new or revised procedures from time to time and replace worn or soiled pages.

In-service education

It is essential for the nursing department to have an ongoing in-service educational program for the nursing personnel. The written nursing procedures can be an excellent "textbook" for part of the training and especially for the indoctrination of new personnel.

In-service education must be regularly scheduled to be successful. It is wise for the director of nursing to schedule weekly training sessions for the nursing staff.

The training not only should encompass the nursing procedures but also should include lectures by the consultants to the home on their specialties and their concepts of care. For example, the consulting pharmacist should lecture on medication techniques, medication reactions, proper handling of pharmaceuticals, new drugs, and the like. Similar lectures should be given by other consultants, such as the dietitian, the medical records librarian, the medical advisory physician, and the physical therapist.

Regularity of the training programs is the key. If they are constantly scheduled, the program will succeed. If they are scheduled only when "time permits," they will undoubtedly fail.

The classes should be given during the employees' working hours, and the employees should be paid for the time. The class should be scheduled so that both the day and the evening shifts are accommodated at the same time. Obviously, more than one class will be necessary to get the information to all personnel. Attendance records should be kept to assist in seeing that all personnel get the training.

Getting the programs to the night shift personnel is always a difficulty. The director of nursing or her delegated in-service training coordinator should conduct a program on the night shift regularly, however.

Restorative nursing[5]

The human body is designed to function best in an upright, standing position. When a patient is confined to a prone position in bed or to a sitting position in a chair for prolonged periods of time, certain physiological reactions take place that can reduce a patient's ability to recover. Without restorative nursing techniques, bedfast persons soon tend to become mentally dull, confused, and disoriented. Their elimination processes become inadequate; the bladder frequently cannot be completely emptied. These factors combined with inactivity eventually lead to poor appetite. The skin begins to break down, especially at the bony protuberances such as the hip, the shoulder blades, the sacrum, the elbow, and the heel, creating decubitus ulcers. Muscle contractures develop and a general deterioration of the body begins. In the prone position, breathing difficulties develop, and finally, all these physiological problems lead to death.

Restorative nursing techniques are designed as much as possible to prevent these problems from occurring. This requires a 24-hour, seven-day-a-week team effort of all the nursing personnel. These techniques, which are as follows, are relatively simple and require little skilled training:

1. Positioning and turning of patient. If the patient is confined to bed, frequent turning helps to reduce pressure buildup that creates skin breakdown. Small pillows can be used to support the body trunk and limbs. Turning the patient on his stomach may help him sleep better at night. Skin massage with body oil on the pressure sites is necessary, too. The nurse's aide should be taught to watch for reddened areas, bruises, abrasions, and scratches while giving this body care. Patients confined to wheelchairs or geriatric chairs should have cloth-covered rubber rings or pads to sit on and small pillows to help keep the body in a normal position. The use of bed boards and foot boards may be necessary. Foot boards help to keep the feet in a more normal position, preventing foot drop.

2. Exercise to extremities. Patients who are able should walk with assistance several times a day, depending on their condition. Patients who are not able to get out of bed should receive regular passive range-of-motion exercise to the limbs. As does correct positioning, these passive exercises help to prevent contractures due to atrophy of the muscle tissue that may begin to develop within just a few days of disuse of the arms and legs. Range-of-motion exercises should be done only by adequately trained personnel and by direction of the patient's physician.

3. Bowel and bladder retraining. This takes great patience on the part of a highly motivated staff. However, if done with consistency, retraining can be quite successful in many instances. Success depends on regularity of staff procedures. The patient should be taken to the toilet or offered the bedpan at preplanned intervals. The goals should be to restore patient dignity and confidence in himself, which will lead to greater independence, and to keep the patient dry and unsoiled, which will aid in prevention of skin breakdown, rashes, and decubitus ulcers. If retraining is successful, linens and staff time needed to change wet and soiled bed clothing will be conserved. In the retraining program, a bowel and bladder retraining schedule form is necessary. Bowel movements and urinary functions are charted along with amount of fluid intake. Both voluntary

and involuntary results are recorded. The success or failure of this retraining depends totally on the motivation of all nursing personnel on all shifts.

Adequate fluid intake is essential to the retraining program as well as being necessary to the general well-being of the patient. Patients should be encouraged to drink at least 2 quarts of fluid daily, and fluids should be offered frequently.

4. Activities of daily living. The major goal of all restorative nursing techniques is to help the patient to regain the maximum possible level of self-help and independence. The degree of performance of these activities may be quite limited in many patients. Simply getting a patient to roll on his side while in bed may be a great accomplishment. Activities of daily living are the normal actions that a healthy ambulatory person accomplishes, usually automatically and without conscious effort, such as the personal hygiene procedures of bathing, brushing the teeth, shaving, grooming the hair, and washing the hands and face; eating; dressing; getting in and out of bed and chairs; and walking. Depending on the nature and degree of the patient's disability, these activities may be quite limited, and his retraining potential may likewise be limited. Patients recovering from a stroke should be retrained in these activities as soon as the physician believes it is safe to start.[6] This retraining should be done only after written orders and instructions are received from the physician.

As in all restorative techniques, the attitude of the staff toward the patient is most important. Encouragement and patience must be exercised together with firmness tempered with understanding. Stroke patients often respond well to retraining in the activities of daily living if skilled personnel are on hand to perform this task, especially during the early recovery stages.

The goal of this restorative technique in the nursing home is to get the patient to the point where he can help himself as much as possible in the activities of daily living. Often the patient's relatives are misled by the staff's encouragement of the patient to work toward independence. They sometimes feel that the personnel in the home are there to wait on the patient, and they look on attempts to have the patient walk to a central dining room, make his own bed, and dress himself as ways to cut down on personnel. The home administrator should be aware of this potential misunderstanding and see that the home's patient care goals for increasing self-help are explained to the relatives by appropriate nursing service personnel.

5. Ambulation. With approval of the physician, ambulation should be included as a necessary aspect of restorative nursing. Gait training with crutches and other mechanical aids should be begun by a physical therapist. After the basics are mastered, the nursing personnel can carry on with this procedure as begun by the therapist. Ambulation in general not only is an essential exercise routine but also enhances a patient's feeling of well-being, especially when he can relearn to ambulate by himself. His horizons become broader when he once again can move about unattended. Patients who are weak and unsteady must be assisted with walking. Ambulation with assistance should be done as often as directed by the physician.

6. Transfer activities. These activities include moving from a bed to a wheelchair, moving from a wheelchair to a toilet stool or regular chair, and transferring from a wheelchair to an automobile. The goal in teaching a patient these techniques, as in all restorative programs, is to get the patient to reach his highest level of independence. Special techniques are required. Personnel should be trained in rehabilitative nursing procedures before they attempt to train the patients.

Restorative and rehabilitative nursing is an ever increasing responsibility of the nursing home. Frequently today because of the need for hospital beds for acutely ill persons, elderly people must be discharged early. Although these patients are no longer acutely ill, they still usually have a long road ahead of them to regain, if they can, the degree of independence they had prior to the hospitalization.

Whenever possible, the administrator should have his key nursing personnel receive special restorative nursing training. These people can then return to the home to teach other personnel, through in-service programs, what they have learned. Good restorative nursing techniques are a mark of a high-quality, patient-centered nursing home.

Geriatric nursing and social components of care

There are many challenges to be met in geriatric nursing. It has been said that the practice of geriatric nursing is not as glamorous as is the nursing practice in a hospital setting. It has been said that the nurse in the nursing home seldom sees the thrilling experiences of modern miracle medicine, which daily returns patients to their normal homeostasis and thus to vital, productive living. The hospital-oriented nurse may argue that her work is more important to society, that assisting a physician to save the life of a 6-year-old child is far more meaningful than giving medication to a senile nonresponsive old person. It is a fact that the nursing home does not provide the intellectual stimulus found within the hospital, where the physician-patient-nurse contact is the daily routine. It is true that the geriatric nurse is more often than not professionally alone, not having other professional nurses at her side to assist her in testing decisions and to reinforce her when she is in doubt. It is true that because of the infrequency of patient-physician contact, the geriatric nurse carries a heavier load of responsibility and decision making. For these reasons, geriatric nursing is not the field for every nurse. It takes a special kind of person who has confidence in herself and great empathy for weak, often confused, frequently disagreeable, older patients in the nursing home setting. The nurse must hold the dignity of the human being in the highest esteem because, I believe, God has created man in his own image. She must be able to do this no matter how repugnant her duties with certain patients may be.

The field of geriatric nursing is indeed a challenge. It requires people with unique qualities and strengths. There is no room in this special field for the misfit who may finally arrive at the nursing home after years of drifting from one hospital to another, presenting questionable references. The administrator and the director of nursing must be sure that each person employed to give care to the patients is truly well qualified and dedicated. A high degree of care must be exercised in checking into the background and qualifications of the nursing applicant. Likewise, before putting a new nurse in charge of a unit or shift, the director of nursing must be assured that the newcomer is thoroughly trained in the home's policies and procedures and motivated to give good geriatric nursing care.

Although geriatric nursing is challenging, it can be very rewarding personally. The rewards are small and often slow in coming. They present themselves in many ways: a silent smile of thanks from a patient whose pain has been eased; a glimmer of recognition from a confused or disoriented patient; a positive response from a stroke patient, coming slowly but surely, to a well designed patient care plan; the knowledge that the nurse has that she may have been able to show a dying patient, forgotten by others, his last bit of human love in his final days.

The geriatric nurse has something that the hospital nurse never seems to have: time. This does not mean that her day is not filled with rushing. She frequently finds that her day has gone and her work remains, so that she must work an hour or longer beyond her normal eight-hour shift. The time she has is long-range time.

In the general hospital setting, patients must leave as soon as they are medically well, to make room for others with urgent needs. Often the hospital nurse is not able to identify with the patient. The patient is referred to as the "duodenal resection in 119, bed 2." The nurse meets his medical and nursing needs under the direction of the physician. Little time is available for meeting social and psychological needs. In fact, they may never be known, since they usually do not represent a barrier to the "production line" of the hospital. A part-time nurse, working one or two days a week, may return to find an entirely new group of patients. Often this leads to a technical approach: caring for the disease or injury and not the needs of the whole patient. Usually, only if there is a placement problem at the time of discharge, do these social and psychological needs emerge. At that time, the problem may be referred to the social service, and the nurse may disengage herself because of the demands or needs of the other charges.

The geriatric nurse does not have the production line pressures. She has time. She can know the patient by his name. She can learn his likes and dislikes, his strengths and weaknesses, his fears and his expectations. There is time for planning. It may be planning for reaching a higher level, planning for a return to home, or planning for a peaceful death. The nurse can know the patient's relatives or friends, if he has any, and can usually work with these people in the total team effort to help the patient. There is time to listen and time to explain, and there is time to understand. There is time to work toward meeting all the patient's needs. These experiences can be very rewarding to the highly motivated nurse.

The American Nurses' Association has issued a set of standards for geriatric nursing developed by the Committee on Standards for Geriatric Nursing Practice. These nine standards or guidelines can help the administrator and the director of nursing better understand the role of the geriatric nurse. They are also of extreme value to the nurse herself. Since they relate specifically to her unique relationship to her long-term patient, they provide insight about how she may apply her knowledge of basic nursing arts and skills to the nursing home patient. These standards can help instill and reinforce confidence in the nurse and give her direction in her highly complex position.

I. The nurse demonstrates an appreciation of the heritage, values, and wisdom of older persons.

Rationale:

The nurse has some understanding and appreciation of the social and historic settings in which older people have developed, and how these factors may affect their behavior and values. This enables her to respect the older person as an individual and provides for enrichment of the nurse's life. Such an appreciation also provides ways in which the nurse can point out how the present generation has built on their foundation, thus helping to keep older persons in the present.

Assessment factors:

1. The nurse helps older persons share their experience and talents with the present generation.
2. The nurse respects the older person's right to practice religion as he desires.
3. The nurse accepts the older person's desire to cling to a particular item, such as a piece of jewelry or a photograph.
4. The nurse accepts the older person's right to wear the clothes he is accustomed to wearing, such as a night cap or long underwear.

II. The nurse seeks to resolve her conflicting attitudes regarding aging, death, and

dependency so that she can assist older persons, and their relatives, to maintain life with dignity and comfort until death ensues.

Rationale:

If the nurse does not recognize and seek to resolve conflicts regarding aging,
death, and dependency, functioning can be impaired and personal satisfaction
not be achieved from her work. These conflicts are resolved to enable the nurse
to enlarge her capacity to express empathy and compassion.

Dying and death are common emotional and stressful experiences. Preparation
for death is an imminent developmental task of old age. The older person is
more frequently exposed to dying and death. The nurse needs to assist older
persons, personnel, relatives, and other persons who are experiencing dying,
death, and bereavement to express their feelings, thoughts, and rituals.

Rituals provide a socially acceptable way of coping with emotion; therefore,
the nurse enables the older person to participate in rituals meaningful to him.

Assessment factors:

1. The nurse recognizes that the dependency-independency conflict is perpetuated
   throughout life.
2. The nurse recognizes that many of her own attitudes concerning death and
   dying are learned from the culture of the society in which she lives.
3. The nurse freely shares her feelings with colleagues or other individuals
   about her attitude toward aging and death.
4. The nurse recognizes the many ways of coping with death.
5. The nurse calls the appropriate religious adviser or provides for last rites.
6. Upon request or other indication, the nurse assists in the preparation for
   dying, making of will, plans for burial, and notification of other persons.

III. The nurse observes and interprets minimal as well as gross signs and symptoms
associated with both normal aging and pathologic changes and institutes appropriate nursing measures.

Rationale:

In older persons, pathology may be ignored because their symptoms may be
ascribed to the normal aging process. Older persons do not attend to and are
frequently not able to express or recognize the importance of symptoms. They
have lived with some symptoms, such as pain, for a long time and have adapted
to it so that they either ignore or exaggerate the symptom.

Sensory and cognitive changes are often slowly progressive and may be ignored
until the adaptive response of the aged may interfere with functions or health,
such as a personality change due to progressive loss of hearing.

Assessment factors:

1. Falling, irritability, or slight speech changes may be a sign of cerebral dis-
   turbance.
2. Confusion may be caused by medication, dehydration, or excessive fatigue.
   Mild confusion may be the first indication of pneumonia.
3. Edema may result from prolonged sitting or it may be a sign either of a
   cardiovascular problem or electrolyte imbalance.

IV. The nurse differentiates between pathologic social behavior and the usual life
style of each aged individual.

Rationale:

In all human beings, there is a continuum of behavior which is within the range
of normal. It is difficult to discriminate between that which is normal and that
which can be dangerous to the individual or others, such as the right of the

person for privacy and its extreme, which is withdrawal, and a person's right to independence and its extreme, which may also be pathologic.

Assessment factors:

1. The nurse visiting in the home may observe poor maintenance of the home and a lack of cleanliness. The nurse assesses the situation to determine whether this has always been the person's life style or that his behavior has changed.
2. Many older persons who have been useful and needed throughout their lives may resent being given "busy work."
3. Withdrawal may or may not be a coping mechanism.
4. An older person who is used to independence and self-direction who becomes mildly confused and is placed in an institution, may be agitated—trying to phone, ordering others out of his room, and so forth. The nurse must not automatically see this as senility, but rather determine whether it might be an effort to maintain a life style that is being threatened.
5. The nurse provides for healthy outlet of normal sexual drives within the individual's life style and environmental settings, such as opportunities for heterosexual activities.
6. The nurse assists older persons to develop and maintain their social contacts, both inside and outside the institution or dwelling. This may take the form of telephone calls, birthday cards, et cetera; these activities may be provided by voluntary services.

V. The nurse supports and promotes normal physiologic functioning of the older person.

Rationale:

The nurse helps the older person to experience a higher level of wellness and seeks to prevent iatrogenic conditions.

Assessment factors:

1. The nurse makes use of selected foods, fluids, exercise, and habit training instead of cathartics, enemata, and other artificial means for bowel regulation.
2. The nurse uses back rubs and gentle massage and other nursing measures as possible alternatives to medication to encourage sleep.
3. The nurse is aware of the increased dryness and fragility of the older person's skin so that less frequent bathing is indicated.
4. The nurse allows sufficient time for the patient to perform his activities of daily living at his own pace.

VI. The nurse protects aged persons from injury, infection, and excessive stress and supports them through the multiplicity of stressful experience to which they are subjected.

Rationale:

Aged persons have a decreased margin of compensatory reserve and, therefore, are more vulnerable to secondary problems as a result of stressful experiences.

Assessment factors:

1. Because the older person frequently has a variety of chronic illness, an acute episode will often exacerbate a chronic illness. When pneumonia occurs, the older individual frequently develops cardiac decompensation or his diabetes becomes unregulated. The nurse must recognize early symptoms or even the potential for decompensation and provide the preventive rest and dependence.
2. The nurse uses appropriate precautions to prevent self-mutilation, suicide, and assaultive behavior.
3. When an older person has a fractured femur, unless early mobility is pro-

vided, he frequently develops complicating conditions such as incontinence, confusion, social withdrawal, and decubitus ulcers.

VII. The nurse employs a variety of methods to promote effective communication and social interaction of aged persons with individuals, family, and other groups.

Rationale:

Communication is essential to mental health and social well-being. Older persons need all kinds and a higher intensity of sensory stimulation. They frequently experience barriers to communication, such as language difference, aphasia, deafness, edentulousness, or sensory loss.

Assessment factors:

1. Older blind persons may be able to use talking books and other devices.
2. The nurse uses touch as a nonverbal means to communicate purposefully an idea or feeling.
3. The nurse uses eye contact, special effort to get and hold the older person's attention, a pitch of voice, and/or objects which improve her communication with older persons.
4. The nurse uses clocks, calendars, newspapers, and reading materials, thermometers, and holiday decorations to assist in the orientation and stimulation of older persons to time and events.
5. The nurse plans and creates situations so that interaction is encouraged, such as placing an older person in a wheelchair near the nurse's desk so that he can observe, or thoughtfully selecting roommates or caring personnel.
6. The nurse is aware of obstacles that will break communication between the nurse and an older person, for example, a person in authority enters the room.
7. Music is a universal language; therefore, it may be used on an individual basis or as group activity to promote interaction.

VIII. The nurse together with the older person designs, changes, or adapts the physical and psychosocial environment to meet his needs within the limitations imposed by the situation.

Rationale:

The health of the older person is greatly influenced by his environment; the nurse uses this environment as a therapeutic tool. His environment may be monotonous because his mobility is reduced. The nurse, therefore, provides for variety in his environment.

Those older persons who have increasing dependence still have a need for maintaining a degree of mastery of their physical and psychosocial environment.

Assessment factors:

1. The nurse provides a variety of materials for the older person's creativity, manipulation, and sensory stimulation.
2. The nurse suggests the installation of hand rails in buildings used by aged persons.
3. The nurse changes the location of a patient's bed so he may look out of the window.
4. The nurse provides opportunities for learning which expand the horizons of older persons.
5. The nurse teaches the family to avoid many sudden changes in the environment. Often the most simple change of furniture is upsetting.

IX. The nurse assists older persons to obtain and utilize devices which help them attain a higher level of function and ensures that these devices are kept in good working order by the appropriate persons or agencies.

Rationale:

Devices are essential supportive measures to facilitate function. A nonfunctioning or defective device is potentially dangerous. To help older persons be more independent, the nurse teaches them to secure, to use, and to maintain their devices.

Older persons have a proportionately greater need for one or more assistive devices to facilitate functioning; therefore, the nurse needs to be well informed about resources for obtaining and maintaining these devices.

Assessment factors:
1. If a hearing aid is required, the nurse considers the problem of cost and, if necessary, contacts a community agency. When a hearing aid is fitted for the older person, the nurse assists him in his adjustment to it by recognizing fatigue and that it takes time to get used to it.
2. The nurse uses other resource persons to help design and fit wheelchairs and to adapt and maintain this equipment.
3. Following a cerebral vascular accident, the older person may need to adjust to using a cane, foot-drop brace, hearing aid, and special eating devices.
4. The use of some devices, such as a hydraulic lift, may be primarily for the benefit of personnel; and the older person may need a great deal of reassurance and instruction to perceive the mutual benefit obtained.
5. The nurse makes use of appropriate community resources, such as the Ileostomy Society, for additional assistance.[7]

PHARMACY SERVICES

The retirement facility that does not provide a health service is not involved with pharmacy services beyond perhaps maintaining a registry of local pharmacies that provide individual residents with delivery service or special discounts. Residents give themselves medication, and the facility is not involved in this aspect unless it becomes a problem.

Methods of providing institutional pharmacy service

The consideration of pharmacy services in this discussion is confined to institutional pharmaceutical services. The facility has three basic choices to make: (1) to hire a full-time or part-time pharmacist, obtain a license from the state to operate a pharmacy, and provide adequate space and security for the stock and records; (2) to arrange for an affiliated hospital that has its own pharmacy to provide the services; and (3) to arrange with a local pharmacist in the community to provide service from his shop and act as consultant to the home.[8]

Requirements

The federal government requires that the facility assume the responsibility to make sure that adequate provisions are made for obtaining prescribed medication for patients promptly.[9]

If the facility chooses to employ a licensed pharmacist to administer the pharmacy service, the administrator must see that the pharmacist is responsible for the control of all bulk drugs and that he keeps the required records of their receipt and disposition. Moreover, the administrator and the pharmacist must establish and record in writing the policy that the pharmacist is the one who dispenses the drugs from the home's pharmacy to designated nursing personnel on receipt of written prescriptions from licensed physicians.

Written prescriptions. The federal guidelines require that medications be administered to patients only after written orders are received from a licensed physician, with the exception that verbal orders can be taken if (1) they are immediately written down and signed by the nurse taking the order from the physician and (2) they are countersigned by the prescribing physician within 48 hours.

Emergency pharmaceutical policy. The administrator together with the pharmacist and the director of nursing must also establish and record in writing policy and procedures for the emergency withdrawal of drugs from the pharmacy when the pharmacist is not available. The policy and procedures must conform to local or state laws and standards. The federal regulations require that the home maintain an emergency medication kit available to the nursing staff if the home does not have a home-based pharmacy. The contents of this emergency kit should be selected by the home's medical and pharmaceutical consultative staff members.

Stop orders. The federal guidelines call for automatic stop orders on medications if specific limitations are not already established by the prescribing physician. The policy on stop orders must be developed by the home's medical advisory physicians and must be in writing. These stop order policies must be developed by drug type, such as analgesics, cardiovascular drugs, barbiturates, diuretics, hypnotics, and antibiotics. The advisory physician must set an automatic stop order time for each type. At the end of this period, the nurse must contact the prescribing physician to ascertain if the medication is to be continued and must get written confirmation of a continuance. Stop order times range from a few days to 30 days, depending on the drug type. This policy is a necessary safeguard followed in both hospitals and other health care facilities in order to prevent overmedication of the patient.

The federal regulations require that the nurse review medications at the minimum of once a month with the patient's physician. Documentation of this review must be made in the patient's chart, and changes in medications also must be properly recorded and handled by the nursing personnel.

Administration of medications. The federal guidelines are specific on the details of administration of medication. Some of the requirements are as follows:

1. Medications must not be administered by the patient unless specific orders are given for supervised predischarge training programs by the patient's physician. They must be administered only by appropriate nursing personnel according to the laws and regulations of the particular state.
2. Appropriate systems must be developed, such as medication cards, so that during the preparation of individual doses, a check may be made against the physician's orders.
3. Medication must not be "borrowed" from one specific prescription for one patient and given to another patient.
4. Any drug reaction or error in administration must be reported immediately to the patient's physician, and a record of the event must be made in the patient's chart.

Labeling and storage of drugs and biologicals. The federal government requires that all medications be stored in locked medicine cabinets that are well lighted and ample in size to prevent crowding. Medications specifically for external use only and poisonous drugs must be stored apart from other drugs. Drugs and biologicals requiring refrigeration must be kept in a refrigerator in a separate box with its own lock. The refrigerator must be located in or near the nurses' station. Narcotics, barbiturates, amphetamines, and other dangerous or controlled drugs must be kept in a second locked box or drawer within the locked medicine cabinet. The box or drawer must be designed so that it cannot be removed from the cabinet.

As to labeling of medications, the requirements call for several definite items: (1) patient's full name; (2) physician's name; (3) prescription number; (4) name and strength of medication; (5) date prescription was filled and expiration date of drug, if appropriate; and (6) name, address, and telephone number of issuing pharmacist. If the label becomes damaged or illegible or if it is incomplete, the medication must be returned to the issuing pharmacist for relabeling. Medications must be kept in their original container as issued by the pharmacist for each individual patient. There can be no transferring or borrowing of medications by the nursing staff between patients' individual prescriptions.

Narcotics, hypnotics, amphetamines, and other legend drugs. The guidelines state that both federal and state laws regarding these drugs must be strictly observed. The administrator should have the consulting or staff pharmacist regularly give in-service instructions to the staff concerning the handling of these controlled drugs. The home should have clear, written policies and procedures about their storage, accounting, administration, and disposal. The theft of these drugs is sometimes a problem in some homes. The administrator is responsible for ensuring that both the director of nursing and the consulting or staff pharmacist regularly review the details of these policies to be sure that they are being followed.

The home must maintain a narcotics record, with separate sheets for each type and strength of narcotic. These sheets must show the name of the patient who received the dose, the date and time the dose was administered, the name of the patient's physician, and the signature of the person who administered the drug. The sheet should be designed to show accountability for each dose, with a place for recording a beginning and ending balance. These forms must be preserved for state and federal inspections.

Drug profile. One of the many valuable contributions a staff or consulting pharmacist can make to the home is the individual patient's drug profile. This is a record of each patient's medication regimen ordered by the physician. With it, the pharmacist can assist the home and the physician in preventing the *synergism*, interaction of two or more medications, that produces undesired reactions and other incompatibilities of medication in individual patients. The profile should show the patient's drug sensitivities, if they are known, and his various diagnoses, and it should provide space to list individual prescriptions prescribed with the directions for administration. By providing this profile, the pharmacist can be of great assistance to the home, the physician, and consequently, the patient, if he notes drug incompatibilities. It is one more safeguard in the good care of the patient, which should be the goal of the home and the physician.

Drug reference data. Every home should ensure that each nursing unit has a current copy of the *Physician's Desk Reference* (PDR) and the *ASHP Hospital Formulary*. These books, revisions of which are issued regularly, are essential reference data for the nursing staff. The PDR describes each drug, with a photograph of the capsule or tablet to help in identification, giving its usual prescription data, its uses and actions, its reactions and potential side effects. Such reference data is essential to good drug administration procedures.

Other drug reference books and literature may be obtained through the staff or consulting pharmacist as needed. An excellent source of information about pharmacy services for the home administrator is *Pharmaceutical Services in the Nursing Home*.[8] This booklet also has a list of selected references and a list of sources of audiovisual training materials. The administrator should likewise obtain copies of all federal and state laws, rules, and regulations relating to drugs and biologicals. These booklets should be available to nursing personnel for reference, and the home's policies on pharmaceutical service should incorporate these laws.

MEDICAL ADVISORY COMMITTEE AND MEDICAL DIRECTOR
Physician advisory service

Hospitals have, by tradition, required that the physicians who are granted the privilege of practicing in the facility, organize themselves into a self-governing, regulatory body. The major purpose of this medical regulatory body is to assure the governing board of the hospital that recognized and accepted professional methods of medical practice are being carried out by the individual physicians and that the individual patient is receiving proper and necessary care. A secondary role of this organized medical staff is, through its various committees, to act as an advisory group to the hospital owner, administrator, and various departmental leaders. The staff is grouped into several committees, each with specific responsibilities to oversee the professional work of the individual physicians.

Although the governing board (owner) of the hospital is ultimately responsible for the care given the patients, it delegates this responsibility to the organized medical staff. This delegation is necessary simply because no one except a physician is qualified to determine the quality of work of another physician. The governing board, through written bylaws, rules, and regulations, motivates the medical staff to organize for self-regulation. The physicians themselves are motivated to cooperate because an appointment to a hospital medical staff is required before the physician can admit his patients. Without hospital admission privileges, the practicing physician is not able to care adequately for his patients. From this comes the willingness to participate in the process of peer review.

In the nursing home setting, the owners have the same responsibility toward the quality of medical care that is given their patients. However, they do not have the influence of denial of staff membership to a physician that the hospital enjoys. The nursing home staff appointment is not necessary for a physician's success in practice. Therefore, it is virtually nonexistent except in rare instances. The physician tells the family that it is time to move the patient from the hospital to a nursing home but leaves the responsibility of choosing the home to the family in most cases. Most nursing homes, anxious to get patients, try to cooperate with the family in admitting the patient, and thus most admissions are arranged for by the family or agents of the patient. Physician cooperation is necessary since the nursing home requires a physician to be responsible for admission medical reports, but the family or agency initiates the admitting process. This is in direct opposition to the situation in a hospital, which admits a patient *only* on direct orders from the patient's physician.

Since nursing homes do not motivate physicians by need to assist them in the review and oversight of the medical care of the patients, they must find other methods of obtaining physician advisory services. Often, physicians will volunteer to advise as a service to the home or the community. Sometimes the county medical society will provide the services. Frequently, however, the medical advisory staff expects a fee for this demand on their already busy schedule. This is a justified request.

Most nursing homes have what is known as open staffs. This means that they allow any qualified and duly licensed physician to care for patients in their homes. The administrator should be cautious in using the open staff concept without some safeguards and qualifications. Certainly the home should require that the physician be a member of a local hospital's medical staff and thus approved for practice in that hospital by his peers. It is essential that the attending physician have local hospital privileges so that prompt hospital admission can be made when necessary.

Medical advisory committee. To help the administrator with the problem of the qualifications of the medical staff and to act as professional advisor on the overall medical management of the patients, a medical advisory committee composed of at least two licensed physicians is necessary. This committee should assist the administrator and his staff in developing and putting in writing the *medical care policies* for the home. The physicians should meet at least quarterly to review the medical progress being made and to discuss and assist in resolving specific medical care problems of the home. Although they are not responsible for the individual medical care of each patient, they can point out to the administrator specific problems they discover and can assist him in finding solutions.

After initially developing the patient medical care policies, this committee should review them periodically, at the minimum of once a year, and revise them as necessary. At certain times the administrator should involve the consulting pharmacist in these advisory committee meetings also. Other consultants and home staff members should likewise be asked to participate if their participation would be helpful.

Utilization review committee. Early in the 1960's, the concept of utilization review was adopted as a principle for hospitals by the Joint Commission on Accreditation of Hospitals. The concern was to review the use of acute care hospital beds to be sure that hospital admissions were truly necessary—that the patient could not be served equally as well as an outpatient—and that the patient truly needed an acute care bed (as opposed to a long-term care bed) and to encourage better management of patient hospital stays, producing more efficient use of beds. This need was brought about by the shortage of acute care beds, waiting lists for admission, and overcrowding of general hospitals. Medical staffs were encouraged to adopt the utilization review method to assist the hospital in patient care efficiency.[10]

With the implementation of Medicare and the subsequent establishment of the extended care facility, federal regulations called for a utilization review committee to be established in Medicare-certified homes. The goals were similar to those of the committee in the hospital: to see that the money being spent for the care of patients certified for Medicare was being applied in the most efficient manner and that the patient was really in need of extended care.[11]

On paper the concept is good and still functions well in many extended care facilities in the country. However, many nursing homes have recently become disenchanted with the Medicare program, and utilization review committees have been critical of the fiscal intermediary's overruling physician judgments.

To become certified as an extended care facility, however, the home must have an effective utilization review committee that meets the requirements of the law. The committee must meet at least monthly with the purpose of reviewing, on a random sample basis, the medical case histories of patients at the facility. The patient's physician is consulted when necessary, and his opinion is given considerable weight in the final decision of the committee. When the committee determines that the patient is no longer eligible for federally financed benefits because of his changed condition or needs, it recommends termination of benefits.

Medical review. The utilization review committee's work should not be confused with the efforts of the medical review team. Required by federal regulations, the medical review team surveys homes covered by Title XIX of the Social Security Act (Medicaid). These are homes offering skilled nursing or intermediate nursing care to medically indigent persons. The medical review team is not controlled by the home. It is under the direction of the single state agency responsible for administering the Title XIX regulations.

The purpose of this committee is to best utilize the health care dollar by seeing that the patient is placed in the proper level of care. The team is headed by a physician who is assisted by appropriate professional staff such as registered nurses, social workers, registered physical therapists, pharmacists, and dietitians. The team is charged with the responsibility of determining the adequacy of the facility in meeting the needs of the patients and of determining whether the present level of care meets the patients' needs or other levels, higher or lower, would be more appropriate.[12]

Medical director in the facility

Whenever it is economically feasible, a nursing home should seriously consider employing a medical director. Ideally, he has a full-time position, but usually a part-time post is all that can be afforded. Some of the tasks that can be assigned this physician are as follows:

1. Meeting regularly with the medical advisory committee to the home.
2. Acting as a consultant to the administrator and his staff for advice on medical policy between meetings of the advisory committee.
3. Acting as a liaison between the home and the patient's physician when necessary.
4. Reviewing all applications to the home to determine if the home is able to accept the patient.
5. Acting in emergency situations when the patient's attending physician cannot be reached. This should be spelled out in the patient's agreement, and it should be made known to the attending physician that this is the policy of the home.
6. Accepting patients under his care if the family is not able to find anyone to act as the patient's personal physician.
7. Advising administrator of specific patient care problems needing attention.
8. Performing preemployment and annual physical examinations on all employees.

To be successful in many of these tasks, the medical director must have the respect of the local medical community and be interested in the care of the older person.

The medical director can be of great value to the administrator through his consultative services. He can relieve the administrator of many problems that otherwise might tend to go unsolved.

The medical director in a retirement residence with a health center can also provide invaluable assistance to the administrator and the nurses in the health office. Reviewing medical histories and physical examinations of applicants should be the responsibility of the medical director. He can advise the administrator or the persons responsible for resident admissions of the suitability of applicants, according to whether the applicant meets the health qualifications of the home and whether there is an indication of the need for institutional type of care in the near future.

The health care policies and procedures of the residence's health office should be designed with the assistance of a physician. The medical director, of course, should give this assistance. Likewise, he should assist the administrator through consultation on medical-administrative matters and thus assist him and the nurses in the implementation and administration of the health care policies.

One of the most difficult decisions an administrator of a residential center has to make is exactly when a resident is no longer physically or mentally able to remain at the residence. The medical director is the logical person to make this decision, since he knows the capabilities of the center and the problems of the resident. This is never an easy task for anyone. If the administrator has a medical opinion, his job of telling the resident of the decision will be easier.

Relationship between the home and the resident's physician

The administrator is on the horns of a dilemma in his relationship with the physicians caring for the residents in his home: he must keep their goodwill so that they will be inclined to recommend his home, and yet he must be insistant that they visit their patients and keep up with their medical records as called for by icensing regulations of the home.

The administrator must rely heavily on physicians' recommendations of his home to prospective patients. Naturally, having an excellent patient care program with efficient staff will be a major factor in gaining the respect of physicians. The physician as well as the patient and his relatives want to be assured that the patient will receive the care and treatments ordered. The physician soon knows whether or not the home is sincere in its efforts to provide good care. The first step, then, in gaining the goodwill of the physician is to provide excellent care for his patient.

A second way to enhance the physician's outlook toward the home is to make his visits to the home as efficient as possible. The nurse should have the patient's chart and necessary blank forms right at hand for him. She should assist him in the examination of the patient and show a helpful attitude. She should make sure that supplies and equipment he may need during his visit are nearby so that he is not delayed by a search for an item. She should anticipate his visit and have notes on the patient's general condition and complaints. She should be able to give a thumbnail sketch of the patient's course since his last visit.

When calling the physician at his office about a medical problem of one of his patients, the nurse should keep in mind that efficiency and accuracy of her account to him is necessary. She should organize her thoughts before calling him. She should have the patient's chart with her to record the physician's orders or to give him information he requests from the records.

Time is important to the physician. Although the nurse must be sure to give him all necessary information, she should avoid idle conversation and be professional in her discussion. This is true for either physician's visits or telephone calls.

Keeping the physician informed of events of interest to him at the home is another good method. The administrator can do this by writing a brief monthly newsletter, *individually typed*, not mimeographed, to each physician. This may mean that the administrator of a large home must write 40, 50, or more letters a month. This indeed sounds like a formidable, costly task; however, if the task is spread out through the month, the administrator's secretary has to type only two or three letters a day. The letter should be informative and friendly. It should highlight, briefly, the major activities planned for the month; list new equipment purchased; and introduce new personnel or promotions. The letter should include inserts, which can be mimeographed, such as the monthly menu. The letter should always close with friendly thanks for the care given the patients and the cooperation extended to the home.

On the other side of the coin is the administrator's responsibility for ensuring that the physician visits the patients under his supervision as required by state and federal regulations and the home's individual medical care policies. Sometimes the home's personnel are forced to make many telephone calls in attempting to get a few of the physicians to the home for their specified visits. Occasionally the administrator may have to be firm and insist that a physician come. This is the difficult side of maintaining goodwill. If the home, however, has developed a good relationship with a physician, the administrator's task will be easier and the physician, hopefully, will be understanding. The medical director also can be of great assistance in this situation. If the medical director is a respected member of the medical community, he can exert gentle and tactful pressure on the physician to gain his cooperation.

MEDICAL RECORDS

This section is devoted to the discussion of medical records for institutional facilities. Medical records for retirement residences are discussed elsewhere.

Reasons for medical records

With the advent of Medicare and Medicaid, nursing home operators have become well aware of the need to keep good medical records for their patients. Federal and state requirements are quite specific about the type of records required for documentation of care given the patients. Moreover, with today's public well aware of the legal responsibilities of the nursing home operator, it is very important that the home keep *complete* and *thorough* medical records as proof of the quality of care provided the patients.

There are four major reasons for a nursing home to keep these medical records besides the federal and state requirements. They are as follows:

1. The record can provide the patient's physician with documentation of the patient's care and progress. By looking at the record, the physician can recall his previous decisions for course of treatment and medication orders. He can see from the nursing notes and reports from consultants, how the patient is responding to the regimen he has ordered. It offers the physician an opportunity to record, in writing, his orders for future care of the patient, thereby making a permanent record of his professional care.

2. From the physician's orders and the comments of the various consultants, the nursing personnel can see what is to be done for the patient. They can use these comments and orders for the formulation of the patient care plan. The patient's record also documents changes in the patient's condition or the physician's orders, and it is the major tool for the nurse in giving her report to the nurses on the following shift.

3. The record is of great value to the home as a documentation of the care rendered the patient. Third-party agencies responsible for payment of the patient's bill can have access to the record (with written permission of the patient) to verify billings for service and to assure the agency that the care given is proper and adequate for the patient. The patient's record is one of the major reference items used in utilization review and medical review of procedures. The record likewise can be invaluable as a documentation of adequate care in the case of legal questions.

4. The medical record can be used as an impersonal document for research purposes. This is done when there is a need to seek information on certain disease entities for medical research. Also, the record can be used to assist health planning agencies and other responsible medical or paramedical groups in planning for areawide health care needs.[13]

Confidentiality of medical records

The nursing home administrator must ensure that the individual patient's records are kept confidential to protect the patient. Medical records are, in general, considered confidential communications between a patient and his physician. This concept is ancient, stemming from the oath of Hippocrates, which the physician proclaims when beginning his practice. Part of the oath states: "Whatever, in connection with my professional practice or not in connection with it, I see or hear, in the life of men, which ought not to be spoken of abroad, I will not divulge, as reckoning that all such should be kept secret."

This respect for the privacy of the patient should extend to the home and its staff. The nursing personnel and other concerned parties connected with the care of the patient may have access to the record. If they did not have such access, their care of the patient would not be complete. However, those who are privileged to use, inspect, or write in the record are, along with the physician, required by both tradition and legal precedent to respect the confidentiality of the patient's record.[14]

The administrator must clearly establish the aspect of confidentiality in the written policies of the home. All personnel having access to patients' record must be well aware of their professional and legal responsibility to keep their lips sealed concerning the records and the knowledge they gain from their relationships with patients.

Obviously, a patient and his condition may be discussed openly among the home personnel and the consultants. A conversation must be geared toward planning assistance for the patient. When a discussion develops into gossip or when it takes place outside the environment of the home, it ceases to be in the interest of the patient and becomes a violation of the patient's rights.

Laws governing confidential communications or privileged communications vary from state to state. The administrator should obtain legal advice concerning specific details of the concept of confidentiality of the particular state in which his home is located.

Ownership of medical records

The medical record is not the property of the patient or the physician but belongs to the nursing home, which acts as custodian of the material.[14] It is interesting, however, that, although the record itself—the physical document—is the property of the home, the contents of the document belong to the patient or, if the patient is incompetent, to his legal representative.[15]

Inspection of patients' records

Although it may be contrary to the best interests of the individual patient, certain states have laws permitting the patient to inspect his own medical record. It is the usual custom in many states, however, to refuse to allow the patient to inspect the record unless written permission is obtained from his physician.[13]

Nursing home personnel having a professional interest in the care of the patient have the right and the obligation to inspect his medical chart.

There are others who may see the patient's record also. A medical record may be subpoenaed by a court. In this case, the home administrator is served a subpoena duces tecum that spells out, in detail, the records desired and commands that they be brought to the court on a specific day. He must honor this demand. If the administrator receives such a subpoena, he should consult his attorney for assistance.

The patient himself may give written authorization to other parties, such as his legal representative or an insurance company, to inspect his record. Insurance companies frequently wish to document care rendered and will obtain such permission. Although the home does not have to honor a request to inspect a record, it may do so if it is expected that such inspection will not be potentially damaging to the home or the patient's physician. If the home does not cooperate and receives a subpoena subsequently, it then may have to produce the patient's record.[13]

Essential parts of medical records

The standards for nursing homes spelled out by the Joint Commission on Accreditation of Hospitals call for the following essential parts in medical records:
1. Identification section. This is commonly known as the face sheet of the record. It contains sufficient data to identify the patient, his physician, his relatives or responsible agents, and the admitting diagnosis. Items that should be included are the patient's home address, admission date, date of birth, place of birth, mother's name and father's name, sex, and marital status. State requirements should be consulted before this form is designed.

2. Physician's orders, notations, and progress notes. These notes give the admission history and results of physical examination, including an admitting diagnosis and an evaluation and orders by the admitting physician concerning treatment, restorative nursing goals, and rehabilitation potential. These notes should include subsequent orders from the admitting physician concerning the further care and treatment of the patient.

    This portion of the record may be broken down into physician's order sheets, medication orders, dietary orders, rehabilitation orders, and other similar forms. All such forms must be signed by the admitting physician when he issues the specific order.

3. Nursing notes, medication records, and treatment records. These are records of nursing procedures, giving of ordered treatments, administration of medications, and observations of patient reactions to these.

4. Laboratory, x-ray, and consultation reports. As reports are received, they should be made a part of the record. The home medical policies should specify that the charge nurse should notify the patient's physician of all results of test as a double check to be sure that the physician is aware of the results and to obtain any orders he may wish to give as the result of the test or examination.

    Reports of the various consultative personnel, such as dietitian, social worker, physical therapist, podiatrist, and dentist, should also be made a part of the record.[16]

State requirements are usually more specific. They should be consulted and followed in the construction of the contents of the record.

Filing of medical records

Medical records must be maintained as long as the state requirements specify. It is my opinion, however, that they should never be destroyed. In changes of ownership of the home, legal advice should be sought about what should be done with the medical records, although they usually remain as property of the facility.

Records should be completed fully before they are filed finally. All physician's orders should be signed. Discharge summaries should be made and signed by the physician; a final diagnosis for the patient should be included.

Nursing notes should indicate the final disposition of the patient, that is, whether he was discharged to his home, was transferred to a hospital, or died. These should be dated and signed by the nurse writing the note.

All medical records of deceased, discharged, or transferred patients should be completed as promptly as possible. They should be filed in order to safeguard and preserve the contents from damage, theft, or deterioration, in a suitable location on the premises.

Medical records librarian

If the home does not employ a medical records librarian, the administrator should assign the responsibility of overseeing the filing and maintaining of the records to a specific person employed by the facility. This person should receive regular consultation from a person trained in the keeping of medical records. The designated person should review all records when a patient leaves, to make sure that they are complete before they are filed.

The role of the consultant is important. He should assist the nursing department in in-service training and should inspect current patient charts on each visit. He should advise the administrator if he discovers problems in the current records or finds that the record keeper is having difficulty in getting cooperation in the completing of records.

Often, the administrator is able to locate a consultant through the local hospital.

Usually one or two days' work a month is all that is necessary from the consultant unless the home is having difficulties.

AUXILIARY HEALTH NEEDS
Physical therapy

Most states now require licensing by examination before a person can practice the science of physical therapy. In order to take the exam, an applicant usually must have a bachelor of science degree in physical therapy from a school or university accredited to offer training in this specialty. Prior to taking the exam for professional registration, a person must also have a clinical internship under supervision for about four months.[17] Usually a physical therapist associates himself with a hospital department of physical therapy. Sometimes, large nursing home facilities are able to employ a physical therapist on a full-time basis. If a skilled nursing home offers physical therapy, it must be provided by or supervised by a registered physical therapist. This person can be a part-time employee.

A nursing home administrator can usually obtain help from a physical therapist by contacting a local hospital for assistance. A therapist may practice independently, however; he is not bound to work only through a hospital.

In obtaining the services of the physical therapist, the home administrator should exercise the same degree of caution he would in hiring a physician or a registered nurse. He must take steps to verify the background, registration, past work history, and other qualifications of the applicant.

There are at least two accepted methods of reimbursement of the therapist. If the therapist is a salaried employee, the nursing home bills the patient directly. If the therapist works without compensation from the home, he bills the patient himself. The method varies according to accepted practice in local areas.

The physical therapist works from specific written orders of the patient's physician. He may not practice medical diagnosis or prescribe drugs for the patient. He must follow the instructions of the physician whether they are general or specific.[14]

In carrying out the orders of the patient's physician, the physical therapist attempts to restore function to limbs, muscle groups, joints, or other specific parts of the body to the highest degree possible. It is the prerogative of the therapist, on receiving the physician's orders, to develop a therapy program for the patient. He may use special equipment, or he may apply or assist the patient with active or passive exercises, including range-of-motion exercises, or he may instruct the patient in self-applied exercise regimens. The program may include gait training, which is often an important step in helping the patient to regain his ability to walk independently or with the mechanical assistance of canes, crutches, or walkers. He may train the patient in the use of prosthetic devices and braces.

The equipment and size of area for the physical therapy department vary according to the needs of the home. The physical therapist and the medical advisory physician should assist the administrator in selecting the area and equipment. Departments range from elaborate facilities complete with whirlpool baths, full-immersion tanks, ultrasonic machine, and paraffin baths, to very simple facilities with equipment limited primarily to range-of-motion exercise apparatus and parallel bars for walking. The type of facility depends on the goals of the owner and the level of care of the home.

The physical therapist should keep records of the individual treatment and progress of the patients. He should make notations in the patient's medical chart also so that the nursing personnel can amplify his program in their work with the patient.

Homes that do not have a physical therapy department should make arrangements with a local facility for outpatient physical therapy when it is requested by a patient's physician.

X-ray services

It is not usual for a nursing home to have an x-ray department. Usually the patient is transported to a facility providing this service, such as a hospital. If portable x-ray equipment is brought into the facility, it can be operated only by a resistered x-ray technician. Bringing the equipment to the patient is often preferred but may be more costly to the patient or his family. Portable equipment is not sufficient for some tests, so that in many cases the patient needs to be transported to a facility. If films are made in the home, the technician should take the films for interpretation to a radiologist, a physician specializing in radiology.

Policies should be established and put in writing about how the home's staff should handle a physician's request for x-ray films. The report of the x-ray findings should be sent to the patient's physician, and the home should request copies for the patient's record.

The extended care facility may be equipped with diagnostic radiological equipment. If the facility provides this service, it should make sure that all local, county, and state requirements are met. The department must be supervised by a radiologist at least on a part-time basis. Only a radiologist or an x-ray technician should be authorized to use the equipment. Adequate space must be allocated for this department. Safety must be assured: specific construction standards for x-ray rooms must be followed so that x-rays generated by the equipment cannot penetrate the walls of the room and expose personnel to the hazard. Sufficient storage space for films must be maintained. The films, like the patient's records, are the property of the home.

If the extended care facility or nursing home is affiliated with a hospital, it is logical for the hospital to provide radiological service.

Laboratory services

Measures must be taken to provide laboratory services for patients in the home. It is usually less difficult to provide these services than x-ray services, since a technologist can come to the home, obtain a specimen, and return with it to the laboratory for testing. Some skilled nursing homes and extended care facilities may find it convenient to have some laboratory equipment on hand, especially if the home has a house physician or medical director in regular attendance. If a home does have a laboratory, it must meet the standards established by local or state authorities. Whatever methods are followed, policy must be established and put in writing so that the home staff knows what is expected.

Simple tests that can ordinarily be done in the patient's own home can be done by the nursing staff. Tests of the urine may be done by the nursing staff, using the convenient dipstick method. These tests are relatively simple and are easy to read and interpret. The pH of the patient's urine and the presence of protein, glucose, acetone, and blood in the urine can be tested with this method. All these tests give indications about the patient's health status.

Examples of laboratory equipment that might be found in a skilled nursing home or extended care facility are as follows: (1) a Fibrometer or a water bath for measuring plasma coagulation of patients receiving anticoagulant therapy, (2) a small centrifuge for separating the plasma from the cells for this same determination, (3) a supply of test tubes and a hot plate for blood urea nitrogen determinations, and (4) a small spectrophotometer for reading all these test procedures.

All these test procedures can be done by nursing personnel with adequate training by a medical technologist if state laws allow this practice. These tests should be done only on order of the patient's personal physician.

If the facility deems it necessary, a more elaborate laboratory may be set up, provided state laws permit. The facility can employ a medical technologist on a part-time or on-call basis to perform these tests. This may be necessary in a rural area where hospital or commercial laboratory services are not conveniently at hand.

Setting up of laboratory facilities may be a costly procedure for the home. The elaborate equipment may be used infrequently. These factors should be weighed against the better care for the patients that may result.

Dental services

The nursing home should obtain the services of an advisory or consulting dentist to assist in setting up a sound oral hygiene program for the patients and in conducting in-service training programs for the staff. Each patient should name a local dentist for his oral care. However, the home's consulting dentist should agree to be available to meet emergency dental service if the patient's own dentist is not available.

The nursing care policies and procedures should call for the nursing staff to supervise and assist the patients in cleaning their teeth and dentures on a daily basis. Proper oral hygiene is one of the hallmarks of a good nursing home. Patients frequently need assistance in this procedure. They can usually do the oral care themselves, but reminders are necessary.

The consulting dentist should be asked to write dental care policies for the home. These policies should specify the frequency of an oral survey by the patient's dentist. A survey is usually done annually, but the patient's own dentist may specify that it be done more frequently.

The patient's dentist should have the name and telephone number of the patient's personal physician so that he can consult him, if necessary, before giving care to the patient.

When the patient is taken to the dentist's office, a physician's order sheet should be sent along so that the dentist can make notations and give written orders for follow-up care.

Miscellaneous needs

The nursing home administrator needs to know where to obtain the services of ancillary medical personnel that may be needed for the care of the patient. These services usually must be ordered by the patient's physician. Among the specialists needed are speech therapists, podiatrists (frequently necessary with geriatric patients), audiologists, and optometrists. A registry should be compiled of the specialists who are known to be qualified by education and training and who hold proper state registrations or licenses to practice their profession.

Since the services of a podiatrist are often needed, the home should attempt to obtain a qualified practitioner to visit the home regularly to care for the patients' feet.

Written medical care policies should govern the activities of all these allied specialists. These policies must be developed in consultation with the home's advisory physician.

NOTES

1. The golden years—a tarnished myth. The Project FIND Report, Jack Ossofsky, project director, Jan. 1970, the National Council on the Aging, Inc., 305 Park Avenue South, New York, N. Y. 10010.

2. Kleh, Jack: A classification for the aged and other patients with chronic disease or disability, Journal of the American Geriatrics Society 11(7):638-641, 1963.

3. Medicaid; compilation of federal requirements for skilled nursing home facilities, publication no. (SRS) 72-24351, U. S. Department of Health, Education, and Welfare, Social and Rehabilitation Service, Medical Services Administration.

4. Little, Dolores E., and Carnevali, Doris L.: Nursing care planning, Philadelphia, 1969, J. B. Lippincott Co.

5. Adapted from Training manual for a rehabilitation program in a nursing home and an extended care facility, Springfield, Ill., Oct. 1967, Rehabilitation Education Service, Illinois Department of Public Health, Bureau of Health Facilities, Rehabilitation Section.

6. Mahoney, Florence I., et al.: Up and around, a booklet to aid the stroke patient in activities of daily living, Public Health publication no. 1120, Washington, D. C., U. S. Government Printing Office.

7. Moses, Dorothy V., Grant, Marie D., Brown, Myrtle I., Knowles, Lois N., and Lane, Harriet C.: Standards for geriatric nursing practice, revised 1972, American Nurses' Association, Inc., Kansas City, Mo.

8. Pharmaceutical services in the nursing home, ed. 2, Washington, D. C., 1966, American Nursing Home Association, American Pharmaceutical Association, and American Society of Hospital Pharmacists.

9. Conditions of participation for extended care facilities, U. S. Department of Health, Education, and Welfare, Washington, D. C., 1966, U. S. Government Printing Office.

10. Utilization review, a handbook for the medical staff, 1968, American Medical Association, Department of Community Health, 535 N. Dearborn St., Chicago, Ill. 60610.

11. The extended care facility, a handbook for the medical society, Chicago, 1967, American Medical Association, Department of Hospitals and Medical Facilities.

12. Federal Register, vol. 35, no. 96, May 16, 1970, Office of the Federal Register, National Archives and Records Service, General Services Administration, Washington, D. C., 20408.

13. Huffman, Edna K.: Medical records in nursing homes, Berwyn, Ill., 1961, Physicians' Record Co.

14. Hayt, Emanuel, et al.: Law of hospital, physician and patient, ed. 2, New York, 1961, Hospital Textbooks Co.

15. Buttaro, Peter J.: Legal manual for nursing homes, Aberdeen, S. D., 1972, Western Printing Co., Publishers.

16. Standards for accreditation of extended care facilities, nursing care facilities and resident care facilities, Joint Commission on Accreditation of Hospitals, 645 N. Michigan Ave., Chicago, Ill. 60611.

17. Job descriptions and organizational analysis for hospitals and related health services, U. S. Department of Labor, Washington, D. C., 1971, U. S. Government Printing Office.

Chapter six

SOCIAL SERVICES

THE NEED TO BE CONCERNED

The third major area of the nursing home and retirement residence that must be explored is the social component of care. In many instances, this is the area that should be given the greatest emphasis.

A person coming to a retirement residence may be in a state of shock, so to speak, from the events that occurred prior to his coming.

First, he may come reluctantly, through the urging of his children or other family members who have made him realize that his former life style is no longer safe for him. He may still find independent living in a retirement residence—he may still! direct his personal activities, make his own decisions, and come and go as he pleases. However, it is not the same. He may have memories of his former home, its environment, the friends in the neighborhood, and its privacy. He may recall his productive years and his former companions at work or in social and fraternal groups and at his church or synagogue. These may now seem to be only memories, and all these ties may be lost. He may remember friendships now broken by distance or by death.

Second, he may have had some traumatic times in breaking up his house or apartment. Even though he may now have a beautiful apartment in handsome, possibly luxurious, surroundings, he may have had to divest himself of much of his furniture, bric-a-brac, and items perhaps stored away in an attic. Parting with these items, even those long forgotten and only recently rediscovered in a trunk in the corner of the basement, may have been painful.

Third, often a move to a retirement home is precipitated by the recent death of a husband or wife. Thus he may have a haunting feeling of loss and loneliness. More often than not, many tearful hours are spent long afterward over the bereavement. Some people never adjust fully to this parting.

Another problem the aged person may have is fear from the sudden realization that he is no longer young. He may think that in coming to the retirement residence he has taken the first step that can lead only to further loss of independence, physical dependency, illness, and eventual death. Seeing the other residents may only make this more of a fear, for some of the residents may be older and more dependent, perhaps even on the borderline of need for nursing home care.

Another problem is the adjustment he must make to community living. Some are never able to adjust and leave the community after only a few months. Community living is not for everyone. Even though the person has his own private apartment, his life style now may have to be changed somewhat in order to conform to dining hours, dress restrictions, and other community rules. His life is no longer completely his own. He must mix with the other residents who have come from all walks of life with their own particular habits, likes, and dislikes. He may perhaps have to eat in a community dining facility with food that, although nutritious, is not like home cooking. His life becomes more public. Residents and staff see him come and go, see his visitors, and notice his faults. He is now subject to institutional rules and regulations.

All these factors can combine to make adjustment to community retirement living difficult. The administrator must be capable of understanding this and empathizing with the residents. He must convey this sympathetic and understanding attitude to his staff so that they, too, respond appropriately to the needs of the residents. Not all residents have these problems of adjustment to their new way of life, but many do. The administrator and his staff must anticipate this and be ready to respond to fill unmet needs or to listen sympathetically.

The administrator must be able to counsel residents who ask for assistance and to refer residents to individuals who can help them to adjust to their new environment. For example, the administrator may need to help the resident find a suitable bank, someone to help him with his income taxes, or an attorney who can give him legal assistance. The administrator may need to help the resident find a church of his choice or help him become established in a local senior citizens' group.

The administrator of a retirement complex must be attuned to the needs of his residents at all times. He must never be too busy to talk to one of them. His door should be open and he should not place barriers such as secretaries or receptionists between himself and his residents. Whenever possible, he should give the needed time to a resident's problem at hand, trying to solve it or to get the resident help in solving it. His job can never last merely eight hours a day, five days a week. He must be available when there is a need, even if it means missing supper with his family or getting out of bed in the middle of the night to go to the hospital to be with a resident during a medical emergency. Almost everyone working in responsible positions with aged people has these qualities or soon leaves the field.

The administrator of the retirement home, realizing all the negative factors facing his residents, must establish a program of activities to keep the home environment busy and happy. He must utilize the skills of several different professionals to bring about this needed busy and happy environment.

The nursing home patient faces similar negative factors, although they may very well be more acute since he may realize that he is closer to his final days. The patient may have severe physical and emotional problems with increasing, insidious, chronic, and multiple afflictions. More, if not all, independence may be lost. He may no longer be able to walk, see, hear, or talk with clarity. He may see about him people who are confused and physically deteriorated. He may sense that death is near.

The nursing home patient may have a clear mind and may be there only because he is no longer able to lead an independent life physically. He may abhor his new environment. He may hear the cries of the confused. He may lie awake at night in fear of his personal safety and of his fate. He may not be able to understand why he has been left with so little after a long lifetime of happiness.

His life is vastly different now. He is trapped, no longer able to leave the unpleasant situations, get in his car, and drive away from his cares. He may have feelings of doom. His hands may be twisted with arthritis, or his legs may no longer be able to support his body shrinking and wrinkled. He may long for the old days and recall frequently now the events of his former life. He may sit for hours wondering why this has happened to him and may find no answer.

Thus the administrator of the nursing home has a difficult task, perhaps one that is never solved. He must train his staff to help and to serve, to be sympathetic, to love, to be gentle, to be understanding, not to demand, not to chastise patients who can no longer hold their urine, to take the time to listen, and to show respect.

Throughout this entire book, I have used the term *resident* to indicate someone in an independent living environment and the term *patient* to denote someone who lives in an institutional setting. There is a trend today to use the word *resident* for a person in any long-term care setting. This was one of the conclusions of participants in a recent conference on activity programming for the long-term care field.[2] There is merit to this idea. The word *patient* denotes sickness, whereas the word *resident* conveys the concept of a home environment.

ATTITUDES AND APPROACHES OF STAFF TOWARD SOCIAL COMPONENT OF CARE

How does the staff member of a nursing home perceive the patient and his role in the care of the patient? Is his job merely a way to spend eight hours a day to earn a living, or is he excited about the challenges he faces each day in working with the patients. Does he feel that he is contributing to team effort to enhance the life and dignity of the patients? In his paper "Getting the Staff to Pull Together (in the same direction)," Cohen urges administrators to involve the staff in the goals of the facility. He suggests that the administrator allow the staff to be deeply involved in preparing patient care plans by assisting the nurse through staff group meetings in which the leaders are receptive to staff knowledge of patient needs. He offers other suggestions about staff participation in goal setting and involvement of all staff members, not just the activity director, in patient activity programs. If staff members are allowed to become involved in patient care goal setting, they become committed to the success of the goals. The goals are no longer those of the director of nursing, the activity director, or the administrator but become those of the patient care team, which should include all who come in contact with the patient. This means that these goals are not developed by nursing personnel alone. Through group staff meetings, the maids, the workers who deliver food trays, the janitors, the maintenance men, the office staff—all personnel—become committed because they have a part in the development of the goals.[1]

This technique requires a skillful, patient administrator. It requires courage, cooperation, and a willing attitude on the part of the department heads and supervisors. In trying out this technique, using intelligent guidance, the administrator may be surprised at how successful a plan becomes. The morale of both staff and patients is enhanced. The staff members feel accepted and necessary. They are there to do more than just wash a floor or carry a tray; they are there to care for patients. The patients quickly see the new understanding the maid shows when she is called to clean up after an accident. Before staff teamwork is used, the maid may have responded with a gloomy attitude toward this distasteful job, but after she understands the team goals of the home, she may do the job cheerfully, giving an encouraging remark to the patient.

An advantage in the long-term care facility that is not found in the general hospital is *time*. Patients (residents, if you prefer) stay in long-term care facilities on the average of about three years. Some are there for many years. This can be used to advantage in developing the social component of care to its highest degree. There is no rush, no great effort to move on to the next new case. New patients arrive infrequently. There is time for the staff to learn about the individual's likes and preferences, fears, worries, and other social and emotional idiosyncrasies and how to deal with them in the best interests of the patient.

As staff-patient relationships are enhanced, the patients tend to look on the staff as part of their family, especially if they are alone. I have often been told that residents in retirement homes miss the hustle and bustle of the staff during the weekend, when the staff is at a minimum. The same is true during the weekend periods in a nursing home. The maids, the office staff, the maintenance men, and the administrator are off duty. Thus it is very necessary to carry out the social component of care 24 hours a day, seven days a week. All the staff members must practice these techniques at all times. The staff-family concept cannot end at 4:30 on Friday afternoon to begin again at 8:00 on Monday morning. It must be consistently and continually applied by all. Each staff person must be motivated to this end in order to provide an ongoing program of love, devotion, and respect for the individual.

PROFESSIONALS AND OTHERS DEVOTED TO SOCIAL, EMOTIONAL, AND RELIGIOUS COMPONENTS OF CARE

Fortunately, to aid the administrator and his staff, there are several groups of professionals devoted to the social, emotional, and religious components of care. I will discuss these briefly and show how they fit into the care plan of the patient and the resident and how they can fulfill many of their needs.

Social worker

Although state requirements vary, in general the minimal educational requirements of a social worker is a master's degree from an approved school of social work. In order to be considered fully qualified, he must have at least two additional years of continual practice under close supervision.

One of the major functions of the social worker is to help patients or residents and their families to adjust as well as they can to difficulties encountered in failing illness and disablement, such as personal, environmental, financial, or emotional difficulties or a combination of them. It is the social worker's role to help remove these real or imagined problems as they occur.

Social worker's duties in facilities for aged people. In order for the social worker to be successful in his work, he must obtain essential background information about the patient, his family relationship, his attitudes, and his goals or his loss of motivation. He must consider this information when approaching a particular social problem needing solution. To obtain this background information, the social worker relies heavily on interviews with the patient and his family, friends, or advisers. He begins this learning process by obtaining information about the patient's or resident's previous life style, including his usual home environment prior to his coming to the facility, his past work history, his hobbies and extracurricular interests, his family relationships, his relationships with personal friends, his marital status, and from his physician or family, his health history.

Obviously, the social worker can contribute greatly to the formulation and changing of the patient care plan. If he is available to the home on a regular basis, he should be included in the patient care planning conferences. His knowledge of the particular needs of the patients can be a great contribution to the staff.

In the extended care facility, there is great need for a professional social worker. The patient turnover rate is much higher in the extended care facility; patient stays are much shorter compared with those in a nursing home. The need for adequate discharge planning is a real factor and one that a social worker is well equipped to handle. A patient leaving an extended care facility usually either returns to his home or is transferred to a nursing home for long-term care. If he returns home, the social worker can arrange further care that may be necessary, such as home health services, visiting nurse services, homemaker services, and meals-on-wheels services. He is armed with the knowledge of the potential community services available to the patient as he returns to his home environment. If discharge to a nursing home is planned, the social worker can help to lead the patient and his family to an appropriate facility.

When a patient or resident has need of special counseling or assistance in financial or legal matters, the social worker can guide him to someone who can help him.

In some homes the intake of all new residents or patients is handled by the social worker. He screens each person for the administrator to make sure that the home is a suitable environment for the patient's specific needs and that the patient or resident meets the requisites and restrictions placed on the home by its board or by licensing authorities.

Homes may engage a social worker as an occasional consultant, a part-time employee, or a full-time employee. This depends entirely on the philosophy and goals of the home and the state and federal regulations. Although a full-time social worker is a costly addition to the budget of any home, his services are valuable time-savers for the administrator and the director of nursing, who usually have to perform these tasks without such a staff person.

The social worker should make regular entries on patient or resident records as needs arise. He should have access to the medical records of individual patients. He should have the authority to contact patients' relatives, friends, and physicians as social needs arise.

Social history form—tool of the social worker. The social history form is a valuable information-collecting device that should be a part of the patient's medical chart. This form should be prepared by a staff member in an interview with the patient or the family of the patient prior to the admission whenever possible. The form should be designed to give the home a better understanding of the patient as an individual person. It should include background social data on the patient; these data are important factors in designing the initial patient care plan. Specifically, the form should include information about the patient's cultural, ethnic, and educational background; his previous occupation; how he has reacted to his current situation; his marital status; recent losses of loved ones; and his relationships with existing family members. A major part of the form should be devoted to notations of the patient's current attitude toward his illness or disability and how he feels about coming to the home. His goals and expectations or doubts and fears should be noted.

In obtaining this information, the social worker, if on the staff, or someone else designated by the administrator, should interview the patient if possible. If this is not possible, then the staff person should talk with the patient's family. If there is no family, others can be helpful, such as close friends, agency caseworkers, the patient's clergyman, and his physician.

In-service training from the social worker. The social worker can be a very valuable member of the faculty of the home's in-service training program. His role should be to interpret for the nursing staff the social and psychological needs of older people in general and of the home's patients specifically. He can make the in-service programs meaningful by using case histories of prior patients or by discussing some of the nonconfidential problems of one or more of the present patients.

The social worker should be able to interpret some of the patients' overt actions so that the staff can better understand and subsequently better know how to respond to these actions.

If the home does not have a full-time social worker, the in-service program should be one of the duties of the consulting social worker.

Preparing the patient or resident for admission. Another function of the social worker should be to assist the patient in preadmission planning. If the home has a waiting list, patient admissions can be preplanned in a somewhat orderly fashion. The social history form can be completed in this waiting period. The social worker has an excellent opportunity sometimes to see the applicant in his own home setting. Usually, the applicant is more relaxed in these familiar surroundings. The social worker can also learn much about the person just by seeing his current environment.

In this preadmission programming, the worker can learn of problems that need immediate attention pending the transfer or admission to the home. He can solve some of them in the interim by engaging the assistance of community home health agencies, the visiting nurse association, and similar organizations. (This outreach concept is discussed further in Chapter 7.)

There may be problems that the social worker himself can solve. Giving the applicant assistance in the completion of the preadmission forms and medical reports can be quite helpful. The worker may spend time in discussing the contract with the home and financial arrangements necessary and may thus answer many unrealized questions and alleviate doubts and hesitancy on the part of the applicant. He can help the applicant prepare for community living by discussing the home's rules and regulations, daily routines, meal arrangements, and provisions for health care that can be expected if the facility is a retirement residence.

He can assist the applicant with his plans for moving and disposing of his furniture and excess personal belongings. This is often one of the major problems faced by a person entering a retirement residence. An interested person (interested professionally—not motivated by personal gain) who can give advice and help with certain arrangements can be very helpful.

Postadmission counseling. The social worker, especially in a retirement residence, can provide postadmission counseling to the new resident. The main purpose of this is to help the resident overcome the difficulties of adjusting to his new environment. During the first several months, the resident may have many experiences that are small, seemingly trivial, but that are traumatic for him and steadily pile up small mountains of doubt and dissatisfaction about the new habitation and way of life. Some of this can be avoided with wise preadmission guidance. However, the new resident may feel lost for a while until he is able to establish a base camp at each level of his new mountain. The social worker can ensure that some of the other residents help the new member to adjust and can tactfully steer him away from the unfriendly cliques that are encountered in some group living arrangements, advising him of potential dangers.

The new resident may be quite dependent on his newfound friend the social worker during his first few weeks at the home. The social worker should slowly disengage himself as he sees the person building new relationships with the other residents.

During the early period, the social worker can assist the new resident in arranging the necessary business ties for banking, legal assistance, shopping, and the like.

Preplanning funeral arrangements. Although the subject may never come up, a resident or patient may want assistance in making prearrangements for his funeral and cemetery location. The administrator should assist aged people, at their request, in making these plans with funeral directors. If there is a social worker on the staff, this can be one of the jobs he can perform with understanding. He may suggest to the resident or patient that he obtain religious counseling about the subject, if indicated.

Making the trip alone to the funeral director's office to make these plans may be quite traumatic for a resident. Having a professional social worker by his side may give him confidence. The social worker can also make sure that the resident makes wise and practical arrangements within his means and that the transaction is completely ethical.

The student new to gerontology may be surprised at the cool, matter-of-fact, realistic way many older people handle these decisions for their personal destiny.

Whatever arrangements are made should be recorded and signed by the resident or patient and placed in his records. The resident should be encouraged to acquaint his relatives with his plans so that they respect his wishes, understanding that they were decisions made with clear thinking.

• • •

Many homes cannot afford a full- or part-time social worker and must rely on consultants. Whether or not the home has a social worker on its staff, the duties and functions described in this section must be performed. It is up to each home administrator to ensure that the needs of the patients or residents are met adequately by some staff person.

Activity director

Every nursing home, personal care home, extended care facility, and retirement residence should have an activity director as a full-time paid staff member. This person should be experienced and skilled in group work and have a thorough understanding of the capabilities and limitations of older people.

The activity director is a person designated by the administrator of the home to oversee the patient activity department. In many instances, this person is a former nurse's aide who was given the opportunity to have some advanced training in this field while working and who has demonstrated an extraordinary ability to work with older people. This person must have leadership ability and must be able to tactfully motivate the patients so that the program is successful.[5]

Toni Merrill has written an excellent book for use by the untrained worker entitled *Activities for the Aged and Infirm.* This book should be in the library of every activity director. It is designed to help the nurse's aide newly appointed as activity director quickly develop self-confidence in the new role.[5]

It is not uncommon for the home to designate someone from the nursing staff to serve in this capacity. However, it is essential that this person have no other duties. He cannot function as an activity director if he must work part of his day in direct patient care. He must be given time, space, materials, funds, and cooperation in order to be successful.

If there is an association of activity directors of nursing homes in the community, the home's director should join it. Since he has a common ground with the other directors, mutual learning can take place and sharing of ideas can develop.

Quite often state agencies sponsor training seminars for activity directors. The home should pay the costs involved to send the director to these programs.

Activity programming. The activity program is a major component of social care. In the past, some home administrators have not been cognizant of the necessity of this most important aspect of care. Some homes were merely warehouses for old people who were thought to be senile and undesirable and incapable of being emotionally and intellectually stimulated. Administrators were satisfied to see that these patients were kept clean, dry, and fairly presentable when visitors came. No thought was given to much care beyond this point. The administrator and staff were complacent when they saw that the patients were sitting in their chairs in the sun. After all, they may have thought, these people are confused and can no longer enjoy life. Let them be content to stare for hours at a time out the window or sit motionless close to a blaring, out-of-focus television set. If they want entertainment, it may have been reasoned, they can find it themselves. After all, they are retired now and do not want to be disturbed. They would rather sleep than be entertained or be given baskets to weave that no one would want when the project was finished.

Fortunately, this attitude no longer prevails in most homes. Today, the modern home administrator is well aware of the vital need of activity as a method of therapy. State and federal regulations require patient activity programs as part of the rehabilitation process. Workshops are frequently held locally and regionally by educational institutions or other agencies for activity directors in which ideas can be shared and further training in this concept of patient care can be received.

It is a recognized fact that patient activity programs can enrich a patient's otherwise lonely life and can forestall further mental and physical deterioration. Patients who are kept active during the day rest better at night. Good activity programs often improve the problem patient's morale and well-being so that he becomes less restless and demanding. By providing a paid activity therapy staff with a sound, continuing program, the administrator may find that less auxiliary nursing personnel are needed because there are fewer difficulties with these otherwise problem patients, who may have been problems because they were trying to act out their frustrations caused by inactivity.

In the nursing home setting, a physician's order should be sought for permission for the patient to engage in activity programs. Likewise, the family should give permission for activities that take the patient out of the home.

Good activity programs, intelligently administered, can teach patients new skills. They may again gain interest in life and their environment. Even the most senile patient may be helped by being involved in simple activities or group activities. Although it may seem meaningless to the untrained person, simply involving or including an apparently hopelessly confused person in an activity can stimulate him.

The activity director in a nursing home must be able to tactfully, gently, yet firmly persuade patients. Some patients may say that they do not want to be bothered. They may say that because they are embarrassed that they are no longer physically capable of performing many tasks. However, they may really blossom out and become involved if the right, positive approach is utilized. Most people respond once they realize that there are interesting things to be done.[3]

Although the activity director should be the motivator for the programs in the home, the whole staff should be committed to the patient activity program therapy. Programs of activity must be scheduled during the day and evening, including the weekend. It is obvious that no one person can do this alone. The whole staff must be involved and have an interest in keeping both scheduled formal programs and informal interaction continuing during the waking hours of the patients.

Through in-service programs, the activity director can teach the staff simple ways of helping patients to continue with activities when the formal programs are not scheduled. For example, patients can assemble together in a multipurpose room for early evening television watching followed by a bedtime snack. Also, they can play bingo on Saturday afternoon, with an aide calling the numbers. Activities that do not require elaborate materials and equipment are best for these times. The staff members should realize that this process can help to give them more time to concentrate their nursing and personal care on those patients who need it. While one aide keeps 15 to 20 patients involved, the rest of the staff can work with the remaining patients who are not able to participate.

The activity director may be able to find some patients who can be motivated to help in working with other patients. For example, a patient who enjoys playing cards may be able to motivate three or four other patients to play. Another patient may enjoy reading aloud to a group. Those patients who can be leaders may enhance their self-esteem through helping others.

Group exercises. Unless contraindicated by the patient's condition or physician's orders, simple exercises can be helpful and entertaining. These exercises can also help the patient to maintain physical function, muscle tone, and general body strength. Background music such as marches is helpful, but the leader should take care to keep the various exercises at a pace that can be easily maintained by most of the members of the group. The exercises should not be strenuous. They should be designed to assist the patients in maintaining motion of extremities and coordination of hands and fingers. These exercises should be done from a sitting position. The exercises may include raising arms to a position straight out from the body, spreading arms out to form a T, raising arms straight up over the head, and bringing arms back to original position. Similar simple extremity and trunk-twisting exercises can be done with moderation.

Deconfusion and motivation exercises. Deconfusion or memory retraining programs can be carried out with success by the activity director or the nursing staff. Small groups of six or less patients respond better than do larger groups. Individual attention is often necessary. Larger groups may hinder the leader in attaining the goals. A patient with an advanced case of chronic brain syndrome is not a good condidate for this retraining. A patient who demonstrates transitory periods of confusion and periods of clarity is best helped by these techniques.

Methods and techniques vary. One successful approach used at the Peoria State Hospital in Peoria, Illinois, involves 2 one-hour sessions a week for a total of 12 sessions. Each hourly meeting is devoted to the discussion of items of direct interest to each specific patient. The leader begins with very basic items such as the patient's name, his location, his age, the current date, names of staff members and other patients, names of relatives and friends, and previous residence. In order to reinforce previous sessions and help the patient advance, the approach is repetitious. As the patient's mind grows in clarity, the leader progresses in later sessions to more complicated items such as memory games and discussions about the geography or history of the region or the United States and about current events.

During this course, the leader also attempts to motivate the patient to reach higher levels and thus be able to enjoy his life more. He attempts to motivate the patient through discussion of personal hygiene, table manners, past hobbies, skills, and goals. Every attempt is made to communicate love and willingness or desire to help the patient progress. The patient should be motivated to improve his lot in life as much as he can personally.

Although as psychologists indicate, lasting motivation must come from within an individual, it is a known fact that every person usually needs a little push once in a while to get going again. Through this program, if it is well designed and led with ability, the patient may improve. Many may gain a new self-esteem if the techniques are successful, and they may take on a new outlook on their lives, desiring to improve even further. Motivation is a powerful force: the will to live. Many patients in whom it is rekindled fight to reach self-care levels, and some win this fight.

A major goal of the activity director in everything he does for the patient is to rekindle the desire to improve. Older persons can learn new skills if they have the desire. They can be motivated to help others. For example, they can get together in a group to make cancer dressings for an agency in the community. An objective of the activity director is to get the patient to stop brooding about himself and to get going again at the best pace he can within his capabilities. The idea is to enrich the patient's life through activities and to prevent his escaping from life by silent disengagement. As his life is enriched and his self-esteem and self-confidence return, the patient tends to forget the constant aches and pains from his infirmities. As he relearns to reach out to help himself, he progresses both mentally and physically. As he relearns to reach out to help others to the best of his ability, he forgets his own problems; (there is always someone less fortunate, in more pain, with less faculties, and more incapacitated than he is). As the patient regains his self-confidence and self-esteem and begins to reach out to help others, socialization with others occurs and companionships develop with other patients.[4]

The approach of an effective activity director is not to do tasks *for* the patient; it is to do them *with* the patient. All the other personnel in the home are there to do tasks for the patient. The concept of self-motivation and self-help is brought to fruition by getting the patient to want to participate. This cannot be a one- or two-man job: all the personnel of the home who normally do things *for* the patient must, in this dimension of care, do things *with* the patient. Everyone from the administrator on down must practice this for the social components of care to be successfully applied in a nursing home or retirement residence.[5]

Cost of the activity program. The administrator must see that adequate funds are available for the purchase of equipment and supplies for the activity department. Initially, caution should be exercised in purchasing elaborate and costly equipment. As the program takes shape and the patients' or residents' capabilities are learned, necessary equipment can be purchased. Money for supplies, though, must be available immediately.

Many useful items can be donated by the staff and patients' relatives. Many items that are normally discarded can be used to great advantage, such as bits of yarn, material, plastic bottles, cord, wire, and foam packaging scraps. The home's activity director should make a list of the things needed and post it for all to see. If the home is located in an industrial area, it usually can obtain scraps from manufacturing of goods on a donation basis, such as leather scraps, pieces of plastic upholstery, packaging materials, and certain shipping containers. The director should make sure that these items are safe for older people to use and that they do not have chemical contamination on or in them.

The activity director should be aware of costs. He should participate in the makeup of the annual budget for the department. He should be aware of the budget and thus be ready to work within its framework.

The cost, of course, is directly affected by the size of the home, the type of patient, the goals of the home, and unfortunately, the funds available. The latter may be limited; therefore, the activity director must be resourceful, utilizing donated items whenever possible.

Volunteer

Selection of the volunteer. Many homes are able to find people in the community who are willing to assist the activity director and other personnel as a volunteer. Since many hands make the home's total programs much more effective and functional, a volunteer program, if adequately directed, is a helpful adjunct to the home.

The volunteer in the home must be screened. To be a volunteer is a privilege, not a right. The home should investigate the volunteer's background and ask for an application with references. Furthermore, the volunteer should be told that he is invited to help the home on a probationary status for a while.[5] The volunteer should understand that, just as an employee is, he is subject to the rules of conduct set by the facility. It should be made known to the volunteer at the onset of his service that the home has the right to ask him to leave when the best interests of the home and the patients would be served.

The volunteer in the home can serve in many areas besides the activity department. Most of the jobs given to volunteers are designed to contribute further to the home's social component of care. With proper guidance, the volunteer can be of immense help in working toward the social care goals.

The volunteer's presence reflects a different kind of love for the patient. Although the paid staff can demonstrate love, kindness, affection, helpfulness, and understanding toward the patient, the patient consciously or subconsciously knows that this person is being paid to provide this care. The volunteer is not motivated by pay. Whatever his motivations may be, the patient thinks of him as being motivated by *caring* for him. The volunteer thus plays an essential role in the social component of care from that standpoint alone.

Volunteer director. In larger homes a director of volunteers may be needed. This director may be a paid staff member. However, usually the president and committee chairmen of an organized auxiliary oversee the volunteer department. The administrator can organize such a group, getting them to draft bylaws and be self-governing within the framework and rules of the home. The bylaws should be specific in mentioning these rules. The auxiliary through its bylaws can be self-regulating. Counseling or dismissal from the auxiliary can thus be done from within the auxiliary itself.

The bylaws should set up committees that have different functions in the home. Some of the committees can work outside the home in fund raising, membership solicitation, public relations in behalf of the home, and liaison with parent church or fraternal groups sponsoring the home.

The committees that work in the home can be organized to help the patients in activities; visit patients who are lonely or have no family; assist with specialty needs of the patients, such as personal shopping, letter writing, and calling relatives; assist at mealtime in feeding patients and provide assistance in the central dining room; and sew and mend patients' clothing and also repair the home's linens.

There are countless jobs that can be done by volunteers. Whatever the job is, if it is done well, it enhances the patient's life in the home.

Youthful volunteers are excellent. They can provide the patients with much joy simply by their effervescence. They can bring interesting stories to the residents of the outside world as seen through the eyes of the young. By simply talking about their school activities and their own personal goals in life, they can contribute much to the patients' day. Most older people enjoy the young; they feel particularly flattered when the young show that they care about them. Often church and service groups have young people who can be invited to serve. Sometimes local schools have social studies programs that involve field work in personal service. The administrator should investigate this.

Recognition of volunteer service to the home. The administrator should make sure that proper recognition is given to the home's volunteers for their service. One method is to have an annual awards and recognition dinner for the volunteers.

Ideally, the home's board of directors should oversee the meeting with the board chairman as toastmaster. Seated with him at the head table should be the administrator of the home and the president, officers, and committee chairmen of the auxiliary.

The auxiliary chairman should be called on for an annual report of the activities. This report may include such items as total hours of donated service, funds collected, disbursements of funds, and special items of equipment obtained by the auxiliary for the home. This may also be the ideal time for the auxiliary chairman to present to the home a check representing the financial assistance obtained by the auxiliary during the year.

The board chairman should respond by presenting service awards to the members of the auxiliary. The evening should also include a time when the board chairman and the administrator thank the volunteers for their needed assistance. The administrator could possibly relate specific stories told to him by the patients or their relatives concerning the devotion to the home by the volunteers. He could perhaps read a letter he has received from a relative expressing thanks for assistance given a loved one by a volunteer or read a few notes of thanks from several patients. He should give his personal evaluation of the volunteer program, stressing what the individual volunteer services have meant to the home.

This is also a good night, for obvious reasons, to seek publicity for the home in the local newspapers, on television, and on the radio.

Volunteer and public relations. A side aspect of a good volunteer program is the good community relations it can bring. Properly motivated volunteers usually spread the news of the excellent care that is being given to the patients. They are a part of this care system and are thus proud of the good results. The good work of the home may be discussed over coffee, at club meetings, at card parties, and elsewhere. For homes giving good patient care, the volunteer can be an excellent public relations agent in the community.

Most nursing homes are dependent on their public image for patient referrals. Volunteers are usually positive in talking about the home, since as a visible member of the home's volunteer program, they have already publicly endorsed the home's program. Although there are always a few volunteers who display a negative attitude when they are away from the home, no matter how excellent the program is, most of them usually speak of the positive results of the home's program.

Volunteer and confidentiality. In the bylaws of the auxiliary, there must be strong, forceful statements regarding keeping the confidentiality of the physical and mental problems of the home's patients. Just as employees must be cautioned about discussing patients away from the home, so must volunteers. This is especially true in smaller communities where both the patients and the volunteers may be prominent people, known to many. Volunteers must respect the patients' right to privacy of their medical conditions.

Communication with the volunteer. The auxiliary president and the home administrator should make sure that the volunteers are given regular communication from the home such as a monthly bulletin. This can be a simple mimeographed news sheet printed at the home and mailed inexpensively. The purpose of this bulletin should be to keep the volunteers up to date on the home's activities and the work of volunteer committees and to reinforce the volunteer's interest in the home. Although this can be done by one of the committees of the auxiliary, the home administrator should contribute something to each issue. His contribution should be newsy, not filled with statistics, and should be complimentary about the continual good work of the auxiliary personnel. Occasionally he can offer suggestions about how to talk with a patient, including the do's and don'ts, good topics, and statements and topics that should be avoided; highlight important forthcoming events or report on the successful results of an inspection by a licensing authority; introduce new employees, announce new staff promotions, or explain changes in policy.

Occasionally, the chairman of the board of directors should contribute something of interest or major importance, such as the announcement of an expansion program, major equipment purchases, or planned building remodeling or renovation.

The news bulletin should be issued regularly, not hit or miss, and have a deadline for submission of material. It can be designed to be sent to leaders of civic groups, physicians, prospective volunteers, and even patients' family members if deemed wise. Telling people of the good aspects of the home is essential to continued worthwhile public relations.

Arrival of a new volunteer to the home. Proper orientation of the new volunteer is necessary. If the home has an auxiliary, the new volunteer should be given a copy of the bylaws and be invited to attend the meetings. A staff member, either the activity director or the administrator, should take the new volunteer on a tour of the facility. He should be introduced to key staff personnel and all the employees in the specific area in which he will work.

If there is no formal auxiliary with its own rules and regulations (by-laws), the home should have its own guidelines or do's and don'ts printed and given to the new worker. In either case, someone, preferably a staff member such as the activity director, should take the time to review these guidelines with the volunteer so that there is no misunderstanding.

Sometimes a volunteer leaves the home soon after he comes and does not return. This may be caused by the fact that no one properly oriented him or gave him specific duties. If the volunteer is just turned loose by the staff person doing the orientation and told to go out and find something to do, he may lack motivation. He may quickly become discouraged. The volunteer should have specific duties and be given definite days and hours he is expected at the home. If he does not show up, he should receive a telephone call to remind him of his importance to the home.

During the orientation, the volunteer should be reminded that he begins work in the home on a trial basis. This should be described as a two-way street: the volunteer may elect not to stay, and the home may elect not to keep him. This *must* be explained at the onset of the orientation.

In the orientation, someone who is professionally able should explain to the volunteer some of the more obvious patient problems. For the uninitiated person, exposure to these patients may be depressing or frightening. Someone, perhaps the director of nursing, should join the orientation session for a while to explain some of the problems of aged patients in general to help the beginning volunteer better accept what he might otherwise misunderstand. Merrill's book *Activities for the Aged and Infirm* includes an excellent section on the volunteer in the home.[5]

Clergyman

Religious services. To some elderly people, the religious aspect of their life is of little consequence or is nonexistent. To others, it may be such a strong motivating force that they seek out a retirement residence or nursing home under religious auspices. In either case, the need or nonconcern is usually the result of their former life style. If they were religiously oriented, they will probably remain so and perhaps show an increase in their need for religious activities and environment.

A nursing home or retirement residence may not have space for a chapel by itself. Certainly, though, the administrator should make sure that a certain area is available on a regular basis for religious services. A multipurpose activity room can be used as a chapel. All that is really needed are chairs for the patients or residents, a table, and a lectern. The clergymen who visit the home usually are able to supply anything else that may be needed.

Home chaplain and visiting clergyman. A home sponsored by a religious organization may have a full- or part-time chaplain on the payroll of the home. He may have an office and be available on a daily basis. In other cases, the sponsoring church body may lend support by having the pastor or an assistant of the church spend part of his time at the home. If the home is of one particular faith in sponsorship or ownership, arrangements should be made with other clergymen to satisfy the needs of the residents who are not of that faith. If such a home has a chaplain or a visiting minister from the sponsoring body, this person should be the one who arranges for other clergymen to visit.

Homes that have no religious ties must meet this obligation also. Frequently, arrangements for visiting clergymen can be made through the local ministerial alliance association in the town. The administrator can call a local church to find out who is in charge of this association. This group can make sure that someone or several persons on a rotating basis are assigned to visit the home. The association can also give emergency religious counseling assistance as it is needed.

The administrator should offer a stipend to the clergyman who is assigned to visit the home and is on call. This may be arranged individually or through the ministerial alliance association, whichever is more appropriate. The clergyman provides a service to the home as well as to the resident. He should receive payment for the service.

No patient should be denied the right to speak with a clergyman of his choice. Sometimes, however, there is no person of the particular faith available. The home's chaplain or visiting clergyman should be asked for assistance with this problem and should see the patient and attempt to help him.

The home administrator should respect the different religious requirements of his residents. He should make every reasonable attempt to cooperate with the visiting clergymen and should make sure they are called when residents request visits.

• • •

It is the administrator's role to find the proper person or agency to assist the resident with his particular need. He is not expected nor should he attempt to counsel patients or residents in all areas. He must, however, see that the need is met by competent people.

NOTES

1. Cohen, Stephen Z.: Getting the staff to pull together (in the same direction). In Directions '70, American Association of Homes for the Aging, Washington, D. C.
2. Knee, Ruth I.: Winds of change, report of a conference on activity programs for long-term care institutions, American Hospital Association, 840 North Lake Shore Drive, Chicago, Ill. 60611.
3. Activity director's guide, Springfield, Ill., 1971, Rehabilitation Education Service, Illinois Department of Public Health.
4. Lucas, Carol: Recreational activity development for the aging in homes, hospitals and nursing homes, Springfield, Ill., 1962, Charles C Thomas, Publisher.
5. Merrill, Toni: Activities for the aged and infirm, Springfield, Ill., 1969, Charles C Thomas, Publisher.

Chapter seven

RELATIONSHIP OF THE HOME
TO THE COMMUNITY

CARE OF NONINSTITUTIONALIZED AGED IN THE COMMUNITY
Nonresident department of the home

Several years ago I made the following statement to a group of students in a class: "Every nursing home administrator has a duty to the noninstitutionalized aged in the community." Although not all the students agreed with me then, it still remains my opinion. This opinion was strengthened when in 1969 during an administrative training seminar cosponsored by the College of DuPage in Glen Ellyn, Illinois, the Rev. George Vander Schaaf, administrator of the Good Samaritan Home in Flanagan, Illinois, presented a paper entitled "Do Waiting Lists Bother You?"[1] Vander Schaaf raised a stirring question: Who can help these aged persons who are waiting, perhaps on "hopeless waiting lists," for admission to the home? He believes that the home for the aged can and should attempt to reach out with its programmed services of care through the establishment of a nonresident department. The goal of this feature of the home is to help aged people remain in their home, living independently but with support from the home. His program includes a meals-on-wheels service: volunteers take a hot meal daily to the homes of persons no longer able to prepare it for themselves. He points out that this one delivery could provide not only the hot noon meal but also sufficient food for a cold supper at night.

Vander Schaaf describes another service of the nonresident department: the home health service. The department assigns registered nurses to leave the home periodically to visit the persons on the rolls. Other services that can be overseen by this nonresident department include homemaker services, minor home repairs, assistance with shopping, bringing the aged person to the home to participate in activities, and telephone security calls. Vander Schaaf suggests that the department be supervised by a social worker who is familiar with the existing community resources.

In many communities, these services are already available, quite often supervised by the local visiting nurses' association. Where formally structured programs already exist, the home need not duplicate the service. However, the nonresident department or the administrator should be aware of these services so that home applicants unable to be admitted immediately can get the needed assistance through the home's referral.

The main thrust of this concept is that practicing administrators do indeed have a duty to the aged in the community. A valid argument against this concept, however, is that nonresident departments cost money. The money may perhaps come from the charges made to patients; thus the patient in the home subsidizes this "outpatient" cost. Most nursing homes are not in a position to extend themselves financially, since their budgets are already stretched as far as they can be. There simply is not enough of a margin in the average nursing home's budget to establish a nonresident department. Dedicated people like Vander Schaaf, however, do not stop at this point. They seek out agencies and social and fraternal organizations to sponsor these extra costs. Even if the home cannot extend itself, the administrator should care enough to alert the existing community agencies when the home cannot meet the need.

Neil Gaynes, a nationally known leader, educator, and consultant in the care of aged people, has carried out further the concept of meeting the needs of the noninstitutionalized aged people in the community. He states that the professional nursing home administrator may very well be the only practicing gerontologist in the area; there may be no one else who has his specific knowledge in the needs of older people. Gaynes, therefore, also believes that the home administrator has a duty to the aged people who are not institutionalized.[2] Even if the home itself does not have the financial ability to develop this concept, the administrator can personally do something to help in the framework of the community. If services are nonexistent and there are aged people with needs unmet, he can make this fact known to governmental leaders and civic groups as well as to local service clubs.

In many communities there are existing agencies with programs aimed toward keeping the older person in his home, where he truly would rather be, as long as possible through supportive services.

The concept of keeping the older person in his home as long as possible is excellent. It should be used by the administrator of the retirement residence; the residents can remain in the independent-living setting of the residence with assistance in daily living needs and health supervision. Retirement home administrators must investigate fully the federal funding available and motivate local civic groups to develop programs to present or potential fund receivers. No one wants to go to a nursing home, no matter how excellent the care is, if there is the slightest chance that he can remain in his own home safely with outside assistance.

Day-care programs

Although some state licensing laws make it difficult to have day-care programs, the idea of providing day care is essentially sound. Day care is a service that a home can offer the community. Often a working couple have an aged relative living with them. During the day while they are both out of the home, they may fear for the well-being of this older person. When they are at home, they can provide the necessary supervision and personal care. While they are away at work, however, they may worry that their charge may become injured, fall, catch his clothing on fire from the stove, or leave the home and become lost.

If state laws permit, homes can be excellent day-care centers for these individuals. Reasonable charges can be made for this service, which may include a hot meal at lunchtime and supervision of the aged individual throughout the day. A home having a well-organized activity department can easily add these persons to its groups.

The home should not find this difficult. Some states require that a bed be available to the person if he needs to take a nap or becomes exhausted. If this is a requirement, the home should give serious consideration before offering the service.

Day-care "patients" can be a helpful adjunct to the existing program of services to the patients. Usually they are in better physical and mental condition than many of the patients. Therefore, they can help motivate the less fortunate people in the home. They represent the outside world. They can bring in stories of their own personal experiences and perhaps stimulate the home's patients with news of the latest events in the town.

When a family considers that a responsible sitter may cost them about $15 to $20 a day, depending on locality, for the care of their relative in his own home, they may be happy to pay a reasonable rate for day care in a nursing home, which includes the noon meal. At the close of the day, the relatives can come to the home to take the person back to his home environment.

The older person usually looks forward to this opportunity. He feels more secure. He has companionship and the opportunity to join in the structured activity programs of the home; this gives him self-esteem. He has the company of the patients and the staff at hand; this gives him the opportunity to join in with group activities that he ordinarily would miss.

The day-care program may also be a way of helping the older person adjust to the fact that eventually the relatives in his home will no longer be able to help him stay there. Either his own needs will increase or the environmental needs of the household will change, and the needs of the younger members of the family will become more significant. If the person has gotten used to the staff and the daily routine of the home, the necessary change to the nursing home may be less traumatic after the initial adjustment period.

Even if the home does not have a formal day-care program, it can, I believe, expand its activity center to let senior citizens in the community participate in the events, at least for part of the day, with limitations and guidelines. Well aged people can contribute much to the home as volunteers. In reality it is a mutually beneficial situation. The home benefits and the older volunteer benefits. The older person's sense of worth is enhanced, and he also contributes to the goals of the home.

The commitment to day-care programs requires boldness on the part of the board and the administrator, for it carries known risks. However, if the board is community oriented and truly wants to help older people, the decision will be made with less hesitation. Some of the risks are obvious: the home may be responsible if the person in the day-care program wanders away from the home; legal problems may be created if the person becomes injured; and the person may have a behavioral problem.

The policies for the day-care program must be well defined and approved by the board so that the administrator knows the limitations. It is likewise necessary to develop and write down policies for obtaining the health history of each applicant before he is accepted. This history should be obtained and the medical examination done by the person's physician. The physician should send to the home an indication that the person has been adequately screened for communicable diseases, written permission for the person to engage in the home's activity program, written orders for supervision of medication if the patient needs any during the day, and the medical diagnosis of the person's current problems.

Adequate written records should be kept for each person so that the home is able to act in the event of an emergency. The record should list the person's physician and the telephone numbers of the places where the relatives can be reached during the day.

Although day care is not ordinarily a profitable venture, it can perhaps satisfy another unmet need in the service to elderly people in the community. It must, therefore, be given careful consideration by the home's owner.

PUBLIC RELATIONS

In most instances the home's status in the community is of paramount importance in keeping the home filled. Often there is competition among homes for the patients needing care. Frequently the family is left with the decision of which home to use. The home's community image may well be the determining factor.

A good public relations program begins within the walls of the home. The staff members themselves project the image of the home to the patients, their relatives and visitors, and the friends and families of the staff members. A worker who is well motivated and believes that the goals of the home are worthwhile and are being met usually conveys a good image. He supports the home when it is criticized by his friends. He speaks proudly of the home's record to visitors. He supports the home and the staff because he believes in its goals and sees them succeed.

The home administrator should help the staff develop this feeling of responsibility to the home through the techniques discussed throughout this book. It is important to remember Cohen's concept of involving the staff in making decisions and setting patient goals[3] and McGregor's Theory Y, that work is as natural as play and that if a man is committed to an objective or goal, he will exercise self-direction and self-control in his activities to achieve that goal.[4] These two concepts alone can build confidence in the home so that the employee supports its programs both when he is at work and when he is away from the home.

There are a variety of ways in which the administrator can develop good public relations. He should take advantage of national promotions, such as senior citizens' month, that focus attention on the problems of aged people. During such promotions, the press carries articles about older people. This is an ideal time to hold an open house so that the public can see the home's program of patient care, meet key staff members, and see the patient activity programs in action. The activity program itself can be newsworthy. If the home's patients are taken on an outing to a local park, the local newspaper should be sent an advance release of the event. Handicraft exhibits, too, can be newsworthy. Feature stories on certain residents may likewise be of interest to the local press. A photograph of the home's oldest resident smiling over a birthday cake with his relatives in the background is usually of interest to the newspapers in the area.

Although larger homes may be able to employ the services of public relations firms, most are not. This task falls on the shoulders of the administrator and his staff for the most part. Sometimes, members of the home's board of directors can be helpful in maintaining the image of the home in the community, but most often the administrator spearheads the action.

ADMINISTRATOR AS COMMUNITY GERONTOLOGIST

The word *gerontology* means the study of aging. A gerontologist, therefore, is one who is a participant in the study of aging. Certainly, the administrator is involved in this science. He must be well equipped to practice his profession; therefore, he must read about the field, talk with fellow administrators, attend special seminars on aging and home administration, and participate in professional associations. The study of the theory and the practical experience qualify him as a gerontologist. As Gaynes states, the home administrator may be the one person in the local area who truly understands the needs of older people. Of course, that is not to imply that he is the only one who cares. This is far from the truth. Almost every community has groups of concerned citizens. Many cities are blessed with professional gerontologists who head up senior citizen community centers or who work for various agencies helping aged people. In some of the smaller communities, however, this is not the case. There are concerned citizens but little formal knowledge of what is needed. This is where the home administrator can help. He can seek out groups offering to work with aged people in the work of their various committees. He does not necessarily have to do this on home time. He can do it as his contribution to the community just as other business leaders serve voluntarily on various community service projects.

However, the home's board of directors should see the good that can be accomplished by the administrator's community service and support him, understanding his role as a leader in the community efforts to solve the needs of aged persons of the area. The board members should take pride in the fact that they have a man who can extend himself to the community in voluntary efforts. The board should also recognize the secondary effect that this service activity can have: the enhancement of the public's image of the home and its administrator. If the administrator is recognized as a leader in meeting the needs of aged people through his involvement in community projects, the public will believe in the goals of the home. A good administrator should never let himself become so involved with the details of the home that he cannot find an hour or so a week for this outside activity. If he is indeed too busy to get involved during the daytime hours, he certainly should be able to find an evening or two a month to get involved.

To get started, he might talk with the local civic leaders to learn of unmet needs that they hear about. Also local church, clergy, and service clubs may know of unsolved problems. He can get involved with local or state health and welfare agencies by offering to serve on their advisory boards or can seek nomination to serve on a board of directors of the local senior citizens community center. If no such center exists, he should attempt to get a local group of interested citizens to start such a program. Help in this area, can be obtained by writing the Administration on Aging in Washington, D. C., to learn of the name and address of the state agency administering these several titles of the Older Americans' Act.

Since the administrator is a gerontologist, he should consider teaching as another way to help the community. In many communities, there is a college or university that offers courses in home administration. There may also be adult education classes in preparing for retirement. It may be possible for the administrator to participate in these programs on a part-time basis in night school. His specific knowledge of the field can be of use to the student interested in entering the field of health care administration. Another way in which he can contribute to the welfare of the field and, therefore, to society is to write articles on home administration for the many professional journals. Well-developed manuscripts are accepted and published. This can be of great benefit to his fellow administrators.

There is much that an administrator can do to help his community if he takes the time to give of himself beyond what is normally expected of him.

NOTES

1. Vander Schaaf, George H.: Do waiting lists bother you. Unpublished paper presented for credit at Long Term Care of the Aged and Chronically Ill Patient, educational institute sponsored jointly by the Illinois Association of Homes for the Aging, the Metropolitan Chicago Nursing Home Association, and the Indiana Association of Homes for the Aging in cooperation with the College of DuPage, Glen Ellyn, Ill., Nov. 1969.

2. Neil L. Gaynes, Neil L. Gaynes and Associates, Consultants in Care of the Aging, Chicago, Ill.
3. Cohen, Stephen Z.: Getting the staff to pull together (in the same direction). In Directions '70, American Association of Homes for the Aging, Washington, D. C.
4. McGregor, Douglas: The human side of enterprise, New York, 1960, McGraw-Hill Book Co.

RULES AND REGULATIONS OF A RETIREMENT COMMUNITY

A retirement facility is something more than a hotel, yet something short of a nursing home or similar institution. In the institutional structure of a nursing home, the board of directors through the administrator requires the patients to live within a set routine that governs their coming and going, where and when they may smoke, when they are to bathe, when they may have visitors, and other areas. Residents of a retirement facility are well, ambulatory aged people who have none of these restrictions. As in a hotel, they have the freedom to make decisions about their lives that cannot be extended to those in institutions. Yet the administrator of the retirement facility has a greater duty to his residents than does the manager of a hotel because of the nature of his clientele. They are seeking a higher degree of security than that provided by a hotel, and they need the security.

In order to provide this security, the board must develop a set of rules and regulations that can be used as guidelines by the residents and staff. These rules are necessary for the well-being of the individual residents as well as the total group. It must be remembered that these people are well today and can continue to function adequately with watchfulness on the part of the staff. Furthermore, there may come a time when more care than can be given at the facility is necessary. Guides must be established for decisions in this regard. Another factor to be considered is that the retirement facility is a community of people brought together in social interaction at meal times, during activities, and during other leasure times on an informal basis.

So that the residents can live their lives with minimal restrictions, the guidelines established by the board must be liberal; yet they must be sensible for the well-being of the residents individually and as a whole.

The following set of rules and regulations is patterned after one now in use in one retirement facility. Of course, they should not be copied and used as they stand. Every facility should develop a set that is geared to the specific needs of the home. The following rules can be used, though, to provoke thought about what is practical and necessary for any retirement complex.

RULES AND REGULATIONS

Retirement residence
Best Homes, Inc.
ANYWHERE, U.S.A.

Welcome to the retirement residence

Our hope is that your life with us will provide you with a new spirit of living. It is our desire to see that you are comfortable and safe. My staff and I are pledged to your service toward these goals.

My door will always be open to you should you have a question or a suggestion for us. If you prefer to use our suggestion box, it is located just outside my door. When writing a suggestion, please sign your name so that I can answer you.

We have prepared this little handbook so that you may find adjustment to your new home easier. Some of these points are listed specifically for your safety. Please read it through carefully. . . then talk with me if you have any questions.

Sincerely,

John Doe

ADMINISTRATOR

DINING ROOM

MEAL TIMES

Breakfast	7:30 A.M. to 10:00 A.M.
Lunch	11:45 A.M. to 1:00 P.M.
Dinner	First setting—4:45 to 5:45 P.M.
	Second setting—6:00 to 6:30 P.M.

You may come to the dining room for your meals at any time during the above listed serving hours.

GUESTS

Feel free to invite your friends to come to dinner with you.

The charges for guest meals are posted at the cafeteria line.

If you wish, you may pay the cafeteria personnel for the guest meals at the time the meal is purchased, or you may charge meals by signing a guest meal charge ticket, which will be prepared by the cafeteria staff. This may be signed in advance of your guest's meal if you wish. Charges will appear on your monthly bill.

When you are having guests in for meals, please notify the food manager in advance whenever possible. The food manager may be reached through the switchboard.

SPECIAL DIETS

Your physician may want you to have a special diet. If this is the case, please contact the nurse in the health office, who will arrange this for you. Your special diet will be reviewed by the consulting dietitian, who will contact your physician if necessary. Please always arrange special diets through the health office. If you would like to discuss your special diet needs with the dietitian, contact the food manager or the health office.

TEMPORARY TRAY SERVICE FOR MEDICAL REQUIREMENTS

The design of the residence makes room meal service an impractical and costly procedure. It can be arranged temporarily, on recommendation of the nurse or your physician in keeping with a *temporary* medical condition. Please contact the nurse for assistance. It will assist us in serving you better if you will let the health office have as much advance notice as possible. Although we will always accommodate your needs, at least one hour's notice prior to the regular serving time is most helpful. Charges will be made for room meal service that is given for reasons other than medical conditions.

MISSED MEALS

If you find that you will be away from the residence for a seven-day period or longer, please notify the administrator. He will see that you are not charged while you are away. We are sorry that we cannot allow credit for missed meals for periods of time less than seven days.

HEALTH OFFICE

Shortly after you arrive, the chief nurse will help you select a local physician. She will arrange for an appointment with him as soon as possible. This is done so that your health maintenance needs and medical emergencies can be cared for by a local physician who is familiar with you and your medical requirements.

Please keep the health office staff informed of any health changes. After each physician visit, please drop by the health office to give the nurse a brief report of your physician's findings. This is required so that we can better respond to your needs in the event of an emergency.

Please advise the health office of all future appointments with physicians, dentists, or other medical or paramedical specialists. As soon as the appointment is known, notify the nurse so that adequate scheduling of transportation personnel may be made. The nurse will make sure that free transportation is arranged for local visits. There are transportation charges for trips beyond the local area. Of course, emergencies will always be handled, but if you forget to tell the nurse of the appointment until the day of the visit, she may not have enough time to arrange for free service.

The chief nurse will issue you a medical identification card. It is security for you. If you are injured, it provides an information source for the persons caring for you. When they telephone us, we can give them the name of your physician and further data from your medical files at our office. It also is your proof of our payment responsibilities for your medical expenses.

For prescription service, you are free to choose any local pharmacy. Costs of medication are at the resident's expense.

Each resident is encouraged to see his physician as often as necessary. A physical examination at least annually is in your best interests and is requested by the administrator.

EMERGENCY CARE

A staff nurse is available at all hours to assist you when necessary. Never hesitate to call her if you believe that you have a problem. The nurse will be glad to contact your physician for you if it is necessary. You may reach your nurse through the emergency intercom system; you may call her on the telephone or, if she does not answer, call the operator; or you may drop by her office or visit with her when you see her in the hall. Please do not hesitate to talk with her any time you believe her assistance is needed.

EMERGENCY ASSISTANCE

Every apartment is equipped with two emergency communication systems. A switch, located in the bathroom, will summon aid when activated. Likewise, the speaker system in the bedroom may be used for this purpose. Those having telephones can call the operator and ask her to get help. A resident hearing calls for assistance from within another resident's apartment should call the health office immediately and report it.

INTERCOM SYSTEM

The speaker in your bedroom may be used for communication with the switchboard operator for any purpose. To ensure privacy in your apartment, you should keep the lever in its privacy position. No one can hear you through the communication system when the lever is in that position.

MAID SERVICE

A maid will visit your apartment once a week. Her assignment is the general cleaning of your apartment, including the care of floors and fixtures. She will also change the linens. Since she is working on a tight schedule, do not overtax her by requesting that she assist you with personal daily chores, such as washing dishes.

If more frequent service is needed, special charges will be arranged by the housekeeper.

LAUNDRY AND DRY CLEANING

Self-service washers and dryers are located in convenient places throughout the residence for your personal laundry needs. A modest charge is made to pay for the cost of utilities.

A dry cleaning and laundry collection station is located in the housekeeping office. A local cleaner provides this service. You will be billed at the end of each month. Finished garments are to be picked up at the facility's store.

SAFETY

Your happiness, health, and well-being are our primary concerns. The facility has been designed throughout with safety in mind. Your cooperation, however, is essential for the achievement of a complete, successful safety program for all the residents.

The following rules are necessary:

1. Do not smoke in bed at any time.
2. Be sure that all ashes are extinguished with water before emptying the ash tray into the wastebasket. Check ash trays before retiring for the night.
3. Place your trash in the container located in your corridor or in the trash chute in your building. Notify the housekeeper or operator if the container is full. Call the housekeeping department for the removal of large packing boxes from your apartment.
4. Be sure that your stove and electrical appliances are turned off before retiring or before leaving your apartment.
5. Let us replace your light bulbs for you in the receptacles in your apartment. Please call the switchboard operator to ask for assistance with this.
6. If one of the facility's appliances, such as stove, refrigerator, washing machine, heating unit, or intercom, fails to operate or operates incorrectly, contact the switchboard operator at once.
7. Do not attempt to lift heavy objects or to climb ladders. Let us assist you with these matters at all times.
8. In winter, after a snow, we will clear the walks as soon as possible. Likewise, we will clear the drives quickly so that you may use your automobile if you wish. Please give us an opportunity to make them safe for you, however, before you attempt to use them.
9. Advise the switchboard operator of any suspicious person seen on the premises. Make sure that you close all outside doors behind you. Keep your doors and windows locked.
10. Inform the administrator's office during the day or the switchboard at night of any unsafe condition that you may notice within the residence.
11. Keep clothing and linens away from the heater in the bathroom. Do not store flammable items, including pressurized spray cans, on shelves near these heaters.
12. Electrical extension cords are often hazardous. If you find it necessary to use an extension cord, please contact the housekeeping office, which will assist you in this matter.
13. If you find that the temperature in your apartment needs to be adjusted, please contact the telephone operator, who will arrange for assistance.
14. Frayed or old electrical cords to lamps, radios, and other items are dangerous. Such appliances should be repaired or discarded. We will be happy to replace these cords for your safety. There is a nominal charge to cover the cost of material and labor.

FOR BETTER SECURITY

Occasionally a workman, delivery man, or other stranger will knock on a door other than the front doors and ask to gain entrance. *Do not let him in.* Tell him to go to the front entrance, where he can properly identify himself. If he is given permission to use one of the other doors, one of the staff members will be dispatched to let him enter.

TELEPHONES

A telephone can be installed quickly in your apartment if you wish. Please contact the administrator's office if you wish to have a telephone installed.

You will be given a monthly service charge for your telephone. No charges are made for local calls or calls to other telephones in the facility.

If you do not wish to have a telephone, you may use any of the pay telephones located in the main lobby or come to the switchboard and have the operator place the call, for 15¢ per local call.

The switchboard operator will be glad to receive messages from your friends if you do not have a telephone. The switchboard operator will make sure that you are contacted if you have a message. We will do our best to locate you if we cannot reach you in your apartment. If we fail to reach you, please remember that we have tried our best.

GUESTS

You may have overnight guests if you desire. Ask the housekeeper for assistance with any needs. There are nominal charges for extra linen and fold-away beds.

CHILDREN

Children are welcome to visit you. For your comfort and that of your neighbors, we ask that you remind the children that this is a retirement residence. Children are not allowed to move about the buildings and grounds without adult supervision. Please do not allow them to run in the corridors. This is requested for the children's safety and for the needs and safety of other residents.

GRATUITIES

All employees of the residence understand that they are not to accept gratuities for services rendered by them. There is an annual Christmas collection for the employees that is gathered by free-will offerings of the residents. It is split equally among all employees.

PROBLEMS WITH EMPLOYEES

Each employee works under a supervisor. If you have a problem with an employee, contact the administrator's office or the employee's supervisor. The administrator or the supervisor will discuss the problem with the employee. We request that you assist us in maintaining good supervisory practices by not criticizing or giving instructions directly to the employees concerning their methods or manners of work. We assure you that prompt attention will be given by the employee's supervisor to any problem that you bring to our attention.

BILLINGS

You will receive a monthly bill covering the next month's life care charge plus any miscellaneous charges that have accumulated over the past month. We would appreciate receiving a check for payment of the bill as soon as possible. If there is ever any question regarding your bill, please feel free to discuss it with the administration.

CHANGES IN YOUR CONFIDENTIAL STATISTICS FORM

You must notify the administrator's office, in writing, of any changes in your confidential statistics form, such as changes of name, address, or telephone number of your relatives, friends, or others whose names you have given previously. It is essential that we keep this information current. Be sure, too, to give the administrator written notice of changes of persons previously named as executors and any changes in funeral arrangements previously given us on this special form.

RESIDENTS' COMMITTEE

The residents' committee is a group of five elected resident representatives. Three residents are elected in the summer for a full year, and two are elected in the winter for an equal term. There are no officers. They meet with the administrator on an informal basis monthly to discuss community activities and problems and to offer suggestions.

ACTIVITY ROOMS

The residents are invited to use the various activity and hobby rooms at the residence whenever they wish. You may reserve one of these rooms for a private party by contacting the housekeeper in advance. The pool room should be used for reasonable periods so that all those who wish to may have an opportunity to play.

NEIGHBORLINESS

Please respect your neighbors' privacy and right to peace and quiet by not playing your radio, television, and stereo too loudly.

PERSONAL POSSESSIONS

Every reasonable care is exercised by the facility to safegaurd your possessions. We cannot assume responsibility for them, however. We ask that you keep your windows and doors locked, particularly when you leave your apartment. Valuables such as jewelry, securities, and large amounts of cash should not be kept at the residence. You should obtain a safe-deposit box at a local bank for the storage of these items.

Your apartment will be cleaned on a regular schedule. You will know in advance when the maid will unlock your door and proceed with the cleaning. Because of the large number of apartments that must be cleaned daily, we must ask your cooperation with this matter.

ABSENCES FROM THE RESIDENCE

For your convenience and safety, we ask that you notify the switchboard operator when you expect to be absent overnight or longer from your apartment. This is essential so that we may know where to reach you in case of an emergency and may assure ourselves of your well-being.

Please note that the facility's health care plan covers you while traveling anywhere within the limits of the continental United States. Trips outside the country are not covered, and special short-term trip insurance for illness and accidents should be obtained.

TORNADO ALERTS

From time to time we receive tornado alerts through the office of Civil Defense. In the event of a tornado alert, we suggest that you go to your apartment. If a tornado warning is given, indicating that a tornado is imminent, the safest place for you would be in your bathroom.

BYLAWS OF A RESIDENTS' ASSOCIATION

For a retirement facility to be successful, it must have a method by which the residents can have a voice, collectively, to respond to the management of the facility. I am not suggesting that the residents be allowed to have a vote or veto power over the management function. The board has selected the administrator and has delegated to him the necessary authority to manage the home. However, the wise administrator listens to his residents so that he is able, within his authority, to respond to their needs and desires.

A residents' council is an excellent sounding board and allows the residents to voice objections or to better understand policy. I have talked with a great many administrators who favor this idea. Most of them have found this to be a great help to them and their staff in programming.

It is necessary to establish a firm principle, however, that this council does not have any administrative or legislative powers. It should function as an advisory group. The administrator should make it quite clear that he has the final word in all the decisions but that the suggestions of the residents' council carry weight in his decision making.

Following are the bylaws of such a council. It was designed for a population of residents of about 200.

ARTICLE I
  Name
  The name of this organization shall be the Residents' Association of the Retirement Residence.

ARTICLE II
  Purpose
  The purpose of the residents' association is to function in the interests of the residents and the board of directors to sustain a cooperative community environment for the benefit of all the residents and to speak on behalf of the residents, individually and collectively, for promoting a more satisfying and happy community life. To this end, there shall be

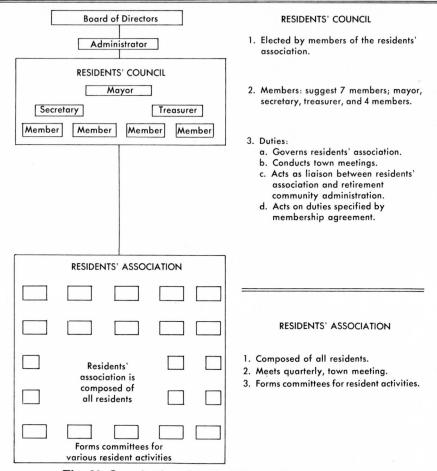

Board of Directors

Administrator

RESIDENTS' COUNCIL

Mayor

Secretary   Treasurer

Member Member Member Member

RESIDENTS' ASSOCIATION

Residents' association is composed of all residents

Forms committees for various resident activities

RESIDENTS' COUNCIL

1. Elected by members of the residents' association.

2. Members: suggest 7 members; mayor, secretary, treasurer, and 4 members.

3. Duties:
   a. Governs residents' association.
   b. Conducts town meetings.
   c. Acts as liaison between residents' association and retirement community administration.
   d. Acts on duties specified by membership agreement.

RESIDENTS' ASSOCIATION

1. Composed of all residents.
2. Meets quarterly, town meeting.
3. Forms committees for resident activities.

Fig. 20. Organization of residents' council and association.

close cooperation between the administrator of the retirement residence and the residents' association.

ARTICLE III
Jurisdiction

The jurisdiction of this residents' association shall be limited to the purpose as set forth in article II.

ARTICLE IV
Membership

All residents are members of the association, with the right to vote, to hold office, to serve on committees, and to transact whatever business may come before the association and its meetings.

ARTICLE V
Officers

1. The officers of the resident's association shall be a chairman, vice chairman, secretary, and treasurer.
2. The chairman shall preside over all meetings of the council and the association,

appoint committees, and generally perform all duties incidental to the office of presiding officer.

3. The vice chairman shall act in the place and stead of the chairman in case of absence or disability.
4. The secretary shall keep the minutes of all meetings, shall keep and maintain all necessary and pertinent documents and records, and shall post all required notices as well as the minutes of each meeting.
5. The treasurer shall keep such financial records as may be necessary, shall keep all funds that come into the hands of the association, and shall make such disbursements thereof as may be proper.

ARTICLE VI
Residents' council

1. The executive agency of the association shall be the residents' council, composed of the four officers of the residents' association and three other councilmen.
2. Association officers and councilmen shall serve for one year or until their successors take office.
3. In case of a vacancy for any reason, the remaining members of the council shall fill such vacancy for the unexpired term. If the office of chairman should become vacant, the vice chairman shall succeed thereto, and the council shall elect a new vice chairman from among its own members, to serve as such until the next general election.

ARTICLE VII
Meetings

1. *Town meetings.* There shall be a quarterly town meeting of the residents' association held in January, April, July, and October.
2. *Special town meetings.* Special town meetings may be called by the council, or at the request of the administrator, or by a petition signed by 25% or more members of the association.
3. *The residents' council* shall meet monthly.
4. *Special council meetings* may be called by the chairman, at the request of the administrator or on request of any two members of the council.
5. *Roberts' Rules of Order* shall govern all town meetings and council meetings as far as practical.
6. *Quorum.* Thirty percent of the residents' association shall constitute a quorum for town meetings. Three members of the residents' council shall constitute a quorum for council meetings.
7. *Secret vote.* It shall be the privilege of any member to request a secret vote on any subject or matter before the meeting. The presiding officer shall ask if any members desire such a secret vote before putting the question in any case and, if any member expresses such desire, arrangements shall thereupon be made for such secret vote.
8. *Order of business.* The order of business at the residents' association and council meetings shall be as follows:
   a. Reading of the minutes
   b. Reports of officers and standing committees
   c. Reports of special committees
   d. Special orders
   e. Unfinished business
   f. New business
   g. Adjournment
9. *Annual town meeting.* The annual town meeting of the association shall be held in January of each year, at which time the council members shall be elected to serve for the coming year.
10. *The administrator* or his appointed representative is an ipso facto member of all meetings of the residents' association, the council, standing committees, and special committees and may attend such meetings or not as he sees fit.

ARTICLE VIII
Elections

1. At the October town meeting, the chairman shall appoint a nominating committee to present to the association at the annual meeting a slate of 14 candidates for the seven positions on the council.
2. During the annual meeting the nominating committee shall report these 14 names. Nominations may also be made from the floor.
3. The members of the association shall then vote by secret ballot on the nominated names, and the seven persons who receive the highest number of votes shall be declared elected to the council.
4. The resident receiving the highest number of votes shall be named chairman; the next highest, vice chairman; the third highest, secretary; and the fourth highest, treasurer. In the event of a tie at any level, the members of the association shall vote a second time on those tied for that office, the winner getting the office and the loser(s) falling immediately behind him in rank to fill other offices.
5. Present members and officers of the council may succeed themselves.

ARTICLE IX
Committees

1. *The residents' council.* The residents' council shall be the executive agency of the association and shall manage and direct its affairs. It shall act as a liaison committee to represent the association and its members in all matters in which the management of the residence may be involved or may have an interest.
2. *Standing committees.* Library, dining room, entertainment, bulletin board, education, decorations, religious activities, hobbies, and hospitality.
3. *Special committees.* Special committees may be appointed by the chairman for needs as he sees fit.

ARTICLE X
Financial matters

1. *Solicitation of funds.* There shall be no solicitation of funds without the knowledge and approval of the council and the management.
2. *Residents' activity fund.* Collections of fees for movies and similar community-sponsored projects and sale of materials made by resident committees shall be funded in a separate account. The purpose of this fund shall be to reimburse the retirement residence for the costs of these projects. Surplus money in this fund shall be used for promotion of resident entertainment activities. Expenditures from this fund must be approved jointly by the residents' council and the administrator.

ARTICLE XI
Comments or suggestions

Constructive comments or suggestions concerning life at the residence in accordance with article II shall be presented in writing to the residents' council, signed and dated by the author. Such suggestions shall be considered by the council and, when found to be of sufficient importance, submitted to management.

ARTICLE XII
Amendments to the bylaws

These bylaws may be amended by majority vote of the entire association membership at any meeting called for the purpose or at any regular monthly meeting, provided such proposed amendment shall have been posted on the bulletin board for at least two weeks prior to such meeting.

ARTICLE XIII
Approval

These bylaws shall become effective from the date of approval by the board of directors and the management and by the residents' association.

GUIDELINES FOR THE RESIDENTS' COUNCIL

1. The council may review matters affecting the residents' life at the retirement residence and may make recommendations to the administrator.
2. The council's action shall be in the form of recommendations only. The council cannot make binding decisions about the administration or operation of the retirement residence.
3. The council cannot discuss specific residents, nor can they have access to information about specific residents' physical or financial status.

INDEX

Employees; *see* Personnel administration
Employment application, 36-37
Engineer, chief, 73-74
  job description, 73-74
Escort service, 117, 136
Exercises, 140
  deconfusion, 169-170
  group, 169
  motivation, 169-170
Extended care facility, 9, 115
  definition, 8
  licensing, 2
Extermination service, 64, 93-94

F

Financial management, 5-6; *see also* Budget
  accounting, 11, 20, 32-33, 48, 49, 53, 71,77
  auditing, 11
  authority in, 7
  borrowing practices, 10
  budgeted hours, 33
  business office manager and, 45-47
  business office policies and procedures in, 48-54
  business office subgroups in, 47-48
  controls, 29
  income and expense statement, 32-33
  liabilities, 10
  payroll report, 33
  reports, 12, 29, 47
Fire extinguishers, 62-63, 100
Fire safety, 21, 57, 62-63, 97-107
  construction standards, 98
  drills, 106-107
  early-warning detection devices, 98, 100
  evacuation planning, 98-107
  fire department notification, 99, 100
  fire extinguishers, 62-63, 100
  personnel fire and disaster plan, 102-106
  personnel training, 98-107
  resident evacuation plan, 101-102
  smoking and, 101
  sprinkler system, 98
Floors, 80
Food service, 87-97
  baking, 95
  cafeteria (buffet), 95
  cleaning function, 96-97
  complaints, 88, 89
  consulting dietitian, 88-90
    -manager relations, 89
  contracting for, 57-58
  convenience foods, 94-95
  cooking, 94
    in resident's apartment, 88
  cost control, 92
  diets, 122, 135

Food service—cont'd
  employee meal policy, 96
  environmental sanitation, 93-94
  equipment cleaning, 96-97
  food-handling techniques, 93-94
  food preparation, 94-95
  frozen foods, 94-95
  insect and rodent control, 93-94
  inventory control, 93
  literature on, 91-92
  locking system, 97
  management function, 90-94
  management techniques, 90-91
  meal count, 92
  meal tray, 95-96
  meals per day, 88
  menu planning, 91
  organization, 90-97
  portion control, 96
  purchasing, 91-92
  record keeping, 92
  in resident's rooms, 122-123
  sanitation in, 93-94
  serving function, 95-96
  silverware cleaning, 96
  storage, 94
  table service, 95
  waste disposal, 97
  work area cleaning, 96-97
  work schedules, 92
Food service manager, 89, 90-91
Free-rein leadership, 27-28
Funeral arrangements, 121-122, 136, 166-167
Furnishings log, 70-71

G

Gardening by residents, 78
Gardens, formal, 78; *see also* Landscaping
Geriatric nursing, 142-147
  American Nurses' Association standards, 143-147
Gerontological Society, 11
Goal delineation, 8, 9-10
Golden Years—a Tarnished Myth, The, 111
Grounds maintenance, 77-78
  contract for, 77
Group-centered leadership, 27-28
Group exercises, 169
Group planning, 20

H

Hawthorne experiments, 28
Hazard prevention, 62, 77
Health office, 113; *see also* Nursing office
  in apparent death, 121-122